POWER SHIFT

POWER SHIFT

◆

The Transition to Nuclear Power in the U.S. Submarine Force As Told by Those Who Did It

By Dan Gillcrist

Foreword By Don Walsh

iUniverse, Inc.
New York Lincoln Shanghai

POWER SHIFT

The Transition to Nuclear Power in the U.S. Submarine Force As Told by Those Who Did It

iUniverse books may be ordered through booksellers or by contacting:

iUniverse
2021 Pine Lake Road, Suite 100
Lincoln, NE 68512
www.iuniverse.com
1-800-Authors (1-800-288-4677)

ISBN-13: 978-0-595-38574-4 (pbk)
ISBN-13: 978-0-595-82953-8 (ebk)
ISBN-10: 0-595-38574-5 (pbk)
ISBN-10: 0-595-82953-8 (ebk)

Printed in the United States of America

This book is dedicated to all the intrepid crews
of the United States Submarine Service

"Sign on, young man, and sail with me. The stature of our homeland is no more than the measure of ourselves. Our will is to keep the torch of freedom burning for all. To this solemn purpose we call on the young, the brave, the strong and the free. Heed my call. Come to the sea. Come sail with me."

—*John Paul Jones*

Contents

Foreword. xi

Acknowledgments. xix

Introduction 1

Are you crazy?. 7

Sub Culture 16

Rickover 57

Transition. 97

Apples and Oranges 130

Full Circle. 155

Ditty Bag 183

Glossary 217

Contributers 227

Biographies of those Interviewed. 231

Endnotes. 249

Foreword

Individuals and institutions are basically wary of change, even though they understand intuitively that it is inevitable. This wariness is generally not a bad thing; it provides a degree of inertia that moderates the rate of change. It also serves to make it a carefully considered process. Most often this caution is not resistance to the new but rather a healthy questioning process on how change is applied, as well as how fast it is to happen. History is full of examples of transformations made in haste that led to unfavorable outcomes. Thoughtless *new* is not always better than a working status quo.

Moderation of the pace and degree of change in military organizations is particularly important. They continuously evolve and change generally at a rather stately pace. In the military where both political and military policy makers are frequently changed, there is a temptation for each new leader to put his/her mark on the organization. However, it rarely happens since institutional inertia requires a broad consensus and concurrent support from all players involved.

But there is a delicate balance here. Change made too rapidly can be bad but so can change that is never made because of institutional resistance. As in all things there has to be balance between the 'quick and the dead' institutionally speaking.

Of course, there are those who simply do not want the status quo to be disrupted. They are unwilling or unable to adapt to new circumstances. By not participating in the change process they get left behind.

It should be recognized that cultural change in the military almost always results from technological change. New machines and devices facilitate better ways of doing things. People need to be trained how to operate and maintain new things. Then military planners have to employ them to find out how warfare doctrines must be changed. Because this is all people-intensive, their existing culture must change along with the technologies

But cultural changes in military organizations come hard. These inevitable transformations are as old as the history of arms. Warfighting institutions often resist the new and more efficient, preferring to remain comfortable with existing way of doing things. Armies resisted replacing the horse with motorized machines. Much later, the US Navy had these problems as naval aviation displaced the 'battleship navy' as the primary striking element. Looking backwards it is hard to understand how the generals and the admirals could not have eagerly embraced the greater efficiency and lethality of new technologies.

With respect to the US Navy's Submarine Service, it was a half-century old when the first nuclear submarine joined it. It took just two decades to replace the diesel submarines with nuclear ones. Not even the most dedicated diesel boat sailor could argue against the advantage of that 'infinite battery' that lets you remain submerged "until it's time to reenlist the crew". But many of the 'smokeboat sailors' were uncomfortable with the velocity and substance of the change process that is the subject of this book. Those not chosen or who did not want to join this new submarine navy were indeed left behind.

From the time *USS Holland*, the Navy's first submarine went into service in 1900 until WWII, change in the submarine service happened at a relatively slow pace. In those years submarine service was not a recognized full career path for naval officers. After a few early years there they would 'surface' and join the fleet. Furthermore, the senior leadership of the Navy did not have a clear or realistic doctrine for how to employ submarines in wartime scenarios.

During WW II, both the air and submarine navies came into their own. The effectiveness of the fast carrier task forces and their striking power settled the 'airplane vs battleship' issue for good. The USN submarine actions in the Pacific quickly showed the immense impact these small ships had on the enemy. It was a costly campaign for both sides. The Submarine Service had the largest casualty rate, nearly one-third, of any US armed force. But for the Japanese, nearly two-thirds of their merchant shipping and half their navy was sunk by submarines. For a nation absolutely dependent on seaborne shipping, this was an unmitigated disaster for Japan.

After WWII, the importance of naval aviation and submarines was no longer a matter of speculation by a few forward thinking strategists, as was the case in the years of the 20's and 30's. Now these branches of naval warfare were recognized career paths that could lead an officer to the top jobs in the Navy. Both institutions had developed a rich warrior reputation and tradition during the war years.

In the postwar years from the mid-40's to the mid-60's the Submarine Service experimented with many new technologies and operational techniques. A major direction was the "Greater Underwater Propulsion Program" (Guppy) that used captured German technology and USN innovations to create a faster, quieter diesel submarine. Two new classes of attack submarines were put into service. In addition, several submarines were either converted or constructed for a variety of missions. Some examples were the nuclear warhead Regulus missile subs, the radar pickets, antisubmarine 'killer' boats, troop carriers (UDT, etc.), and even a seaplane tanker. In addition there were experimental subs for study of high-speed hull shapes, acoustics experimentation, oceanographic research and deep diving investigations.

However, because all these innovations involved the basic diesel submarine, there was no significant cultural impact. Of course no good officer or sailor wanted to stay on a specialized boat too long. Then it was the Guppies and fast attack boats that were the 'front line'; the subs doing the really interesting Cold War missions. But the point here is that technological change has been a continuing part of the submarine force for the half century since WWII ended. Submariners not only lived with it, they thrived on it. Better tools meant a better job…

Operationally, the Submarine Service was learning how to do new things including highly classified special missions in the Cold War. Compared to the surface navy and naval aviation, submarine operations were governed by few tactical publications and written doctrines. Training of young submarine warriors was an apprenticeship largely loaded with a tradition-based oral history. Submarine captains had a great deal of latitude to use their boats as effectively as possible in any given situation. 'Rudder orders' from higher authority were very rare. Self-reliance was a prized attribute and a desirable reward for those selected for command.

Beginning the late 1940's, it became apparent that nuclear energy could be applied to submarines. Building on previous work in the Navy Department, and in a remarkable show of will and carefully assembled personal power, Captain-to-Admiral Hyman G. Rickover forced a change upon the US Navy that has no historical equal. Here was a massive technological revolution that also forced a profound cultural change. It was the most extensive institutional reformation in the history of the Navy's Submarine Service, an organization that was, after all, no stranger to innovation.

The cost in human terms was high in many cases. For officers, some careers were distorted and destroyed while others soared. It was a somewhat brutal filtering out process. Admiral Rickover's personal interviews with candidates created a legendary body of stories from those fortunate enough to be selected as well as from those who were not. He wanted nothing but the best…as he defined "best".

For enlisted men, there was more opportunity to 'move across the pier' to the nuclear navy. Not all the jobs on nukes required nuclear power training. However many were unwilling to give up the diesel boat life and eventually left the submarine navy as the number of those boats decreased.

In defense of 'Rickover's Navy' the conversion of the submarine service to nuclear power was a remarkable and relatively swift evolution. In the late 1940's the idea of nuclear power for anything on land or sea was seemingly futuristic. But to propose that the first major application anywhere would be inside relatively small submerging warships was nothing less than revolutionary. Yet a submarine was the one application where a 'perpetual powerplant' would pay huge operational dividends.

In 1955 Rickover's persistence paid off when *USS Nautilus (SSN 571)* got underway on nuclear power. She was the first nuclear powered warship in the world. It was a triumph of will and technology.

I was fortunate to serve as an officer in the submarine service during those transition years, 1956–1970. A witness to change…

When I went through submarine school at New London in mid-1956, there was a small group of officers there being trained for *Nautilus* and the newly completed *Seawolf (SSN 575)*, the only operational nuclear subs in the Navy. All were already qualified in submarines having served for several years in diesel boats. And the first nuclear captains had commanded diesel boats. Rickover was staffing his navy with veterans. A very experienced cadre was launching a revolution in submarine warfare. These were Rickover's 'best'.

For those officer volunteers who did not get Rickover interviews or who had failed them, there was another path for diesel officers. This was on board the Fleet Ballistics Missile submarines. The FBM's had diesel-trained submariners as missile officers and navigators. Here there was a change-of-career opportunity through on board self-study programs that could prepare a lucky few to finally get an interview and be selected for nuclear power training.

Of course, I was an early volunteer. Who would not want to sail in and eventually command the first true submarines? Regrettably, I never got an interview; my poor academic performance at the Naval Academy years before probably shut that door for good. So I remained in the diesel boat navy as it withered away in favor of an all nuclear submarine service.

Fourteen years after submarine school I was fortunate to get command of one of the last diesel submarines, *USS Bashaw (AGSS-241)*. According to "Janes Fighting Ships" it was possibly the oldest operating submarine in the world. She was a great boat, with a superb crew.

Ultimately, I took her to her final 'home port'—the Mare Island Naval Shipyard. Just off San Francisco we took her to test depth for the last time. It had been 25 years since she had made dive #1 in 1943. We collected all the medicinal liquor on board, made a tub of punch in the forward torpedo room. Once each member of the crew had a mug in hand, I got on the 1MC and made a toast to a grand ship that had served her country well. We surfaced and went up the Bay to Vallejo where *Bashaw* was decommissioned. A sad time but it was all part of that inevitable process of change that we knew and understood.

The point of this little sea story is that diesel boat sailors 'owned' their submarines. It was more than a duty station or a place to serve out your time in the service. It was home and your shipmates were an extended family. As the nuclear submarine navy took on form and scale, many of us wondered if this hard-won sense of community would reemerge there.

Submarine service from the 50's to the 70's was a time of remarkable transition. I was very fortunate to be part of it. The most impressive fact is how fast an entirely new submarine navy was built and manned. It took just two decades. Necessary technological development, industrial base mobilization and educational infra-structure required were without equal in military history. Adding to all of this was the concurrent development of a completely new class of very complex submarines, the FBM's backbone of the nation's strategic deterrence. It is a true wonder that it all went so well.

Furthermore, Admiral Rickover's absolute insistence on safe powerplant operating procedures resulted in virtually no serious nuclear incidents over a period of nearly a half-century. By comparison, one only has to look at the nuclear accident record of the Soviet Union's submarine navy to appreciate our Navy's unrelenting attention to safety.

There were transitional costs. As will be seen in this book, the personal and emotional stresses on the people who did all this were enormous. Their stories are told verbatim here with all their triumphs and tragedies. And perhaps most of all, told with pride.

I cannot think of a better person than Dan Gillcrist, former TM2(SS) diesel boat sailor, successful businessman and gifted writer to do this book. This project was his idea and he personally underwrote the costs of its preparation. I have had the pleasure of spending many an evening with him sitting by his outdoor fireplace in Santa Fe, New Mexico. Over brandy and cigars, I have heard his stories and professed love for the submarine service. This was a book he had to write, he had no choice…

He probably takes exception to the word "write". He will say that all he did was to do interviews and organize the actual 'voices' of the men who lived and worked in those times. He has made simple a very difficult literary device for writing history. That is, how to incorporate many spoken styles into a single format without losing their 'flavor'. From admirals who transitioned from diesels to nukes to enlisted men who served single enlistments in both types, they are all here to describe what they experienced.

The intense pride in being a member of the US Navy's Submarine Service comes out on every page. Go to any crew reunion, even for submarines long gone to the scrapyards, and you still see the pride and affection these men had for their shipmates and their boats. Older men now, they relive the best days of their youth through their memories of time in the submarine service. And I believe they are also proud of the submariners of today who have forged a new culture and tradition system over the past half century of power shift.

Power Shift has captured this state of mind. It is a great and unique contribution to the literature on submarine warfare. A story not told before. In a larger context it provides a good case study of how major technological and operational change is brought about in a military culture. I was glad to have been in the community for those exciting years; a witness to and participant in a history so ably captured by Dan Gillcrist.

Acknowledgments

My first 'thanks' goes naturally to those I interviewed at length. They had to go through the polishing and edit stages which required a lot of their time. There were many 'submissions' via the web site, nearly all of which I have included. Thanks to the 90 or so submariners who responded.

This brings up the third thank you—my big sister Anne Gunshenan. She graciously fixed up the bad grammar and the many nits which I refer to as my "which's and that's". I informed her that I did not wish to change the style and spontaneity of either the submissions or the interviews. However, she advised that some might be embarrassed by their grammar, spelling and syntax—she prevailed. So, you submitters will not be getting scolding calls from your old High School English teachers.

Leslie North did all the transcribing and did a surprisingly good job particularly since so much of our submariner language consists of esoteric words she probably never heard.

Mike Barr was very helpful on a number of occasions. In spite of my expressions of concern about wearing out my welcome, he was always willing to help. He was of particular help in keeping me out of trouble concerning references to nuclear powered submarine facts and nomenclature, since I had very little knowledge about them.

Whenever I was stumped with a definition for the Glossary I simply posted my problem on Ron Martini's BBS and I would always get prompt and correct answers from the many posters there. Also, with respect to Navy protocol, customs and the like my brother, RADM Paul T. Gillcrist USN (retired) was always there, answering my questions and encouraging me.

Not only was Mike McLane enthused about the project and one of the contributers, he was the last to read the manuscript for any remaining nits.

Gray Coleman, a literary lawyer, helped me navigate the 'rocks and shoals' of the Byzantine world of copyrights and publisher's contracts.

Barbara, my wife of 42 years, thought this project was a great idea and continually encouraged me. Since it was on my mind, nearly constantly, for the last several years, I am surprised she never once told me that she was sick of hearing about it. Dave Oliver, an experienced writer knew the syndrome and actually expressed his condolences to my wife.

My friend Don Walsh, a man of many credentials not the least of which having been CO of Bashaw AGSS-341, was generous enough to sit for an interview, write the Foreward and added to a Ditty Bag segment about going deeper than test depth. I am honored to have him aboard.

Upon the suggestion of my friend CAPT. Dave Marquet, I sent a copy of this manuscript to VADM Al Knoetzni. At the time he was Deputy Commander, U.S. Fleet Forced Command and on the board of the Naval Institute. Admiral Knoetzni has been exceptionally supportive of this book.

Introduction

The purpose of this project is to gather opinions and anecdotes associated with transitional issues as a result of the shift in the United States Submarine Service from diesel to nuclear powered submarines. I thought it would be interesting to include here the email geneses—the very first glimmer of the project:

At 11:13 6/21/02–0700, I wrote my brother and Don Walsh:

> "I was asked recently what I meant when I signed off on an email to a civilianfriend who is helping the military, "DIESEL BOATS FOREVER!" So I replied with a brief explanation about the cultural change which took place in the transition from diesel to nuclear power. His reply was, 'I thought it was something like that'. I think this topic is quite interesting and I am considering writing about it. However, I get that nauseating feeling that I'm way over my head and that someone else is better equipped for the project. In any event, I'd like your reaction to the subject and, if I write something, I'd need it vetted carefully by you both if you don't mind. I'd need it correct. Also, this in no way would suggest that anyone is better than anyone else! But it is undeniable that this change in most ways was pretty dramatic."

I forwarded this to my friend Ron Martini who hosts a great submarine site—Rontini's BBS—and, he has the distinction of being the first submitter. Here was his response:

> "How very interesting. Don't forget that there is a 'camp' on both sides of the fence on the issue about which one is best also. DBF (Diesel Boats Forever) guys from the old school will tell you that a DBF is the only true submarine and if the bilges aren't filled with that wonderful dirt, sea water, diesel fuel, hydraulic oil smell, then it isn't a real submarine. Also comes the problem of fresh water. They abhor guys who can take a couple showers/ week and wash clothes regularly, rather than the old sink full/week guys. The issue of hot-bunking comes to mind also. I think it's basically a jealousy issue. The nuke guys don't seem to rub it in as much and I think they realize the DBF boys must be still suffering from HVCS (Head Valve Cycling Syn-

drome) to actually be thinking that 115 degree Engine Rooms are the only way to fly. The only benefit that I can see, and it is strictly a moral issue whether it be a benefit or not, is that DBF's were allowed into more heinous ports of call than the nukes.

Many issues to confront Dan...

Ron Martini"

The basis for the information herein was through a number of interviews and also from submissions through the web site www.gundeck.com. Since the shift from diesel to nuclear power took place generally from the mid 50's through the mid-70's, it was important, for actuarial reasons, to begin this project as soon as it was conceived. A 30 year old diesel boat Captain in 1955 would have been 77 when I began the project in 2002. It is necessary to note that this important part of the history of the U.S. Submarine Service could not be written without the opinions of those submariners who experienced the change. Historians in the future will have a difficult time indeed reconstructing this period because there are scant statements and writings from members of "the silent service". I believe it is unique in naval history that a naval community—namely the United States Submarine Forces—is basically prohibited from talking or writing about their Cold War operations. It is safe to assume that everyone from the Cold War era will be long gone before secrecy restrictions will be lifted. Only then will naval historians who are still interested in the topic, be able to document the operations. Since no one will be writing memoirs of any interest, they will not be including this non-secret topic i.e. the transition from diesel to nuclear power.

Nearly all submariners from this period have opinions about this 'cultural' change. I have taken pains to have this book reflect the views of all the submariners who were generous in granting interviews and all those who submitted material through the web site. Every entry has been attributed, usually accompanied by which boats served on and when. Of course each interview is identified as to person, place and date. The first interview with RADM Chuck Grojean led to one with a friend of his and so on. There was no organized plan for interviews. I just spoke with whomever I could, one interview leading to the next—in each case by referral. I think I covered the subject thoroughly with VADM Pat Hannifin, a WWII submariner who started on S boats and, incredibly, ended up on a Ballistic Missile boat! I ended with RADM Mike Barr who started on *Snook*, shooting Mk14 torpedoes. He retired in the mid 90's his last job as COMSUBPAC (Commander Submarine Force, U.S. Pacific Fleet). They are like bookends on the transition period with Barr giving us insight on the mature, nuclear power submarine force of today. It is my plan to continue to accept submissions, on my new web site www.subpowershift.com, from those who I may have missed during the first pass, or those who read this book and wish to make a submission. In a few years I will make all the underlying materials of the project available to the Navy historians at the Navy Yard in Washington, DC. There is considerable redundancy particularly with respect to the issue of division between the crew forward a.k.a. nose coners and the nuclear power trained sailors aft. I have attempted to condense the feelings of both halves of the division.

There are many lengthy quotes lifted from the interviews throughout the book. To avoid the cumbersome acknowledgment using complete names and ranks I simply identified each quote with the appropriate names—I mean no disrespect to rank, it is just easier on the reader.

Here is a list of those principals interviewed, in chronological order, with their proper ranks:

-Rear Admiral Chuck Grojean, USN Ret. Held at his office at The Pacific War Museum in Fredericksburg, Texas on 8–29–02

-Command Master Chief Jeff VanBlaracum—Sub Squadron Three
In my office in Santa Fe October 19, 2002

-Capt. Bob Gautier, USN Ret. Held on 2–21–03 in his wine room at his home in San Diego. My brother Paul, a retired Rear Admiral—fighter pilot—was present.

-Vice Admiral Pat Hannifin, USN Ret. Held on 2–21–03 at his home in Solana Beach, CA.

-Vice Admiral Chuck Griffiths, USN Ret. Held at the Army Navy Country Club, Arlington, VA on 3–5–03.

-Admiral Jim Watkins, USN Ret. Held at his office at the U.S. Commission on Ocean Policy in Washington, DC. on 3–6–03.

-Rear Admiral Dave Oliver, USN Ret. Held in the lobby of my hotel in Alexandria, VA on 3–5–03.

-Rear Admiral Mike Barr, USN Ret. Held at his home in Santa Fe, NM, on 4–25–03.

-Capt. Don Walsh, USN Ret. Held at my home in Santa Fe, NM October 2004

Each interview was transcribed and sent to the person interviewed for review and editing. It was their chance to add or eliminate words and to clean up and polish the transcript. I found that several of them chose to eliminate statements critical of fellow officers, even though the criticism was well earned. While I can understand why someone would not wish to hurt the feelings of a fellow submariner or his family, it does not advance the quest for good honest history, so that was a bit disappointing, but it was their call which I honored. In one case of an officer not interviewed, I was sent a section of a memoir with the condition that nothing negative could be said about another submariner! I happen to like this fellow very much, so I simply responded that, for his peace of mind, I would use no portion of his memoir. Apparently there is some unwritten code of civility among the naval officer corps that discourages saying anything bad, however true, about another. The fact is that we submariners have had some bad leaders among the many excellent COs who served in the submarine force. My suspicion is that we submariners have faired better than other arms of the services in this respect.

I did not check each statement in each interview for accuracy, but I am completely comfortable that each person told it the way he remembered. If a reader finds that someone was off a little on a hull number than 'forgive us our trespasses' and just cross it off to 40 year old memories.

My friend Don Walsh, Captain USN (ret), was kind enough to agree to write the Foreword to this book. He is a former diesel boat submariner who began his submarine career on board USS Rasher (SSR 269) and ended as CO of Bashaw (AGSS-241). He has been very supportive of me and this project and, in spite of great subsequent fame as a world renowned ocean explorer, has never lost his interest in, and affection for, the US Submarine Force. For those who may not know or remember, he was Officer In Charge of the Navy's Bathyscaphe Trieste which, on January 23, 1960, submerged to the seafloor at the astounding depth (deepest place on Earth) of 35,800 feet below the Pacific in the Marinas Trench!

There is a subject I must cover here since it involves all the inputs from those interviewed as well as those who made submissions. It is secrecy. This book manages to cover the topic of the transition without revealing things like classified test depths, speeds, operations and the like. In fact, I don't really know any of that. I do recall, regrettable, how slow my underpowered, two diesel engine submarine was. Its test depth was not classified and common knowledge. I recall my brother Paul commenting, "They don't call them The Silent Service for nothing!" That moniker, by the way had nothing to do with noisy submarines. What it refers to is the reticence to say anything outside the crew which could have the remotest possibility of providing information which could endanger another submariner. I found it interesting to note that even though I am a former submariner, no one in all the interviews and all the many submissions, ever volunteered something classified—not one. Keep in mind the Cold War is over, the Russian submarines can't get out of their own way; much less pose a threat to our Navy. It would be easy, now that the Cold War is over, to rationalize mentioning a collision with a Soviet submarine for example, or a near-nuclear accident averted by an attentive crew or, more currently reveal who we are now surveiling and whose coastal waters we are patrolling. The code of silence is apparently deeply embedded in us all. I think we are unique in this respect and, while it does not serve "history" well, I agree with the policy and assume future historians will sort it all out with the help of the Freedom of Information Act.

Tom Clancy's best seller, *Hunt for Red October,* caused quite a stir in Washington and in the submarine community when it was released. I'm sure many thought that someone spilled his guts to the author. That may be true, I'll never know. What I suspect is that he was smart and for the most part, simply put two and two together for the book. The other book, which was not fiction, made an even bigger stir—*Blind Man's Bluff*—which was far more revealing with respect to how nuclear-power submarines operated against the Soviets in the Cold War. There were submariners at the time with whom I had contact that were furious with whoever talked to the two authors. Many of us got chummy e-mails from them. You will see later in Jim Watkins's interview where he infers that those authors only scratched the surface. I am certain that is true.

There is another element that I experienced personally, and that is a quality of many nineteen and twenty year old men. They are bullet proof—immortal. For submariners I suspect this is in large measure due to their extraordinary training, self confidence and experience. They sometimes don't even know they are in real danger, so confident they are in their submarine and their fellow crew members. I remember feeling very, very safe on my submarine during the three years I lived on it. It seems ironic and very strange in retrospect, since we did Cold War operations in a modified fleet boat with only two main engines.

I realized this not long ago. My brothers and I wrote a book about our experiences at sea, my part was about life on a diesel boat. An old shipmate e-mailed me and said, "I can't believe you did not even mention the time we nearly got run over by a Russian tanker. Remember, we were in a big storm (and in a bad place), at periscope depth, Sonar could hear him; we could hardly see anything, when the guy on the periscope yelled out, "Holy shit!" The ship was close and closing so fast that the OD ordered us deep and he lost control of the dive. The stern was at well over 600 feet with a huge up angle." (Our test depth was just over 400 feet). I responded that I honestly forgot the incident. *Forgot the incident!* Now, at age 66, the mental picture scares the hell out of me. I believe that probably there are many hairy stories which have been forgotten simply because we, at age twenty and highly trained, didn't consider them a threat. No big deal...'What's tonight's movie, anyway?' (See Ditty Bag for related stories—Test Depth)

Reading the manuscript of this book gives me a great deal of satisfaction because it has captured for submarine history an important transitional period which, it appears, was not being recorded. None of the principals of the transition whom I interviewed indicated that they had already been approached. In fact every one of them was excited about the project, saw the need and timeliness of the interviews and was happy to accommodate me. Indeed, each one suggested I interview some friend or contemporary as well. The idea that some historian, fifty years from now, would attempt to write down what we thought about the transition and what it meant was appalling to me. Since historians gather their information and draw their conclusions from memoirs and other pieces their subjects write, I feel, as I suggested above, they would have a difficult time with members of the Silent Service since they tend not to write about themselves.

Are you crazy?

"I saw the submariners, the way they stood aloof and silent, watching their pig boat with loving eyes. They are alone in the Navy. I admired the PT boat boys. And I often wondered how the aviators had the courage to go out day after day and I forgave their boasting. But the submariners! In the entire fleet they stand apart!"
James Michener—*Tales of the South Pacific*

Hanging in my office is a WWII recruiting poster of a sailor, white hat cocked back and an understandable grin on his face with a beautiful ruby lipped brunette reminiscent of a 1940s movie star, in his arms. Back then the dolphins were embroidered on the lower right sleeve which cannot be seen in the poster, so what distinguishes him as a submariner is the war patrol pin the gorgeous brunette is fondling admiringly. The artist's tongue was, no doubt, firmly touching the inside of his cheek. Neither I nor any shipmate ever got within a heevie throw of anyone looking like her. Across the bottom it says, "He volunteered for submarine service." The implication seems to be that while you had about a one in four chance of dying with all your shipmates, you'd at least do well with the ladies if you got back! I can't help smiling every time I look at it.

Surely there are as many stories about why and under what circumstances submariners volunteered for sub duty as there are members of the "silent service" itself. Everyone has one and most of them are amusing and my guess is that those stories from diesel boat sailors do not differ much from those of nuclear power sailors. All submariners from the very beginning have been volunteers.

In my bond trading business we have our own language. When one of us wishes to reveal something personal or some business secret to another we say, "I'm going to lift my skirts a little." Well, here goes.

A year or so ago Barbara, my wife of 44 years, and I had an argument which she attributed to the fact that I was depressed. My response was, "Of course I'm a little depressed. Hell, I'm Irish for God's sake!" So, to end the argument, I extended the olive branch and agreed to go to a lady psychiatrist friend of hers to, presumably, be declared certifiably sane. Or at least that was my hope. I sat in this lady's office facing her in a straight backed chair and I began to smile and I said, "You know doctor, the last time I saw a psychiatrist was when I volunteered for submarine duty. You see the Navy immediately sent anyone who volunteered for subs to the base hospital shrink. Evidentially the Navy assumed you had to be crazy to volunteer for such duty. We all thought the practice was very funny. In fact it is one of the great inside jokes among submariners." Anyway, this doctor was fascinated with why we liked living on subs and who volunteered for this stuff and we spent the rest of the hour discussing nothing else. I was finally let out with her assurance that I was not crazy, a fact which I immediately cell-phoned Barbara from the parking lot.

Ron Gorance from San Diego (*Razorback, Bashaw, Swordfish, Tang, and Sabalo*) submitted a funny story. Here is the beginning of it:

The U.S. Military came up in the discussion somehow, and I mumbled something about my personal history. 'Submarines? You were on submarines?' He squinted and looked directly into my eyes, pausing like he was trying to plumb the soul of a Martian, and stumbled on, 'Don't you get...ah, y'know, ah . . takes guts, . . I could never do that.'

Did he say nuts, or guts? Either way, my habitual response was, 'It's not so bad. You get used to it. Yeah, claustrophobia could be a problem.

This *Deja vu* conversation happens at Christmas parties and during short airplane flights—anywhere abbreviated autobiographies are expected. It's eventually been part of every one of my permanent relationships. Afterward, I always think, 'I wish I'd said . .,' but then I shrug, 'They could never understand.'

The problem is, he or she, seconds ago, was trading polite grins with an apparently-normal human being; suddenly, it dawns: Normal humans do not sink themselves in a sewer pipe and then materialize on a far shore grinning because it came back to the surface. It is quite natural to wonder whether insanity is a main prerequisite for, or the result of, becoming a submariner.

Further on in his submission he added;

Selection of "volunteers" begins with psychological testing: claustrophobia tests, personality tests, academic tests, intelligence tests, Rorschach tests, interviews, consultations and interrogations. They asked why I had a tattoo. 'Because I had eight hours of freedom from boot camp, four dollars, and two beers.'Right answer! Most of us who made it through screening agreed that they had rejected everyone who had passed, and kept the nuts.

Physical examinations were intended to eliminate candidates over six-foot-four or two-hundred pounds; they could not have flat feet, and needed 20–20 vision. I memorized the eye chart when the guy in front of me read it aloud; we both missed the same two letters on the bottom line and we both passed. I leave flat-footed footprints like a duck's, and I've known many giants riding the boats. As with the headshrinkers' psychological criteria, failing wasn't necessarily failing. The physical was more like the final exam of the psychological testing: those who managed to show innovation and resourcefulness were passed on to sub school. From the late thirties through the eighties, a few men slipped through who were exactly what the silent service needed. I hope things have not changed.

I was looking through my copy of my Service Record recently to determine when I got qualified (6 June 1959), when I came across the form I signed volunteering me for Submarine Duty. I had completely forgotten we had to actually sign a form. It is remarkable for its language.

"In accordance with Art, C-7404 BUPERS Manuel, subject's (me) training is not considered completed upon graduation from U.S. Naval Submarine School. Therefore, he is ineligible for transfer from Submarine Duty until he becomes "Qualified in Submarines" or for a period of twelve months from the date of first reporting to an active duty submarine, whichever is earlier. <u>However, should he be declared environmentally unadaptable for submarine duty, the foregoing restriction will not apply.</u>"

I was under the impression that such obfuscatory language was invented much later than 1959!

In the first interview I asked Chuck Grojean why he volunteered.

CG: "Oh, I thought about it when I was a plebe with the Naval Academy in 1942. I became acquainted with submarines shortly after entering the Naval Academy, and I like the idea of a small command, I like the idea of attaining a command earlier than I would have in the surface fleet, and I really preferred it to flying because I wanted a significant command, other than just to command my own airplane.

But you know, Dan, I really believe that the idea of a ship being submerged under the water with a small group of men has got a greater appeal, probably, than say the technical aspect. The technical aspects of nuclear power, of course, have some appeal, but I believe that it's far overshadowed by the—a real naval officer will want a command, he wants the camaraderie, and he likes the idea of the excitement of being in a submerged vehicle, whether it's diesels or nuclear.

DG: So when did you get out of submarine school, probably in '46, '47?

CG: Well, when I graduated from the Naval Academy, my eyes wouldn't permit me to go into submarines. They wouldn't take me. So I did three years in destroyers and then I honswaggled my way into submarines.

Here was a highly successful submarine warrior and he wanted sub duty so badly that he had to "honswaggle" his way in.

I asked Dave Oliver the same question and he had a completely different and serendipitous response.

"I volunteered for submarine duty because it paid hazardous duty pay, which at the time was equal to half of a young officer's base pay. At the time, you had to walk about a thousand yards from your room down to the Battalion office to indicate your selection, and I intended to be a Marine when I left my room at the Naval Academy. I was walking along with my company officer, who was a lieutenant commander—which is a very senior rank, and the holder a "god-like" figure when you're a midshipman. The company officer, who was a destroyer officer, said, you don't want to be a Marine. You don't want to be doing pushups when you're 50. And I said, "You're right, okay, I'll go into destroyers." And he said, "No, I think this nuclear power thing is going to work, and they pay you more money." And I said, "Okay." And I signed the sheet that said 'Nuclear Power Volunteer.'"

Jim Watkins was my XO on Barbero. *I of course asked him the same question about why he volunteered. Remember this is from a man who became Chief of Naval Operations (CNO)!*

'I'd been aboard a submarine on a midshipman cruise when I was in the Naval Academy, and it was the worst thing I've ever experienced because we lost air conditioning and we slept in each other's sweat on bunks—leather bunks—for about two or three days. And I said, I'll never get into submarines. Forget it. Of course, that was on one of the old boats. And later when I was on the destroyer U.S.S. *Fechteler*, right out of the Naval Academy, after I was there two years a classmate of mine who was in the First Lieutenant's Department, as I was. I was back on the fantail one day and he was back on the fantail of his destroyer next door. We were getting underway in a nest of destroyers, backing out of San Diego, heading for the Far East for the Korean War. So he yelled over to me, "Watkins, you sucker, I'm getting out of this Mickey Mouse outfit. I'm going to submarine school in January." So I said, 'You sonofabitch, I'm going to apply for submarines today', so I did. I went up to the office; got a first class yeoman that was a good friend of mine. I said, "Get me an application. I want to go to submarine school as fast as I can go, see if I can beat out my classmate over there." And, sure enough, I got orders and he was deferred for six months. So I went before he did to submarine school. So my motivation was a little bit different than many others.

Pat Hannifin further advanced my theory that every one of us has a different story.

PH: At the Naval Academy, and when I was a first classman the system of assigning you to a service within the Navy was a lottery system. You drew numbers. There were 800 and some in my class graduated. I drew a number 12. This was the Class of '45, graduating in June of '44. Anyway, so I figured on a submarine, a smaller ship, you wouldn't get lost as an Ensign on a big ship. You'd be given some responsibility early, and on a big ship, a carrier or a battleship or a cruiser, you're just another ensign. And it turned out that's exactly what happened. So I volunteered. Never been on a submarine before. Came from the horse cavalry in New Mexico [laughter]. And—literally, New Mexico Military Institute. Then to the Naval Academy, and hadn't even seen salt water.

DG: Well, neither did Nimitz.

PH: No, that's right. He came out of Fredericksburg, Texas. This was 1944. The war was on, and that was the other reason I wanted to go into submarines. Because I wanted to be in a submarine in wartime.

Right out of the Naval Academy, they sent all of us through aviation indoctrination at Jacksonville. Left there, got married in Roswell, went to San Diego, and was assigned to an "S" boat here in San Diego. "S" boats were built between 1917 and 1924. Leaked like hell at 150 feet—test depth, 200 feet, and—well, that was when they were new. [Laughter] And so I wasn't quite sure that I'd made the right decision, but this was before submarine school because submarine school didn't start till September. There were about 125 of our class who went directly into submarines.

Went to submarine school after the "S" boat, and it was from September till December, came out to the Pacific, made three war patrols on the USS *Balao* SS-285. The *Balao*, which is the boat that they have the sail and all that at the Washington Naval Yard. 285 was the first thick-skin boat. First of a class. I think we may have had a test depth of maybe three or four hundred feet, something like that. But any rate, it was thick-skin. First patrol, up in the Yellow Sea, deepest water 225 feet. Got depth-charged the hell out of us, the boat's 312 feet long, and we had 225 feet of water, and so it was also my first patrol, so another time when I thought, 'I'm not quite sure I'm in the right service.' [Laughs] Anyway, that was my first wartime experience.

Here is Chuck Griffith's unique response…'for the food!'

"Really, what made me do it was listening to these COs that came back (from the Pacific War) to talk to the midshipmen. They gave lectures to the midshipmen en route to new construction. And quite a few of the skippers were moving around because we were building submarines very fast then and in large numbers, and they were moving the guys off the old boats and on to new ones. And I had the chance to hear a couple of those talks, and was very much impressed with them. The fact that they were the least regulation, that they were extremely informal, that they worked hard when they had to and they played hard when they had a chance to play. And they ate better than anybody in the Navy. Well, those three things to me were sellers. I just thought, you know, this is the way to go, and so I put in for submarines and at that time they took about 100 of my classmates—right into submarines from graduation. We were the last class to do that in those days, and the next class behind us had to go to sea for two years before they could put in for submarines. So we ended up being the junior guys onboard for a long time because they didn't crank out any people to relieve us for a couple of years. So we had a large group that went right to submarine training and graduated from submarine training at the end of '45 and went to our first submarines. But that's what made me go.

DG: I've asked everybody that same question, and it's interesting to hear the responses. You're the first one who said the food was better. It really was. No question. We had great food.

CG: That was a seller. That was a big one. Well, the other one I liked was the informality, and I liked the idea of working hard because I believe in working hard, too, when there's work to do. But I also like to have fun, and those all sounded like real winners to me.

Bob Gautier's story "…finally, after three years I finally got in."

BG: Well, when I first got out of the Naval Academy, I actually put in for flying because my number was too low to get into submarines. In other words, we knew that one out of four would go to submarines, but my number was about five hundred and something. So I decided I'd go into aviation, which I really didn't want to do. And then finally, after three years, I finally got in submarines.

DG: So you were a black shoe, (on surface ships)?

BG: A destroyer to start with and then a DE, the *Fieberling*, and then I got in submarines. I went to sub school in '48, graduated in '48 and went to Pearl and went to the *Tilefish*. Which is now long gone, but that was the oldest submarine in the Pacific at the time. Fleet boat, yeah, 307. And so then I stayed in Pearl and got on the *Tang*, but before going to sub school I went to the *Halfbeak*, and my first skipper was Gene Flucky (famous submarine CO during WWII).

And he said, You know how to dive a submarine? I said, No. He said, You get up there; when I say dive the boat, you say, See that button over there? He said, Push that button. And I said, Okay, that sounds reasonable enough. But during the war, when the diving alarm went, the vents opened. They didn't wait till the second blast. And so I was up there and I pushed that button the first Aooga, and then that water came in.

DG: You heard the vents!

BG: The next one was a short Aooga, and I was down that hatch. But that was my first dive on a submarine, with Gene Flucky, and I spent two months doing that before going to sub school.

DG: Since you were on destroyers, could you describe any differences in the esprit or élan of the submarine crews versus the destroyers?

BG: Yep, I got on...I guess it was the *Halfbeak*. We dove and the Main Induction was left open. We got a lot of water, and the chief engineer told Gene Flucky, he said, 'We got some water in the engine room,' and Flucky says, 'Okay, pump it out'. And I thought, 'By God, this was for me!'. [Laughter] Because these guys, you know, they didn't make a big to-do about this thing.

DG: A stuck open Main Induction!?

BG: He was smart, though. I mean, he was good. He was good and I was fortunate to serve with him, and so I've got all of his books—<u>Thunder Below</u>. But then I got out of sub school and I went to the *Tilefish* with Ben Jarvis. I think he made 13 or 14 patrols. He was a big guy. He was about 6–6; he had a 54-inch chest, and I'd come down the hatch and he'd stand right behind me at the dive station and I'd do something wrong, and he'd take that fist, just about a six-inch punch, you know? I'd buckle. He'd say, 'You didn't do that right.' But he was a good guy. I mean, these guys, I was fortunate to go to sea with them. They were real good skippers—they were good ones.

Don Walsh's decision to volunteer was a three cushion pool shot. He wanted to fly but his eyesight stopped that, then it was UDT but his boss talked him out of it. He is further proof of my position that there are as many stories about volunteering for submarines as there have been submariners.

DW: I grew up in the San Francisco Bay Area in the 30's and 40's. From as far back as I can remember I was an airplane nut. While in high school I was in the

Civil Air Patrol and the Air Scouts. When barely old enough I enlisted in the Naval Air Reserve joining VA-62A at NAS Oakland. I became an aircrewman on Avenger torpedo bombers. All our pilots had seen action in WWII and the squadron was a pretty relaxed military organization. Really exciting for a high school kid who barely had a drivers license. All of this fed an intense desire to become a career naval aviator. Annapolis seemed to be the way to do this and I got an appointment through the Naval Reserve.

When I graduated with the Class of 1954, my dream ended. My eyes were no longer good enough to pass the flight physical. It was a real blow; flying was the only thing I had wanted to do in my life. I had no "plan B"...

In those days, we all had to serve two years in the fleet before going into the specialized branches of the Navy: aviation or submarines. The idea was for the new officer to get needed seagoing experience and become qualified as a watch-stander.

My first ship was the Long Beach based *Mathews* (AKA-96) a combat cargo ship in the Amphibious Forces Pacific Fleet. It was good duty and I learned a lot of practical seamanship. We spent a lot of time at sea and the learning curve was steep. Within a year I was the navigator.

Despite great duty for a new naval officer, I knew this is not where I wanted to spend too much of my Navy career. While in Amphibious School at Coronado I had seen the UDT people training around the base. Hoisting a few beers with some of them at the O Club, I learned a bit about what they did. Clearly this was an elite small unit organization. That appealed to me. Also I had started sport diving at this time and thought it would be great to do diving as part of my 'day job'.

After I had been aboard Mathews for about a year, I talked with my captain, Vincent Meola, about volunteering for UDT. He was a real mentor, seeing that I got thoroughly trained as a ship handler and department head. I respected his views and when he strongly discouraged me from asking for UDT training, I gave up on it. He was right. At that time it was not the career path that special warfare is today.

While we were deployed to WESTPAC in '56 I had the opportunity to visit a guy from the class of '52 who had command of a minesweeper at Yokosuka. He was barely a lieutenant but was captain of his own ship. That really appealed to me but I was not sure how far that career path would go. The Korean War was over and it seemed the need for this type of ship was decreasing.

As for submarines, while at the Academy I cannot recall ever having much information or 'recruiting' pressure about this part of the Navy. This was not the case with naval aviation, Marines or the Air Force (West Point and Annapolis furnished officers to the USAF in the years before their academy was up and running). We even had something called "Aviation Summer" about half way through our four years. The "silent service" was just that. And if a submarine visited Annapolis during my four years, I don't remember it. For me it was an unknown part of the Navy. Sure I was aware of their operational history during WWII but that had ended nearly 10 years before.

Now about half way through my deployment on Mathews I had given up on UDT and the Mine Force. Navy air was not possible and that left the Submarine Service. I volunteered and was accepted for the submarine school class that started in the summer of 1956. I had never even been inside a sub and knew little about what this new life would be like. It was a small-unit, elite organization and that was good enough at this point in my career. Fortuitously, I had backed into what was to become the greatest experience of my seagoing life.

Finally, I am going to give my reason for volunteering for submarine duty. It was mostly what I did not want. I did not want to be ordinary—some black gang swabby out in the fleet—I wanted to be something special like my big brothers. My first choice was UDT (Underwater Demolition Team). However, when I was told that I would have to extend my enlistment by several years, I chose submarines. My room mate at NAPS (Naval Academy Prep School) was a submariner I'll never forget—Third Class Electrician named Jim Stewart. Because of his regaling me with his many colorful sea stories about submarine duty, that was my choice. It was one of the best decisions of my life.

Sub Culture

"The submarines are all we have left. Your crews are more valuable than anything else. Bring them back." Cdr. Stuart Murray to squadron submarine skippers, December 8, 1941 aboard the sub tender *Holland* in the Philippines.
(From *Silent Victory* by Clay Blair)

In order to make comparisons between the cultures of diesel and nuclear power sailors there has to be a description of just what the diesel culture was like. It is also important to recognize that what changes have occurred have taken place gradually. The entire crews of the early nuclear powered submarines came out of diesel boats. Over time the infusion of officers and crew straight out of Nuclear Power School, with no diesel experience, grew. Master Chief Jeff Van-Blaracum in his interview talked about some chiefs he worked for who were diesel boaters and that was about 1988. This was the time frame when the last of the diesel boaters had any influence on the nuke culture.

The now aging diesel boat community will hopefully be amused by, but will learn little from, this portion of the book since they all know the culture first hand. In fact they frequently talk about the subject on the internet submarine sites. With the exception of a hand full of very senior chiefs, the nuclear community has had no exposure to the old diesel culture. It is my hope that the current nuclear power personnel will enjoy this section and be able to see a little deeper into their roots. It may also explain why some of their culture is the way it is.

Part of the submarine culture stems from the fact that they are small and most often alone. Only in recent years have battle groups had submarines attached and even those are a small portion of the current submarine forces. In the case of *Barbero* and most all the diesel boats in my memory, we were always by ourselves. That is a formula for less homogeneity and more independence.

I am a big Patrick O'Brien fan and I recall an appropriate quote out of his novel, *Post Captain*, "All ships were to some degree separate kingdoms with different customs and different atmosphere: This was particularly true of those that were on detached service or much by themselves, far from their admirals and the rest of the fleet." This, incidentally, is true for both diesels and nukes.

Don Walsh

I believe that circumstances shape culture. In the submarine navy it was all independent duty. Really independent…As somebody once told me, "Once you pass the sea buoy, there's nobody behind you to tell you what to do". There's no station zero over there at the center of the formation saying there's a guy without a white hat on your deck or that you've got spilt fuel on the side of your hull. You're all by yourself. And most of the time you were required to make your transits undetected. You didn't want anyone else around you unless that was part of your mission.

So there was a premium on self-reliance and a compulsion to 'do the mission'. If something busted and you couldn't fix it that was it. You couldn't borrow a part from the next ship over in the formation. When you left port you had better have all you needed on board.

You did not ever want to be responsible for aborting a mission. Every member of the crew made sure that his equipment was operational and if it went down then the parts were on board to repair it. That sense of interdependence is a lot stronger in submarines than it is in other parts of the Navy. If you had to leave a station, and nobody could cover for you, then you may have gapped a very important mission. Nobody wanted to let down the team; it was a matter of pride. We all know of stories where submarines just sucked it in and kept on station even with some pretty serious casualties. Not life-threatening, but certainly limiting the ability of a sub to perform to full capability. But the jobs got done. So the nature of submarine operations was the "circumstance" and our culture derived from that.

There are several topics which are peculiar to and in some ways define diesel boat sailors. These particular topics are repeatedly referred to—often humorously—by those interviewed or who submitted comments and anecdotes.

Liberty Ports—My friend Ron Martini—a nuke—thought the biggest distinction was that diesel boats "were allowed into more heinous ports". He is correct! Diesel boats basically pulled into any port where they were not likely to run aground. On Barbero we once pulled into Mazatlan, Mexico, a Pacific Coast port south of Acapulco. At the time Mazatlan had not evolved into the trendy, jet set beach resort town it is today. Rather it was a large, sleepy village which had never been visited by a submarine, nor probably any other Navy ship. I say this with confidence because, as a lookout, I observed that a number of the channel buoys' anchor chains had rusted through and the buoys were washed up on the channel edges. Entering that 'port' was an adventure in ship handling. Surely no larger ship would have attempted it. Apart from sport fishing boats we were the only vessel in the port. A minimum of 50 Mexicans stood on the pier and stared at us night and day for the three days we were there, a reflection of the oddness of the submarine and the fact that they apparently had nothing at all to occupy their time.

To give an idea of the informality on a diesel boat, on one liberty six of us went sail fishing and we went ashore in dungarees.

The town's half dozen cabs all lined up quayside ready to take sailors to, as my Irish grandparents would have referred, "a house of ill repute"—apparently one of the basic occupations of the town other than standing on piers.

My friend from Torpedo School and Sub School, Gene Benton, told me of the time his submarine—*Bluegill* SSK 242—was sent to Tahiti. Two days out when the locals revolted against the French rule, they were re-routed to American Samoa (my heart bleeds). They were the only Navy ship there and it was a scene right out of *Mister Roberts* or *South Pacific*. They went ashore in whites and immediately discovered that wonderful South Sea garment—the lava lava. Webster's definition—"The principal garment for both sexes in Polynesia...printed cloth worn as a skirt". Or as Gene called it, "a wrap around table cloth which could be used as a beach blanket or other things which we will not discuss." Everyone bought one and put them on! I am confident that there was no Shore Patrol there, as there were none in Mazatlan or any other small port. The mental picture of a bunch of submariners in Popeye white tops and lava-lava bottoms and flip flops on liberty in Samoa is almost (but not quite) more than one can bear!

I just attempted to Google the Yokosuka Kanko Hotel and, sadly, it no longer exists or it is too disreputable to be listed along with the swell hotels now in the city. That hotel was the center of many "ship's parties". My friend Don Walsh recently disabused me of the notion that officers did not have fun at such occasions. He, at 75 or so has vivid memories of the parties. I am tempted to use the word 'legendary' parties.

We would simply book a couple floors for a few days, each with his own room, and have a 72 hour party. Until that time I did not know there were 72 hour parties—ever—anywhere. Welcome to the diesel boat submarine service! Every room came with a thin cotton bathrobe (kimono) with the hotel name printed all over it—it turned out to be the uniform of the day. We never took them off—well, almost never.

In Japan in the 50s and early 60s the economy was not robust so there were kids who would, for a tip, run errands. The first liberty ashore was the first opportunity to get your blues cleaned of "eau de diesel boat" along with one's body, so after disrobing and getting a 'hotsi bath', some kid would tare down an alley with the set of blues and get them cleaned and pressed in time for the end of the bath and massage process. We never left the ship's party because there were these kids ready to fetch food and booze.

Liberty in Yokosuka was the best I ever experienced. Hong Kong was way too big and you were not likely to run into shipmates or other submariners. In 'Yoko' as we called it, the town was smaller and more condensed. Most of the bars we frequented were in "Black Market Alley". The surface sailors had their bars, the Marines had theirs. In fact I found the Marine hangout by accident. Walking down some street I heard the sound of bag pipes coming out of a closed door without a name...leave it to the Marines to have a nameless bar. My brother Bob, a sea going Marine, sent me a postcard when he heard I was going to WestPac which contained only a quote from Kipling:

Ship me somewheres east of Suez, where the best is like the worst,
Where there aren't no Ten Commandments an' a man can raise a thirst;

I recall whenever we got hungry at "Bar Atomic" (no pun here, really. It's where all the submariners went!), we would get another kid to run to an unknown restaurant for food we simply ate at the bar. My favorite was a large bowl of *yake soba*…my spell check just locked up.

Not all "liberty" was in ports. Below is a picture taken about 1958 during a party on Barbero off Mexico's Pacific coast. I can't recall the reason for the party, but we came to all stop, brought food up and the crew did some skits. In this picture "Doc" Hosea is on the right, our cook—the hilarious—P. B. Spinny is in the center and the author is on the left playing his uke.

Pat Hannifin's interview is a classic, this portion relates to liberty ports:

PH: I took the first submarine around Cape Horn. From Panama we took the Sea Robin down the west coast of South America, around the Horn, up the East Coast, all the way back to Portsmouth, New Hampshire. We did it in the wintertime, but it was June when we went around the Horn. The first submarine that ever went around the Horn.

DG: Why did they do that?

PH: Well, the skipper liked to go to different places, and we were going back to the shipyard for overhaul, and so he convinced the SUBLANT that this would be a simulated war patrol. [Laughs] We stopped in Colao, in Valparaiso, around the Horn, into Montevideo—oh, the Falkland Islands; we went into the Falkland Islands, the first submarine that had ever been in the Falkland Islands. And then to Montevideo and then up—they wouldn't let us stop in Rio. We wanted to, but went all the way around to Trinidad, I think, and then bounced on up to the Bahamas

DG: What was liberty like in the Falklands?!

PH: It was fun. I'll tell you, it's like going into the Hebrides. Houses are built of rock, thatched roofs, a bunch of sheep. And they had a big party for us in the Grange—what we would call the Grange Hall. It was dancing and all that sort of thing. It was fun. We went goose shooting down on one of the islands. It was interesting.

Chuck Griffiths was CO of Wahoo. A part of his interview also talked about infor-mality and liberty ports on the diesel boats. His submarine was rewarded to basically a month to motor around the South Pacific and do what they wanted.

Here are Chuck Griffith's warm memories of his last diesel boat. Read his first sentence carefully. It is hard not to be infected by his enthusiasm for his diesel boat experiences.

Wahoo was just absolutely the greatest thing that could ever have happened to me. I only had it a year because I got called back for interview and went to nuclear power training. But for the year that I had it we were at sea most of the time. After we got out of the yard we did a shakedown cruise to Tahiti, if you can imagine that. That was just wonderful. And then we came back from that and had a few days in port in Pearl Harbor and we took off for West Pac. We ended up with a seven month cruise instead of a six month cruise because we won a contest. It was a contest to see who could come up with more money for the Seventh Fleet stadium gate at the Naval Academy (they were building the new stadium at the Naval Academy in those days.) And it was a contest between the commander of Seventh Fleet and the Sixth Fleet as to who was going to get the most money in.

DG: Where were they getting the money?

CG: The sailors. So we felt that there was a good bet there, so we kicked in twenty bucks apiece and that won for us, and—it was a per capita thing—we won and our prize was a trip to Australia. Well, we capped this West Pac trip with a trip to Australia and, of course, the West Pac trip was special. We hit everything, Singapore and Manila and we had interesting operations and a great special op and it was really great. And then we finished it off with a month in Australia, or what it amounted to an extra month on the trip counting transit time. Great, just a wonderful tour. I got back and very shortly thereafter was sent off to nuclear power training.

On Barbero we seldom docked with the rest of the submarines while in foreign ports. We had a hanger just aft of the sail with two nuclear tipped Regulus missiles and the Navy did not wish to advertise the fact. So, they would put us in the most remote, out of sight pier in the port. We considered this a plus because we had nobody looking over our shoulders. Along side a submarine tender or across a pier from a cruiser everyone had to be in uniform, white hat and all. Protocol, saluting and the rest did not exist in our remote part of the port. We had volleyball nets set up ten yards away from the brow. Mel "Greek" Reader, our Chief cook always managed to scrounge some half 55 gallon drum barbecue pits over which we cooked steaks. That was the first realization that nuclear anything—boats or weapons—were more often than not unwelcome around the world. Even as Steven Patterson relates below, that applied to the United States as well.

Steven Ray Patterson
RMC (SS)
SSBN-655B, USS Grayback SS-574, USS Barbel SS-580, USS Los Angeles SSN-688
1974–1991

Having served on all types of submarines I much prefer the diesel boat. The crews are smaller and much closer knit than the nukes. I had spent 4 years in the surface navy before I went to submarines so I had the opportunity to experience both sides and there is truly no comparison. No one joins for 20 years but I stayed for almost 24 one hitch after another. The submarine service was not as "military" as the surface fleet but they were much more professional in my opinion. The true benefit of the diesel boat is that it can dock anywhere. We don't carry nuke weapons although we are capable, and we do not have a nuclear reactor. When an SSN visit's San Francisco, CA, they must dock at NAS Alameda whereas the *Barbel* tied up right down town within walking distance from Fisherman's Wharf. This ability alone gives them a huge advantage over the nuke boats when it comes to showing the flag and interacting with the local populace in a much more personal way. We could run tours on our boat wherever we were docked and it was always a huge success. We all made many new friends wherever we pulled in. In Lahina, Maui we'd have to anchor out but that did not stop all of the yachts and cruise boats in port from coming along side in a dingy and asking for tours. We gave them a tour of our boat and they gave us a tour of there yacht, a really nice exchange.

Color and élan—I am sure there is ample color on today's nuclear power submarines. In fact one of the funniest submariners I know was on the nukes—Glen Kieffer (see Ditty Bag). But in general I think that diesel boat sailors had a little more time and enjoyed an atmosphere of less rigidity and formality and pulled more liberty than their brothers on the nukes.

The Pearl Harbor Submarine Base in the 50's and 60's had two types of sailors—married and single. Those married usually, but not always, preferred to be in port with their wives and families and those single who, nearly always, preferred to be in WestPac and its exotic, fleshpot ports of call. So, upon arrival back in Pearl Harbor, those hard core single guys (who had gone a little Asiatic in my view and were for the most part Navy lifers) would walk down the piers asking which boat was shortly bound back to WestPac. When they found the candidate, they simply went aboard in an effort to find a married counterpart of the same rate who wanted to stay ashore in Pearl. After a little paperwork and the nod from the COB he packed his sea bag. It amazed me at the time and still amazes me that this was done so casually and with such ease and simplicity on submarines. While this was very commonly done while I was on *Barbero* in Pearl Harbor, I can not imagine it happening now. For one thing boomers typically go out and come back to the same home port and fast attacks don't usually hit the 'fleshpot' ports. Or, that is my understanding. My guess is that with the economic boom in the Pacific Rim, there are far fewer 'flesh pot' ports of call than there were in the late 1950s.

I chose to put this submission under the 'color' category for obvious reasons. This submission is the direct result of Mike McLane telling me—a former TM2—a 'torpedoman joke' with the usual knuckle dragger connotations. They are the 'Polish jokes' of the submarine community and, of course, anachronistic now since no one on a submarine is stupid and the TM rate no longer exists. Here is the joke just for the record:

Torpedoman Class C school

"Good morning gentlemen. My name is Koskowaniwitz, TM-1 and the title of dis course is "Basic Hand tools for the Torpedoman" Moves to table holding many large tools, picking them up as he describes them
"Dis is a 36 inch crescent wrench." (dropping loudly on the table) Holding another aloft
"Dis is a 48 inch monkey wrench" (dropping Loudly on the table)
Holding another aloft—"Dis is a 10 pound maul" (dropping loudly on the table)
Waving his hand over the three tools—"Dees tools may be used interchangeably"

Torpedomen have always been my favorites since one time in Pearl Harbor, at night, and the Division Commander decided to pull an intrusion drill and didn't bother to advise anybody on the ship who could have taken actions for safety purposes.

Here is the story: Our small arms petty officer (TM2 Luke Congelton) had the duty, it was about 2000, and he had just finished cleaning one of the Thompson submachine guns. He was storing it in the small arms locker which, on SS 565, was located at the base of the bridge access ladder in control. He heard a noise of somebody coming down the ladder, turned, and saw somebody coming down all dressed in black (more than a little unusual in Hawaii).

Luke pulled the Thompson out of the locker, slammed in a magazine and racked the bolt back. As the man turned around at the bottom of the ladder, Luke stuck the muzzle into his nose (or tried to). The guy raised his hands so fast he broke one finger on a ladder rung.

First thing I knew of it, Luke was marching him into the forward battery shouting, "Mr. McLane, I caught this guy trying to get aboard." I stuck my head out of the wardroom and saw them coming toward me with the guy in the lead, hands still up and banging off various pipes, valves, and lights. The Thompson was at the base of his skull and the bolt was still fully back. (I couldn't see where the safety was.) I couldn't imagine what 20 rounds of .45 cal would do to the HP Air and hydraulic lines if the gun went off, to say nothing of the back of the guy's head.

Meanwhile, the Division Commander came down the torpedo room hatch ready to gloat over a successful intrusion. (The guy in black had simulated putting the topside watch out of commission so the DivCom wasn't announced as arriving.) The DivCom turned white and froze when he saw what was going on. I had Luke SLOWLY point the Thompson up and insure that the safety was on. Everything "unwound" from there.

Bottom line, torpedomen (and luck) served us well that night. Shortly thereafter they instituted a procedure to INSURE that all small arms were locked up below-decks before running an intrusion drill.

Here is a letter I came across in my "me" file today. It was to my Marine brother Bob who had asked me about flag protocol on submarines. I choose to include it as my contribution on the subject of submarine culture and its occasional irreverence.

"Actually Bob, we dived the boat with the ensign still up! Something about extenuating circumstances. Much like missing Mass while you are on vacation where there is no church. Do you sense the humor here or are you taking me seriously?

"This is true—it never came down at sea. In port the Topside watch, wearing his unloaded .45 cal. Model 1911, would attempt to fold it up and put it in the Conning Tower for use the next day. By comparison, light years from the Marines with respect to ceremony. Let me give you an illustration of us.

"The boat (Barbero) happened to be in Pearl when a change of command took place. Maybe it was SUBPAC. We were required, for the only time in my four years incidentally, to participate. This is highly irregular for a bunch of oil soaked diesel boat sailors, none of whom had stood at attention in years, much less *marched*. The only time we wore whites was chasing ladies on Hotel Street (in Honolulu).

"Anyway, we 'assembled' on the pier next to the boat. 'Assembled' is as close to 'formation', as you Marines call it, as submariners ever get. You know, dressing right and all that shit. So, the OD, or one of the officers—maybe the COB or someone equally unfamiliar with formations, got us going, generally in the same direction. No two heels struck the pavement at the same time as we headed towards the ceremony. I think the movie STRIPES used us as the basis of the screen play. It was hilarious. We were howling with laughter at the absurdity of the situation as we stepped all over the next guy's whites. We knew we had no business marching to this event. Everyone was bull shitting 'in the ranks'—some, as I recall, were even smoking.

"But here is the good news Bob. We were all VERY good at our real jobs—the jobs that mattered—both individually and collectively. The Navy could not have gotten better people to operate our submarine. No way."
Dan

Fresh Water—When I began this project I predicted that the majority of comments and submissions would be about water and not being able to shower. Surprisingly that did not happen. Fresh water availability and the lack of showers is so obvious and imbedded into the subject that most of the diesel sailors failed to mention it.

Here is my recollection of bodily cleanliness aboard a diesel boat—if you will forgive the oxymoron:

No story about life on an old diesel boat would be complete without describing how the hell we kept clean without showers and with almost no water devoted to personal hygiene. The answer is that none of us were very clean—we were all grubby to varying degrees. For perspective purposes, let's put the Yeoman and cooks and officers on one end of the spectrum and Enginemen and Torpedomen on the other. So, as an illustration, I will describe my weekly hygiene routine. Keep in mind that I was probably in the 80th percentile of cleanliness. I was a TM, but I was a pretty clean TM.

I forgot the day of the week, but once a week I went into the little washroom in the forward part of the crew's mess where there was a shower stall filled with stores and two small stainless steel sinks. I'd fill the sink with water, no more than three quarts and wash my hair. Then I stripped and washed my entire body with soap and a wash cloth (in the same water). Next, I shaved off the week's growth (in the same water). By this time, the specific gravity of my three quarts of H_2O

was changed considerably. I'd then drain and refill the sink with the last three quarts of water which I allotted myself and rinsed my hair, face and body and put on a new set of clothing. It was the second best feeling a sailor can have, and was certainly the best feeling one ever got on a submarine! This conservation of precious water on diesel boats was self-imposed. We were the crew of Barbero, we were literally "all in the same boat," and there was no way any of us would jeopardize the safety and well being of the rest by wasting water.

Eau de diesel boat—If you were to be dropped, blind folded, into a bakery or on a freshly mowed lawn, you would know exactly where you were. The aroma is unmistakable and unique. Any diesel boat submariner, regardless of nationality, will remember the 'aroma' of an active diesel boat until he meets his Maker. It permeated everything you had aboard—primarily your clothing. It left the boat with you on liberty or leave. I was oblivious to the sensibilities of the poor person who sat next to me on the several plane trips I took from Pearl Harbor home to LaGuardia. Believe it or not, we all got used to it.

Numerous attempts have been made to describe the smell of a diesel boat, so I hesitate to attempt it here except to at least give the ingredients without proportions. Diesel oil, diesel engine fumes, food cooking, foods baking, accumulating garbage, cigarette smoke, stale cigarette smoke, wet human sweat, old dry human sweat, hot electric motors, bilge water, hydraulic oil, sea water, salt air, battery acid, battery fumes while charging and finally, human waste 'products'. I'm not sure that proportions really mattered. ALL diesel boats smelled the same—exactly the same in fact.

I recall several times being on leave for several weeks—enough time to be completely rid of the smell both on my body and uniform—and returning to the boat. At the head of the pier I could already smell the *Barbero* even through only three small open hatches.

There is another smell that certainly got to me from time to time and that was the diesel exhaust. If you get a bit sick from some diesel FedEx truck at a traffic light, then you'll need to call 911 if you were on the pier when four huge main engines cranked up. Even at sea if you were running with the wind and slower of course, anyone on lookout or on the bridge or cigarette deck would get a heavy dose of diesel exhaust.

The odors on a diesel boat can not be described without a discussion of how we disposed of human waste products.

Sanitary #1 was a large tank inside of the pressure hull that was topped by a pair of stainless steel commodes. There was a lever on the side of each commode which controlled a spool valve in the bottom, along with a sea water valve to help flush. When you finished your business in the head, you had to open the door since you could not otherwise turn around (well, you could turn around with the door closed, but you could not bend at the waist because it was so small in there) and then you'd SLOWLY pull the lever to the spool valve until the holes lined up and everything dropped into the tank.

When the tank was close to full, the man on watch would open a high pressure air valve and put a pressure into the tank until it exceeded the pressure in the surrounding sea water. Naturally, the deeper we were, the more air pressure was necessary. The watch was aided in this by two adjacent pressure gauges—one for the sea and the other for the tank. Having put a pressure in the tank, he then opened a large valve at the bottom of the tank and the air pressure would expel everything into the sea. When he could hear air escaping into the sea, he knew it was empty and would shut the big valve. Only then could he shut off the air valve. This was only the first part of the process—the 'rewarding' part lets call it.

The second part was a problem—how to get the higher pressure, now left in the empty tank, lowered to that pressure inside the boat so we could again begin using the head. As I said, the deeper we were, the more air was necessary to blow the tank and, consequently, the more air we had to dispose of to equalize the two pressures, i.e., that in the boat and that inside the tank.

There was but one way to equalize—bleed the air in the now-empty, pressurized sanitary tank into *the boat*! At least Electric Boat Company installed a charcoal filter in the venting line, although I doubt the filter was ever changed.

There was one other problem which was actually worse than this, although that is hard to imagine, and it concerned snorkeling. When snorkeling, we ran these two huge diesel engines that quickly sucked great volumes of air out of the boat. The air was, in turn drawn through the snorkel that stuck out of the water. This worked well until either a wave would cover the snorkel or the diving party would inadvertently dip it beneath the surface. In both events, the big head valve would slam shut with the engines still running, and create a vacuum. This was hard on the ears when it occurred, and just as hard again when the situation corrected itself as the head valve reopened.

Each compartment in the boat had a very odd instrument for a submarine—an airplane altimeter! In fact, they were very useful. Each time the snorkel head valve slammed shut and air was sucked from the boat, we could look at the altimeter to see how bad it was measured in altitude. In fact, the one mounted in the engine room was switched to shut down the main engines when the pressure in the boat got to the equivalent of 6,000 feet. Given the size of the diesels and the small volume inside the pressure hull, it didn't take long to get to uncomfortable "altitudes." Imagine a mile-high building with an elevator that got you to the top in a few seconds.

However, the problem with the ears paled by comparison to what this cycling back and forth did to "old Sanitary #1." Every time the snorkel head valve shut, it created a pressure difference between the tank and the boat where the tank was a *higher* pressure. If you did not keep your wits about you, as you went to the head, you ran the risk while leaning over to flush the commode of vaporizing what was just left there all over you and the head. Of course this would not *kill* you; you would just wish it had.

Battery Acid Dungarees—I am no authority on this subject—diesel boat electricians were. You could always tell a submarine electrician on the piers and in the nested submarines provided he was in dungarees.

One of the primary jobs of the electricians was the care and maintenance of the over 250 tons of lead acid batteries on the old *Balao* class submarines. These cells were just below the decks in the Forward and After Battery Compartments leaving just enough room to crawl over the tops of the cells. Like old automobile batteries the electrolyte in the batteries would eventually make its way out and onto the tops of the batteries where the guys were crawling. In addition they had further exposure to the battery acid since they were required to take "gravities" which were measures of the specific 'gravity' of the batteries. This was done with a baster like syringe.

Holes in dungarees seemed minor however when compared to the risks of crawling about on the tops of the batteries with metal objects like dog tags, knives and the ever present Navy sailor's key rings.

Informality

I once heard a carrier pilot's existence described as long hours of complete boredom interrupted by moments of shear terror. The illusion is, naturally, flying in big long circles, then landing on a black night—no horizon, onto a pitching flight deck and low on fuel. Well, we would occasionally get into trouble and scare the hell out of everybody who was awake—heartbeats would soar for a few moments since submarines are pretty unforgiving vessels, but for much of the time, at least on my boat on patrol, we were bored. Our off watch boredom time was usually filled with card games, movies, reading, cribbage and messing with each other's minds—our primary source of entertainment. One other thing about submarines was that everyone was stuffed into this little chamber with its shared hardships and inconveniences and they were all smart, resourceful, self confident and had a sense of humor...a very, very fertile Petri dish indeed. Roger's submission made me remember some hilarious scenes on the boats.

Roger Forgit
EN2 (SS)
USS Tigrone AGSS 419
'71 to '75

Cruising on a boring submerged watch, 10 or so off duty, plus the regular watch in the Control Room and 'Piggy' Watt says to LT. Kenyon, the dive officer, "Mr. Kenyon, if I said you were an asshole, you could put me on report, couldn't you?" Mr. Kenyon replies to the affirmative, while stroking his goatee..." But if I *thought* you were an asshole, you couldn't do anything, right?" asks Piggy. Again, stroking his goatee, Mr. Kenyon replies in the affirmative. "Then I *think* you're an asshole," says Piggy as we all screamed with laughter. <u>That would not have happened on a nuke.</u>

Chief Mel "The Greek" Reeder was chief commissaryman on Barbero for two of the three years I was aboard. I liked him a lot because he was so colorful, a great influence on the crew and so good at his job. I never forgot the man. Fast forward 45 years and we reconnect! He is, I believe in his 80s.
For many diesel boat sailors, "messing" with your shipmates was nearly a full time job. My hope is that this tendency still remains on the nukes, notwithstanding all their additional responsibilities and work loads. We all had numerous examples of this process with which we regaled our civilian friends and families. Here is one of mine...a classic really:

Johnson was a radioman first class who was tall and very skinny. His only form of nourishment, apparently, was coffee and cigarettes, which he constantly consumed. Oh, he'd make every meal, but it was entertainment to him, not an occasion of sustenance. Actually, everyone liked chow time, there was good food and always plenty of banter.

Our chief cook was named Reader. He was a good cook, very excitable and a genuinely good man. The older crew liked to tease him and for some reason we called him "the Greek." The Navy always posted a menu for every meal (not that you had any options). This was done throughout the Navy and Barbero was no exception.

What Johnson would do, since he rarely stood watches and was apparently never hungry, was to wait until third call for the meal and then be late even for that. I'd watch him step into the mess and go straight to the posted menu. Nobody ever read the menu except Johnson, what good would it do? After seeing what was on it, he'd sit down and scan the table to see what had already run out by this late time and, even though he had no intention of actually eating the peas or whatever it happened to be, he would say, "Reader, where are the peas? There are no peas on the table."

Reader having worked long and hard to produce the meal, particularly under lousy conditions, would predictably blow up,

"God damnit, Johnson, you skinny son of a bitch, if you'd get here on time for a change there would be peas—we are out of peas and that's it." Johnson would reply,

"God damnit, Greek, the menu says peas and when I signed on to this f—king Navy, I was guaranteed three meals a day and a place to sleep. You post the menu, it says P-E-A-S and by God I want mine…I'm entitled!"

Johnson just sat there ragging on poor Reader, drinking coffee and smoking. Reader was plenty smart and knew exactly what was going on, and played the game very convincingly. The rest of us would just laugh. It was like dinner theater, except on a sub at sea.

I received this related email a week ago from The Greek:

You didn't know I was a Torpedoman did you? I went in the CCC (program) when I was 15 to get off the farm. They sent me to cook/baker school at Fort Demons, Iowa. When I was seventeen, I joined the Navy. After boots they sent me to Torpedo School at Great Lakes. After school they sent me to the old *Skipjack* SS-184. The first war patrol I made, I was on lookout off Japan. They pick up a plane at 9 miles, cleared the bridge, but I didn't know they dove. I was left in the water. The first lookout down took the bow planes—the last one took the stern planes—every body was looking for me. They hollered, "Reeder's topside!" They surfaced and picked me up. The old man (CO) was at the bottom of the ladder and said "Young man report to the galley, you are on permanent Mess Cooking." They only had two cooks and I had just gotten out of the CCC cooking school. I told the First Class that I was going to strike for cook. The next run (war patrol) I made Third Class. When the war was over I was a First Class. All my buddies I went to school with were Third Class. I was lucky—Mel

Liberty—is always associated with going ashore and getting away from your ship for a time. The crew of *Wahoo* had what I'd call a bit of liberty while underway! Subs in general and particularly *Barbero* seldom went to sea with other vessels. If you consider their missions, this makes sense. We only did it once, when we moved our home port from Norfolk to Pearl Harbor. We went around through the Panama Canal accompanied the entire way by another diesel sub, USS *Wahoo. Wahoo* had the usual complement of four main engines while we had only two, due to our conversion to a missile-launching sub. The obvious consequence of this was that Wahoo was a lot faster than we were. Wahoo, like all of us, hated to poop along at 12 knots when she could exceed 20 all day.

It turned out that the skipper of *Wahoo* was an avid fisherman. He couldn't get enough of it, apparently, because they would run fast all night, get way ahead of us and then shut down their engines and drift all day fishing. Late in the day, we would come chugging over the horizon to catch up, then they would repeat the evolution. I must say that it was very comical each afternoon to see a United States man of war, a rakish looking, lethal submarine, with her rails lined with fishermen! It reminded me of those party boats I saw as a kid, fishing off the south shore of Long Island in the summers.

It must have been a lot of fun for them, because most of the watches were secured for that day's fishing. After all, who needed a helmsman and all the rest? I can just see the cook carrying up all those tuna sandwiches and lemonade for the fishermen on deck. Even as they would get underway as we approached, the captain would actually troll from the bridge! Quite a sight. We saw them once a day, each evening until we arrived off Papa Hotel—the first buoy entering the channel into Pearl. There the two subs fell into line for appearances. I really loved the informality and independence of the submarine service in those days.

Cruising on the surface most of the time

If you love the outdoors and quickly tire of small, sunless, smelly places, then lookout is your watch. You could always tell the lookouts from the rest of the crew. They were the tan, healthy looking ones with the sunglass marks on their noses and temples while the rest of the crew looked as though they could use a month at summer camp. All of the interesting natural things like sunrises, sunsets, moonrises, water spouts, storms, marine life and squalls were only visible to those topside at the time—the lookouts and the OOD. The poor guys below only saw these things when they came up for their "submarine showers" from time to time, so they missed most of it. Lookout sometimes had its tense moments, however.

Once in the mid-Pacific I was on lookout watch when I saw a contact that was clearly a sub. We always knew when there were going to be U. S. ships around us, so this contact startled me—it was clearly not American. I shouted, "Contact abeam to starboard, near the horizon and it looks like a submarine, sir."

"C L E A R T H E B R I D G E, C L E A R T H E B R I D G E," shouted the heads-up OOD. We dove the boat for the first time in earnest and spent the next several hours listening on the sonar, keeping very quiet, exiting the area slowly and wondering, "Who are those guys?" We never found out. Barbero's mission was not to look for trouble but to avoid it, so we exited as discretely as we could manage.

I had many interesting things happen to me on lookout mostly associated with nature. Fluorescent seas in our bow wave and wake, sunsets, whales and dolphins and all the rest but our experiences with merchant ships at sea was disturbing.

From time to time we would pass merchant ships close enough to "glass" them fairly well. On an alarmingly high number of these encounters, I saw that no one was on the bridge! We were so vigilant that we had lookouts up, even during very heavy weather. Apparently these merchant ships had better things to do than watch where they were going—I was stunned to first learn of their carelessness.

Throughout my post Navy life I have watched the news only to see, time and time again, merchant ships running into bridges, each other, aground and generally creating havoc. The stakes, with this sloppy seamanship, were raised considerably with the big tanker spills. Every time I see this kind of stuff I tell my wife Barbara the same thing, that this sort of thing would never happen in the Navy, or at least it is far less frequent. The difference, I believe, is both in the quality of the crews and how seriously Navy sailors and officers take their responsibilities. I've never been aboard a Navy ship where the crew did not take their jobs very seriously.

One night on lookout I was up in the port shears, fighting to stay awake (Barbero had the old un-guppied fleet boat sail). It was tropical, balmy, the middle of the night and I finally gave in and just plain fell asleep, standing there on my little platform. My knees buckled and I began to fall out of the wide, open part of the railings through which we jumped when we cleared the bridge. The boat was on a port roll at that instant and I was past the pipe railing, over the water and in the air, with my feet still on the shears platform when I woke up! I instantly grabbed the pipe railing and pulled myself back into the protection of the shears' rail with my heart pounding and adrenaline surging all over the place! I am confident that since the port roll put my port lookout platform well out over the water, that I wouldn't have bounced off of the tank tops, nor would I have gone through the screws—that was the good news. The bad news was that I wouldn't have made any noticeable noise and my absence would not have been noticed for an hour. Trying to find me in the dark two hours and 25 miles later would have been a challenge to say the least. I don't recall having trouble staying awake after that.

The other fascinating aspect was the sea's wonderful creatures! There always seemed to be dolphins playing in our bow waves. I once saw a whole pod of whales dive under the boat just off our starboard side. A little land bird lit in our sail near the shears while I was on watch one day. It was totally exhausted and stayed all day, regaining some of its strength. It was sad because we were far off shore and the bird did not have a chance. The other lookout and I tried to figure out how to capture the thing, but gave up on the project. In the mornings, the officers' steward would come to the bridge and ask permission to go down on the main deck to collect the flying fish which landed there during the night—fresh fish each morning for the officers. All diesel sailors have these kinds of stories. The absence of them is one of the losses of the nuclear power sailors.

The oceans are a paradox. One moment it is a spectacularly wonderful and exhilarating place to be and the next moment it is a terrifying and treacherous place swallowing up ships. It has always been this way, treating Odysseus and Bull Halsey alike.

Diesel experiences

Dick Brown
ETR2(SS)
Barbero SSG-317, Lafayette SSBN-616B, Amberjack SS-522 and Odax SS-484
Aug 1961—Aug 1967

First, I was sent to the fleet to qualify in submarines. Upon graduation from Sub School, I received orders to report to USS Barbero SSG-317 based in Pearl Harbor. This submarine was a highly modified WWII fleet boat. It was nothing like what I had just learned in Sub School. The forward and after battery compartments were reversed, the diesels had been removed from the forward engine room and the tubes had been removed from the after torpedo room. I quickly learned what the "G" stood for in SSG-317. This boat was one of five submarines converted to carry the Regulus guided missile. The foreword engine room carried missile support equipment and on deck, just aft of the conning tower, was a barrel-shaped hangar to carry two nuclear-tipped birds. I made one patrol on the Barbero and not only earned my silver dolphins but I became a member of the exclusive North Pacific Yacht Club.

This was a great experience. Not only did I feel I was part of our first strategic deterrent force, the predecessor to our Polaris program, but I had already made a deterrent patrol before being assigned to a boomer. But more important than that, I had experienced the diesel submarine navy and was fortunate enough to bridge the gap between diesel and nuclear submarines. I experienced stills that broke down daily and a virtually unlimited supply of freshwater. I experienced the nightly slamming of the snorkel valve and two months of continuous quiet deep submergence. And I experienced risky surface launches with decks awash and precision launches from hidden depths.

Since those good ol' days, I often think about the men who rode the diesel boats during WWII, their many Pacific war patrol successes, and the heavy toll that we paid for victory. My patrol on Barbero took me to Okinawa and Hong Kong, and a long surface run back to Pearl. While crossing the South China Sea, where several of our diesel boats remain on eternal patrol, we received the tragic news that the nuclear fast-attack submarine, USS Thresher, was lost with all hands onboard, off the Atlantic coast. With only two diesels, our "slow boat from China" provided plenty of time to reflect about the ferociously hostile environment in which our diesel and nuclear submarines must operate.

Don Walsh—The surface Navy never really understood what we did.

My first submarine after sub school was the San Diego based *Rasher (SSR 269)*. The number two scoring sub in WWII, after *Flasher*, she had been converted to a radar picket with the addition of a 30 foot long hull section forward of the control room. This was the combat information center (CIC). A massive air search radar antenna was mounted on top of the sail and a height finder radar, the "nodding idiot" was mounted on its own little bottle-shaped pressure hull on the main deck aft of the sail.

The idea of a submarine radar picket came from WWII operations where surface ship pickets (usually destroyers) were extremely vulnerable to enemy action. During the Okinawa campaign the Kamakaze planes heavily targeted these early warning boats. Operating alone they could also be easy prey for enemy submarines. So the idea of putting all the early warning gear on a submarine seemed like a good idea. But there is often a considerable distance between theory and practice.

By 1957, when I reported aboard, the times *Rasher* actually acted as a radar picket were very minimal. The surface Navy never really understood what we did and to some degree neither did the submarine navy. One time we were operating with a carrier task group. All the destroyers were in a big ring around the carrier in the center. The task group commander put us at the rear-most station at the very back of this circular formation. Well, these people are pounding along at more than 20 knots, and they keep calling us and saying "station!" That meant, "Get back where you belong". Poor old *Rasher* was going as hard as we could on four engines and floating the battery on the dinky, our auxiliary diesel. With that 30 foot hull section forward of the sail we were a fast boat but not fast enough. We kept falling behind.

Then the admiral on the carrier decided to do a 180 (degree) and reorient the screen so that everybody makes a 180-degree turn. Then we would have been station one, right in front of the formation. We're looking through the tactical publications books to figure out what the hell that signal was and what we should do. These were surface navy publications and submariners simply were not very familiar with them.

The OD said, "Captain, you really ought to come up here because they all turned around and they're headed for us." Flag Adams (LCDR Alden W. Adams) looked over the situation which seemed like a lot of ships with a zero angle on the bow. "Bleep it! Just dive the boat." So down we went and the whole carrier group rumbled over the top of us. After they were clear, we popped up. Sort of like a duck fishing—it disappears and then boom, it's back to the surface. After this maneuver, station zero said, you're detached, report somewhere else. We don't need you.

We really didn't do very well in that mode, being part of the surface navy. Most of SSR-269's service was with conventional submarine operations. Except we had lots of extra space to store stuff.

Bob Gautier had been on a destroyer prior to diesel boats and commented on the difference between 'black shoe' crews and submariners.

DG: I interviewed Chuck Grojean and he mentioned that one of the differences in the crews was qualification and knowing the whole boat, whereas the black gang (on a destroyer) didn't know what the navigators were doing nor the gunners mates or anybody. So there wasn't that same sort of knowledge of the whole that existed on the boats. Since you were one of the few that had experience on the surface, I wanted to know if you saw a difference.

BG: On a surface ship they did their own thing. I mentioned I was on the *Fieberling*, which was a DE (Destroyer Escort), and the first lieutenant took care of the of the gun sponsons outside. And on the inside it was the responsibility of the Gunners Mates. And, Christ, they wouldn't put any paint on that thing—it really bothered me. So I got to be the First Lieutenant and the Gunnery Officer, so it belongs to me now, both of it, so 'take care of it.' But they were funny. They really were.

DG: There was really more homogeneity on the old boats, I think.

BG: Oh, yeah. Well, when I got on the *Tilefish*, we had a chief of the boat—I'm trying to think what that guy's name was—Chief Jessy Pritchet—but the Chief of the Boat told me, he said, Okay, Mr. Gautier, I'm going to qualify you in submarines. And so every afternoon he'd say, 'Now, today, we're going to do this, and he'd stay after work and do one of the systems.' And he made damn sure that I was qualified. And, you know, that took a lot of time for that guy. But he spent a lot of time educating me to be a submariner. And he was quite proud of that, too. I thought that was good.

DG: Was he asked by the skipper to do that?

BG: No, no. Well, you know, the thing is on a boat, the rank on a submarine was the captain, exec, and the Chief of the Boat. That's how that thing worked. And as soon as you figured that out, you were alright. Because he really was in charge. He was in charge.

DG: That's a really important function, certainly. Did you observe any sort of special color among submariners different from the rest of the Navy? I mean, something you could identify? Were they different and, if so, how?

BG: I think the submariners worked together and they took care of one another. Because, you know, if something happens to the boat, they don't separate the good guys and the bad guys. And so I think that's the attitude that persists in the submarining business.

Another Bob Gautier moment.

BG: When they have these reunions on the *Blueback* up in Portland, we'll sit around the room and these guys are drinking and all that stuff, and we just wear name tags, you know, Bob Gautier or something. Periodically, one of these kids will look and they'll say, 'Weren't you the first skipper of the *Blueback*?' I say, 'Yeah.' And they become very reverent. What they're really thinking is, 'That sonofabitch is still alive!' Yeah, I really had a good time in the Navy. I thoroughly enjoyed the thing.

It strikes me that throughout all the interviews and submissions, not one person said they did not like submarine duty. Most used the word love in fact. Here is what Pat Hannifin had to say.

DG: Well, did you notice—of course, you had nothing to compare to, I guess, at that point, but a certain élan and our spirit?

PH: Oh, absolutely, a great spirit throughout the submarine force. Yeah, which was another reason I was glad I went to submarines.

DG: Can you give some examples or anecdotes of diesel boat culture versus, say, surface ships?

PH: Never served in a surface ship. All my sea duty was in submarines. Other than just observation and discussions with guys who served on surface ships. One of the things I think that made submarines different is that they were an all-volunteer service, and whether it was during the war or diesel boats after the war, you got people who wanted to be where they were, and that wasn't the case in surface ships. And particularly in smaller surface ships. They were there because that's where they were assigned. I'm talking about primarily the enlisted crew. Some of that applied to officers as well. So, there's a culture in the submarine force which goes all the way back to your qualifying in submarines, and it doesn't matter whether it's diesel boats or nuclear boats. You're not qualified until you have the confidence in yourself, and the rest of the ship does, too. That you can do anything that's necessary in case of emergency, whether you're a torpedoman in the engine room or an engineer up in the torpedo room. The expression that someone used before and I use always, the ocean is out there and it is not fair. It's always trying to get in the same compartment with you. And in a submarine flooding is the catastrophe—serious flooding. So you're trained and you have the confidence in yourself and in your shipmates that in case of a flooding accident, or any other kind of an emergency, there's going to be somebody there who knows what to do at the right time and the right place. So that culture exists in the submarine force. I don't think it exists in any other part of the Navy for an entire crew.

DG: I think that I already know the answer to this, but did you enjoy the experience, your submarining years?

PH: Oh, absolutely. Absolutely.

DG: Was it what you expected or was it more?

PH: Oh, more than I expected, and it changed so dramatically from going from the "S" boats to a fleet boat, but then from a fleet boat, a diesel boat to a nuclear submarine. Well, diesel submarines are surface ships that submerge occasionally. With a nuclear submarine, it is a submarine. It surfaces once in awhile. So that's really the difference in the technology, really. I think a greater change than going from prop aircraft to jets. It's even much more dramatic than that because it suddenly became a true submarine.

Nearly everything in this book came from the major interviews and many submissions via a web page where those submariners interested in the project could fill out a form page which was then emailed to me. By a considerable margin, the submissions were from enlisted men. They naturally were responding to the 'All Hands' letter where I asked for their opinion with respect to the cultural changes during the transition from diesels to nukes. Few of them digressed into other pertinent topics about the transition.

By contrast those actually interviewed tended to cover the entire subject, such as why they volunteered for submarine duty (First chapter—Are You Crazy?); the differences between diesels and nukes (the Apples and Oranges chapter); the Rickover chapter and so on. Consequently most of the following entries are concerned with submarine culture.

The following submissions are in random order. I suggest that the reader make careful note of the period of years each one served on the boats. In later chapters you will see, mainly from those interviewed, that the retention rate particularly during the early part of the transition was very low. Chuck Griffiths and Jim Watkins had a lot to do with the program of bonuses for re-enlistment and to keep young nuclear power officers from leaving the Navy.

Some of the following are a bit repetitive, although I did edit out a lot of redundancies. I tried to include all out of respect for fellow submariners who have gone to the trouble of sending in their experiences and views. Most all have something to add.

Ronald C. Kimmel
LCDR
Piper SS-409, Tilefish SS-307, Medregal SS-480, Robert E. Lee SSBN-601, Francis Scott Key SSBN-657
1954 to 1975

My opinions of the cultural differences between diesel boat sailors and nuke sailor are based on observations during my 21 years of naval service.

I believe with the advent of the nuclear submarine came the need for a more intelligent sailor to man her. Submarine systems became more complex to the point of specialization within rates. Up until that time boat systems were relatively simple, i.e. everyone was able to qualify on all systems throughout the boat. In an emergency anyone could do anyone else's job. The complexity of the nuclear power, nuclear weapons, and navigation systems limited this crossover training to basic ships systems. It required people with relatively strong backgrounds in math, chemistry, and physics to operate these systems.

The Navy schools to train these people changed also. As schools became more technical the Navy did away with long schools of 44 and 52 weeks. They found it more cost effective to offer advanced schools as incentives to re-enlistment rather than include it in beginning instruction. Shorter schools based more on operation of the equipment rather than the repair and maintenance of the equipment became the norm. The Navy began to have difficulty finding the numbers of young sailors with the intelligence to complete these schools in the allotted time. The Navy recognized the need for high caliber personnel on submarines. This resulted in the Submarine Force essentially skimming the cream off the top of boot camp graduates.

These more intelligent sailors learned or knew that fitness was important to them in their job, their advancement, and their life. As a result the old routine of getting off the boat and meeting at a favorite bar before going home was dropped in favor of going to the gym or health club and working out. The diets of these same sailors also changed with their life styles. The food prepared aboard was healthier, and with the exception of the fast-food places, the food obtained elsewhere provided a better diet than was available in the 1940s, 1950s and 1960s.

The public attitude toward smoking has impacted the boat sailor of today also. On a diesel boat sailors bought cartons of sea stores when available and smoked throughout the boat. Today there are few places on board where one can smoke. The change is due to the public information made available on the hazards of smoking.

Politicians influenced the sailor's change as well. With the end of the Cold War funding was cut for Navy ship building, training, retention and other programs. The more intelligent sailor recognized this and made decisions to get career training and go out and find employment in the civilian world rather than staying for a 20 year Navy career. The funding cuts resulted in a change to military retirement as well. This too impacted retention and caused even more personnel to leave the Navy after one or two enlistments. Onboard discussions of this subject were influential on young sailors and their decision to make the Navy a career.

I'm sure political correctness also had an impact on the cultural changes of the Navy today. In the period after WWII and through the majority of the Cold War, boat sailors were known and called by their last name or a nickname. Somewhere along the line more formal forms of address became mandatory. Today's address form of rate and name, although correct and formal, cannot help but deter from the closeness between crew members of the past when references of "Shorty," "Animal" and "Warhead" were commonplace.

In my opinion, the end result of all of the above and other facets too numerous to mention is that today's Navy is made up of more intelligent, fitter, and more informed sailors than the diesel boat sailors of the past. I believe the 'can do' attitude of the WWII boat sailor is still ingrained in the nuke sailor of today. This is instilled by the everyday life of living close and depending on shipmates. Although the sailor may have changed to some extent culturally he is still a U.S. Navy sailor and will perform to his best ability when called upon to do so.

Jerry E. Beckley
CWO-4
ASSP-313 Perch, SSG-574 Grayback, SSG-317 Barbero, SSG (N)-587 Halibut
1954–1988

The reason that I have listed my time as 1954, the year that I qualified in submarines and 1988, the year that I retired from the Civil Service is because when I left active duty, I was employed at the Polaris Missile Facility, Atlantic (POM-FLANT) and maintained a professional association with submarines and submarine crews in my work on the A3, C3, and C4 Polaris and Poseidon missile systems. After leaving POMFLANT, I went to Washington to take over a job as the Assistant Program Manager (Logistics) TOMAHAWK Cruise Missile system, where I continued my close association with the Submarine Force, as I was the person responsible for giving the SSN-688 Class submarines the Vertical Launch TOMAHAWK capability. As you point out in your preface Dan, "Not all technological changes prompted cultural changes," however these changes did require a totally different caliber of man in the Submarine Service. These new men were educated far beyond those who served with us on the diesel boats and it began with the Regulus Missile Program. If you will recall, the Submarine Service hadn't changed that much from the WWII submariner until the SSGs and then the SSNs. It did require that the level of education for the Electronic, Missile Techs, Fire Control, and Sonar Technicians, as well as the ancillary rates that were supporting the program such as the Torpedomen, Gunner's Mates and other knukekle busters, be educable They must be capable of converting to a rate where their knowledge (and training) was better utilized. It is my earnest belief that these events ushered in the change you have observed in the Submarine Service. Although I am certain that these changes were not the only reason for the cultural changes, but they did begin about this same time. In addition, you may be able to add officers such as ADM Raborn, who was not a submariner to the list of architects.

The following submission is from a British submariner. I include it only because I conclude from it that, while this is but one submission, the British submarine force's transition from diesel to nuclear powered subs was completely different from ours. They did not experience the intensity and dislocation we did with the phenomanally rapid build up of the Polaris program.

Wayne Byrne
Petty Officer
HMSM Otus, Resolution, Onslaught
1977–1995

Having served on both nukes and diesels, I can say quite reasonably that life on the diesel boat is much busier than on the nuke boat. Nukes have most of the major and the minor valves automated and operated from the control room via the "Systems Console". The diesel submariner would have to operate the valves locally physically by hand. One of the greater differences is that nukes have an abundant supply of fresh water which is manufactured through the separation of salt from sea water. The diesel boat can make fresh water through the reverse osmosis plant, but it is not very efficient. The diesel submariner therefore would not waste water in showering daily. If you cannot tolerate the conditions of a diesel boat you are going to find life difficult.

Anthony J. Craig
STS2(SS)
SSBN 631(B)-Ulysses S. Grant, SSN-691 Memphis, SSN 688-Los Angeles
72 through 78

My sonar division LPO (Leading Petty Officer) on the Grant (blue) was brought up on a diesel boat and would treat us to tales of South American goodwill tours that he had been a part of. His entire demeanor was noticeably different then the rest of our Nuke crew. My LPO was virtually unflappable. You would never see him get excited about the nit-picky issues which I seem to attribute to the nuclear navy but when a crisis developed he was there, solid, steady, and confident. I couldn't have drawn a better role model as a young man and I only wish I could have had a little diesel boat time under my belt to really be able to tell him I understood. I do know that my submarine experience really was a 'dude ranch' version of the life of a DBFer. Showers every day, even at the end of every shift if you were so inclined, clean air, plenty of room. As a trade-off though, we had to look extra sharp like the country club boys we had evolved into.

Sherred Leslie Guille ("Les")
Captain, USN (Ret.)
Charr SS-328, Greenfish SS-351, Wahoo SS-328, Tang SS-306, Menhaden SS-377;
1948–1982

I have not served on a nuke boat, but I have had opportunities to observe SSN operations.

Rickover's program was (and still is) very successful...we currently have one of the most powerful submarine navies in the world. His training and monitoring programs focused on safe reactor operations, quite naturally. The result is that we have not had any reactor-associated disasters.

However I feel that the Rickover-engendered philosophy has created a nuke culture among the officers that is focused too heavily on the rear-end (reactor operations), giving the tactical operations of the boat short shrift. In my opinion, there have been several collisions and groundings resulting from the lack of emphasis on extensive tactical training and experience of submarine officers.

The following is from Les' web site, which he has allowed me to include.

While I was on Menhaden, we worked very hard, especially at sea, but we took time to have some fun, also.

Once, in January of 1971, we were assigned during local ops in San Diego to act as an enemy submarine to the USS Gurnard (SSN-662) while she was doing her work-up to deploy to WestPac.

We were to run submerged on assigned courses, snorkeling at pre-determined times on assigned tracks. Gurnard did not have our op-plan, but she was to try to track us, fire simulated torpedoes, and then open out and regenerate the problem until the end of the exercise. Before we left port, I told my DIVCOM that we would make more successful attacks on Gurnard than her Skipper, Commander Bobby Bell, would on us. He bet me a martini for each successful attack.

At sea we would snorkel as planned, then shut down according to schedule. Each time Gurnard would detect us, then turn to close for the attack. When we shut down and ran on the battery, Gurnard would lose us and roar by. Then, I would order a single ping on the fathometer. When Gurnard heard that, they would turn toward us. By then we had an attack solution, and would simulate a torpedo launch.

We did this repeatedly throughout the exercise...Gurnard never laid a hand on us! When we got back in port, I collected my four martinis from the DIVCOM.

Shortly after, we received a poem from the Gurnard Torpedo Gang written to memorialize the event.

Written by
the
Torpedo Gang
USS GURNARD (SSN-662)

We don't know, but we've heard tell,
The MENHADEN's shooting is mighty swell.
It sure likes to go after big black Nukes,
It has been said they hate those pucs.

Now it is said the diesels are being replaced,
So they are trying to put us to disgrace.
Now we all know the diesel boats smell,
But, we'll have to admit their shooting is swell.

We know one thing, and we know it for sure,
Our solution has got to find the cure.
We had better hurry and find it fast,
Or the MENHADEN will have our ass.

Now the diesel boats enjoy liberty and play,
But they were doing some fine shooting today.
Now on the GURNARD the liberty is none,
and the MENHADEN still has us under the gun.

The Captain is grim; he is wearing a frown,
Because he found out those diesel boats don't mess around.
We hope the Captain will smile again real soon,
Then we do our thing to the MENHADEN before noon.

Now it is noon, the Captain still wears a frown,
Because the MENHADEN shot us down.
Not just once, not just twice,
But four times and that isn't nice.

We're not up to par,
In fact we leave a lot to be desired.

But when we have to meet the test,
We all know the GURNARD can field-day BEST.

One night after Gurnard returned to port, one of the Menhaden crew (SK2 Steve Rose) put on a wetsuit and quietly swam over to where Gurnard was moored (alongside the Nereus), pushing a cardboard box containing a can of white paint and a paint brush. Completely undetected, he painted "DBF" in big white letters on Gurnard's upper rudder, then swam back to Menhaden, pushing the little box ahead of him.
(He was awarded a tin, make believe medal al la Mr. Roberts)

Jack L. Hester
RM1(SS)
USS Rock SSR-274 USS Snook SSN-592
1959–1963

I reported for duty to the USS Rock in San Diego, CA, July 1959 straight out of Submarine School. I was an RM2. It took me about 5 months to qualify onboard Rock. In late 1960 I requested new construction and was issued orders to the Snook pre-comm detail in Pascagoula, MS, reporting onboard in early 1961.

If ever there was any animosity between the sailors that were schooled in nuclear power and those that weren't it would have surfaced in the shipbuilding environment. The guys that were nuclear trained spent countless hours ensuring that every element necessary for successful commissioning were completed. Sometimes they would go days without seeing their families or even having a day off. On the other hand those sailors not nuclear trained usually reported each morning for quarters and then were released for the day. What a breeding ground for malcontent.

However, the Snook was a very fortunate boat in that the COB, TMC(SS) A.E.(Dutch) Kneuer who, as an E-7, was junior to some of the nuke chiefs and the Executive Officer, LCDR J. D. Watkins (who later became CNO) would not allow malcontentment to exist. They were always planning something to bring the crew together, whether it be a picnic or a party or whatever, they continuously strived to keep the "Frame 44" (where the nukes and non-nukes divided on the boat) context non-existent. Every committee formed to act on some action was co-nuke/non-nuke. Everything evolved around co-existence which disallowed for conflict.

The skipper was CDR Howard Bucknell and he supported the XO and COB to the fullest. To me, it was a great crew and we have had a Snook reunion in 1997, 99 and 2001 in an attempt to bring everyone who ever served on this great boat together for old stories and good experiences.

Yes, I'm sure there were cultural changes coming from the diesels to the nukes, but the majority of the guys (in those days) were ALL one-time diesel boat sailors and the comradeship developed on the diesels was still in the heart and soul of most of the sailors. That coupled with the dedication of our COB and XO would not allow for a noticeable difference. I understand that later changed when the diesel boat sailors became fewer and fewer, but I did not experience it.

John W. Schuster
EM1 (SS)
USS Odax SS-484, USS Thomas Edison SSBN-610, USS James K. Polk SSBN-645
Jan 1960 to Sept 1969

DBF/Nuke-Both Worlds: Space, Olfactory Airs, and Camaraderie. Just a few quick observations from one of those who was attracted by, and "bailed" to the Nuke Program.

Space: What a surprise I received when I reported aboard my first Nuke. It was huge. I didn't have to duck once when wending my way aft through the entire length of the boat to Nukeland. In fact, I had a choice of several deck levels. Now the story. When I first reported aboard the Odax, being new man, I was assigned to mess cook and got the worst possible bunk. As I lay on my back, the view was of the ventilation duct 6 inches above my nose. I could sleep on my stomach or my back but not my side. To turn over, I would slide out while grabbing a pipe adjacent to the bunk, keeping my feet in the bunk for balance, turn, and slide back in. Fortunately for me, I had to endure this for only a month when the next poor victim arrived and I moved due to seniority.

Odors: We used to store potatoes in the showers. Most of us back aft types did get preference to use the makeshift shower in the LL engine room when a bad batch of water came out of the still and had to be dumped. Otherwise, the ritual of progressive use of water (face, body, socks) from the same basin full prevailed. The shocking reality came after a run when I opened my locker in the barracks where I had foolishly left a few clothes from the boat which I had no time to wash. The stench of diesel nearly knocked me off my feet. It was then that I realized why some people looked at me and my compadres strangely. Even after much scrubbing, removal of diesel odor was not possible. What a change under nuclear power with a steam distilling plant that produced thousands of gallons of water a day rather than the few buckets we got if we were lucky on the Odax.

Camaraderie: Here was also a noticeable difference. My guess is it was partly due to the size of the crew and the diversity of our jobs. Gone were the days of drawing the 100 psi air system on the back of an envelope for qualifications. On the Nukes, you learned what was required for safety and saving the boat. The systems were too complex and large. No longer could a qualified crewman do anybody's job. And with this, came a slight separation of the closeness experienced by a diesel boat crew. Granted, should a boat sailor be accosted by a surface "puke" the whole crew would be on him. But overall, we formed smaller groups of really close friends. I must say, after 30 + years, I still keep in touch with some of my old shipmates.

In closing I add that I had much more fun on the old pig boat than on the nuke. Operations were far from boring like the deterrent patrols of a "Boomer." I missed getting to the bridge on a moonlit night, listening to the throb of the diesels and watching dolphins swimming in the effervescent water off the bow. Too bad we couldn't have the best of both worlds. If they ever make a "small!!" attack nuke, it could happen. Unfortunately it's too late for me.

Ronald L. Shepherd
MM2 (SS)
USS Nautilus SSN-571
January 1967 to October 1972

While serving on the Nereus, a sub tender in San Diego, we typically wore tee shirts, Levi jeans and ball caps as well as tennis shoes for our uniform of the day. No one seemed to get the least bit excited about this as most of the boats there were diesel at the time and just about everyone wore some mixture of the above for their 'uniform'. A few years later while overhauling the diesels on the Nautilus I used my previous experience on the durability of the Levis vs. the dungarees of the time. The dungarees would tear and rip so easily they were only good for about two shifts of work so those of us in the know wore our Levis. Walking across the parking lot one fine morning about 5:45 am on my way to the boat I was 'accosted' by a first class petty officer who wanted to know what I was doing parading around the Sub Base out of uniform? I tried to explain the situation to him but to no avail. He was going to run me in to the Duty Officer and there would be hell to pay for my transgression. Just as I was entering into the final stages of 'fight or flee' I heard a gruff voice behind me wanting to know what was going on. The first class immediately started into his tirade about my behavior and wanted to know what the Mustang officer cared about it anyway. Well my division officer immediately asked the first class PO where his dolphins were. He said he wasn't a sub sailor. To which my division officer said "Exactly my point son." "If you are not a sub-sailor you have no idea why someone would be dressed like this, but I will tell you this for sure, if you ever stop one of my people again and harass them for what they are wearing I will personally see to it that you will spend enough time in the bilges of my boat to fully understand why they dress the way they do. Is that understood?" The first class said "Yes sir" and that was the end of that. This just shows how, over a period of a few short years, the sub service went from a group of 'untouchables' to 'just another sailor.'

This is an email I received from RADM Chuck Grojean, prominently featured in other chapters.

Dan,

Your idea of a book about the cultural change that took place in the transition from diesel to nuclear power is excellent. I believe that the book could be fascinating, funny and informative.

Having been a junior officer as well as XO and CO on diesel boats and then XO and CO on nuclear submarines during the transition I observed the phenomenon first hand. I also pulled some capers (of which I'm not so proud), that were intended to restore some of the élan that I felt was missing in the nukes.

Good luck with your book.
Chuck

Darrel E. Wagner
MM1(SS)
Catfish SS-339, Casimir Pulaski SSBN-633, Snook SSN-592
October 1962 to August 1974

When I enlisted at 17 in 1962, I was bound for submarines from the beginning. My recruiter touted the glories of the new nuclear Navy, and I was enthralled. Who wouldn't be at 17? Boot camp during the Cuban Missile Crisis, MMA School, and then Sub School in New London. By now I was Nuke School-designated (9901), but had the good fortune to receive orders to the Catfish (SS-339). Made a WestPac run and managed to qualify before my orders came for Nuke School in Vallejo. Drank my Dolphins at the White Hat Club in Yokosuka.

Having qualified SS, SSBN, and SSN, I must say the DBF days were the best. Sure, we didn't get to shower very often, and hot racking was a way of life, but crew camaraderie-wise, it never got any better. Perhaps it was the close quarters and the smaller crew, but everyone knew he could count on his shipmates, ashore or under way. In addition, we were playing Cold War games on a very old (some said expendable) war machine that had seen better days, and was low on the priority list for spare parts to keep it running. We did a lot of jerry rigging, and that probably contributed as well. I remain proud, however, of my 12 years of service, and even prouder that it was all on submarines.

Wviatoslav Steve Seteroff
QMCM (SS) (DV) and later CWO4
SS-396 Ronquil, SS-377 Menhaden, SS-375 Macabi, SS-241 Bashaw, SSN-592 Snook, SSN-594 Permit, SSN-590 Sculpin
1955–1983

The transition from diesel boats to nukes was rather gradual for me because I left to put Snook (SSN-592) in commission early in the nuclear program and the majority to the nose-coners were already qualified, on diesel boats of course. Some of the nukes, had also been in the 9901 program so had served, however briefly, in a fleet unit. Most of the nukes though came straight from the prototype and I can well remember that some of the 'aft' section leaders did not quite measure up to the expected standards. We were used to doing what needed to be done and were less concerned about when liberty call went down, and were very interested in what the yard was doing to our boat, but that was probably a result of each boat having peculiarities and we continued to 'oolie' each other whenever we could find something unique. Many nukes followed along and our culture was fairly homogenous after we were commissioned and solidified significantly after our first deployment, much like a traditional fleet submarine crew. I left Snook to go to New London for three years and was delighted to go to Bashaw (AGSS-241) but alas I was selected to QMC and there were no billets so I went to Permit (SSN-594) and here the difference in culture made an impact. Those of us who were brought up on diesel boats had a clear advantage because of attitude and work ethic. Not to say that there was anything wrong with the rest, they just somehow did not measure up, and I wonder if it was not because of our emerging prejudices. Later, just before retirement, I was a W4 acting as the on-board safety officer on Tridents and fast-attacks on instrumented ranges and noted a very clear difference in the attitude and work ethic that had evolved during the 30 years of submarine service. Life is clearly easier, fresh water is available for bathing, clothes washers are installed, bunking is luxurious in comparison, technological marvels prevail, and stand-off weapons enlarge the engagement area considerably. But these are minor, albeit now physical comforts are expected. The real cultural change I note is the attitude and interpersonal relationships.

Glenn Keiffer
FTB3 (SS) (DV)
USS James Madison SSBN 627(B) and Atule SS 403
June 1962 to Oct. 1968

I enlisted in the nuke program from the beginning. I went to all the schools and then went to the Madison just before it was commissioned. We went down the Cape and fired an A3 Polaris missile. I then made 6 patrols with the blue crew. I then requested and got the Atule down Key West. I knew the Chief in DC who handled all the enlisted submarine transfers. I got whatever I asked for. I went to the Atule and it was a big mistake. See, I was trained for the mark 84 fire control system and knew nothing of the equipment on the Atule. I hated the diesel boat. Loved the time on the nuke. I never remember anyone giving me a hard time on the diesel boat. Never saw the hate that was suppose to exist then. The guys I sailed with on the nuke were old smoke boaters anyway. <u>Give me the nukes any day</u>.

I've always had great respect for Navy Corpsmen. The 'Doc' on any boat always seems to have special status. Wynne Day has had the particular distinction of having been both a submarine 'Doc' as well as a Marine Corpsman! He makes the very interesting statement about the two best duties he had.

WYNNE C. DAY
HM1
RASHER SS-269, SCAMP SSN-588
June 1959 to 1964

I served aboard as an SN and AN on a PA, CVA, and aboard a APA and an LSD as an HM before applying for submarine training. The RASHER was without a doubt the best duty I have ever experienced for unit cohesion—we were a family that worked together well. I trained as a radar/sonar-ECM operator watch stander. After being convinced to attend Nuke school I was assigned to SCAMP. What a letdown! Everyone seemed to have their own empire. I was a Nuke but the HMs were being phased out so I ended up in no ones camp. I reported to shore duty and removed my volunteer status, but still ended up finishing my career aboard the ENTERPRISE, aboard which the same condition existed plus being an outcast of the Medical Dept. too. The next best duty I served with was the USMC (5 years of 24) including a tour in RVN (Vietnam). There the situation was much the same as RASHER and I was now an HMC which was a help too. Please contact me by mail or phone if you would like more detail. Good luck with your book.

Chuck Griffiths

DG: I ask everyone whether they notice some unusual color and élan, among the submarine community.

CG: Oh, definitely. Very noticeable élan. And really there weren't that many submarines in World War II, which, of course, was right when I went in. We reduced from 250 or so, submarines down to about 100 almost overnight. We took all these—some of them brand-new boats, and put them in mothballs and took the crews off and sent them home because the Navy was manned primarily by civilians in those days. And they were all anxious to get the hell out as soon as they could, as soon as the War was over. And so we went from 13 officers in our ward room on the *Cochino* within less than six months, down to seven, with everybody bailing out. But the *Cochino* was brand new, had just been completed at EB. And most of the ones that we kept in, of course, were brand new and they were all the deeper diving boats—deeper test depths—the Balao class.

CG: *Cochino*.

DG: Wasn't that the one that had the accident later on?

CG: Yes, it had the big fire off of Norway, and sunk.

DG: That made me almost sick to my stomach when I read about that.

CG: Yeah, it was something. But, of course, we'd just been guppied, and so we had the big battery and that's probably what led to that, a short in the series/parallel switch which led to that fire. And, incidentally, I had left the ship after having been on it for…three-plus years. I waved goodbye to them as it headed out on that trip. So I wasn't with them for that disaster.

Chuck Grojean in a few sentences put his finger on the fundamental difference between diesel and nuclear power submarine crews.

DG: Was there an élan or esprit on your first boat? Maybe you could make a distinction between the destroyer you got off of and the submarine.

CG: Yeah, I can. I was on destroyers and then I was on PCEC in the amphibious forces, and the camaraderie that existed on submarines was far, far superior to what it was on surface craft.

DG: And I think you just answered this because the next question was did you observe a sort of special color. No, that's a different question. You know what I'm saying by color—among submariners as opposed to other communities?

CG: Yes, no question about it. The submarine force had a lot more—well, first of all, because we'd all gone to submarine school and because technically we all knew what the other guy knew and we all had an appreciation for what the other man had learned and we all had the same kind of language. You know, in destroyers in those days the black gang didn't necessarily know very much what the deck force was doing. And the communicators didn't necessarily know a lot of what the gunnery bunch was doing, but in submarine everybody was getting qualified, everybody spoke the same language, we all had the same problems to overcome in terms of learning our jobs, we all knew that we could do each other's job at any time, and so, yes, there was a much greater attitude of respect for each other, enlisted and officers, officers among officers, enlisted among officers, the racial aspects. **Even when I went in after submarine school in '50, you found that the black sailor, the Oriental sailor, were all one band of brothers**.

DG: Did you enjoy your experiences on the boats and was it what you had expected when you first considered submarine duty?

CG: Yes. I enjoyed it—not only enjoyed it, I loved it. And, yes, it was everything I'd hoped for.

I wish to point out that in nearly 100,000 words gathered in this project not one referred to any sort of racial bias or prejudice aboard United States Submarines. Chuck Grojean's response above was due to misunderstanding my awkward use of the word 'color' where I meant to use it as in 'colorful characters'. Grojean was even referring to the 50s when there was considerable prejudice in the general population. Aboard USS Barbero for three years I recall no comments or incidences of bias—none, and this too was during the later 50s. Moreover, in all my new submariner contacts via the internet, I have yet to hear of such incidents aboard other submarines. We did tend to become closer to our fellow rates such as Engineman or Electricians Mates and speak, always out loud and always humorously, disparaging remarks about each other's jobs. This 'dinner theater' nearly always took place in the crew's mess. As a Torpedoman character in a short story I wrote (Ghost Boat) said, "I went on liberty one time with four Enginemen and if I ever get the urge again I'll just walk out the Main Gate, go straight to the Shore Patrol offices and just turn myself in. I'll save a lot of time and money that way."

If there was flooding around torpedo tube #3 there was no doubt among the crew that whoever was on watch up there would shut and dog the water tight door, shut the flapper valve and begin a pressure in the room and the idea that that sailor was Black, Puerto Rican, a WASP or Asian would never enter anyone's mind.

Jim Watkins talks about his experience.

JW So you talk about a cultural change taking place in the Navy, particularly in submarines. The whole selection process under Rickover was to take the best and the brightest only. You don't even know what operation capabilities those kids have on selection. So that doesn't necessarily mean you're getting the hot-shot of submarine leadership, but it turned out, we learned that you can do both. You can take bright people and also they can turn out to be good skippers. Do we have some questionable skippers? Yeah, I think so, but I think the numbers are small. Even so, all have done pretty well.

*I thought these three poems would be an appropriate ending for a chapter on the culture of the U.S. Navy Submarine Force. Regrettably, the third poem I found as unattributed—I don't even know the title of the verse. The first poem I saw in a wonderful book by Peter Maas—*The Terrible Hours *on page 57, where he was describing how really bad the living conditions were on the early diesel boats, having no refrigeration, distillers, air conditioning, nor any toilets. Submerged, "you were reduced to a bucket half filled with diesel oil." He describes one of my heroes, Swede Momsen, as strumming his ukulele singing defiantly with his men, this hilarious ditty;*

"Submarines have no latrines,
The men wear leather britches.
They hang their tails out o'er the rails
And shout like sons-o-bitches."

The following was written by a submariner, then Lieutenant Commander Richard G. Voge, USN. Former CO of Sealion and Sailfish. He also was Adm. Lockwood's Operations Officer in WWII.

"Old Fuds, Young Studs and Lieutenant Commanders"

Battleships are title B,
That's lesson one in strategy.
They are the backbone of the Fleet,
Their fighting power can't be beat.
They dominate the raging Main,

While swinging round the anchor chain,
And bravely guard your home and mine,
While anchored out there all in line.
They fill the Japs with fear and hate,
From well inside the Golden Gate.

Now lesson two in strategy—
Our subs and planes are title C.
Just send them out on any mission,
And win your battles by attrition.
Where'er you send the subs and planes,
You're bound to chalk up lots of gains—
And losses too, but what the hell,
Who cares about their personnel?
For planes are chauffeured by young studs,
Lieutenant Commanders run the subs.

This is an untitled, obviously contemporary poem which salutes the splendid boats and skippers of the WWII era and carries it through to today's Submarine Service.

Let it never be said, that we don't remember.
What submariners have done, since that day in December.

The sun showed bright, on that Pearl Harbor morning.
When the enemy attacked, with little or no warning.

The Tautog was there, with no time to think.
And splashed one Japanese plane, right down in the drink.

She sent twenty-six ships, to the depths of the sea.
And came to be known, as the "Terrible T."

The Sealion at Cavite was the first to be caught.
She was moored to a pier, but bravely she fought.

Two bombs exploded, through the hull they did rip.
And many brave submariners, died in their ship.

There were many proud boats, like the Perch and the Finback.
The Kraken, the Haddock, the Scamp and the Skipjack.

We remember the Halibut, Blenny and Darter.
And never forget, Sam Dealey in Harder.

Cutter and Seahorse's, torpedoes ran true.
She targeted the enemy, and sank many Marus.

And although the enemy, was quite filled with hate.
"Red" Ramage and Parche, showed many their fate.

"Mush" Morton and Wahoo, never backed down from a fight.
Fluckey and Barb entered Namkwan Harbor one night.

Many airmen were saved, by O'Kane and the Tang.
Some owe their lives, to Sea Fox, Tigrone and Trepang.

We remember the honorable, boat called Barbel.
Before she was lost, she gave the enemy hell.

The Sturgeon, the Trigger, the Pollack had heart.
The Torsk, made the last two frigates depart.

Nowadays the cold war seems to be a big factor.
And submarines are powered, by nuclear reactors.

The proud names are still there, the Tautog did shine.
But her hull number by then, was Six Thirty Nine.

Many boats gave their all, with heroic namesakes.
Like Thresher, Scorpion, Nautilus and Skate.

The Seadragon, Swordfish, Richard B. Russell and Dace.
Have all stood out to sea, and heard the enemies trace.

We remember "Forty-One For Freedom," whose patrols couldn't fail.
The George Washington, Andrew Jackson and Nathan Hale.

Now the Alaska and Nebraska, and other Tridents are here.
They patrol the deep oceans, so aggressive nations have fear.

There are new boats on the line, called Cheyenne and Wyoming.
They will all do us proud, like the old Gudgeon and Grayling.

So take time each day, and think of the past.
Then toast the new Seawolf, for she's quiet and fast.

Let it never be said, that we don't remember.
What submariners have done, since that day in December.

The sun still shines bright, every Pearl Harbor Morning.
But never forget, the enemy attacks without warning.

Rickover

**"The Navy couldn't have stood more than one of him.
But thank God we had him."** VADM Pat Hannifin

Every interview included lots of opinions and anecdotal information about the most famous name in nuclear power—Admiral Hyman Rickover. Not discussing him in this work would be like avoiding mention of a Cape Buffalo at your garden party. He is so deeply imbedded in every aspect of U.S. Navy nuclear submarines, that the interviews are riddled with references to him and his style, his abrasiveness, his rigorous attention to engineering detail and procedures, and his profound effect on not only the nuclear Navy, but upon the United States Navy as a whole.

This chapter will simply convey the responses of those interviewed and those who submitted with respect to this man. Predictably, the stories range from the profound to the humorous. There are a number of books about or including Rickover in the marketplace and this work makes no attempt to compete with them. In fact, I avoided reading any of them particularly that by John Lehman, so as not to poison the well or introduce bias into this project. This is not another biography. These are stories from people who knew him and worked with him.

Chuck Grojean had a lot to say about Rickover in our interview. He even crossed swords a bit with him and lived to tell about it.

DG: So how were people recruited? Was Admiral Rickover passive in that regard?

CG: No, no, no. Admiral Rickover was never passive. That's the most non-passive man that ever existed. Rickover was brilliant in knowing how to create an outfit that was highly desired. He went to the BUPERS and said, I want you to give me the top, the very top cream, of the submarine force. I don't want anything but the top cream. So they would send him a half a dozen guy's names. He would go through and he would interview these, and he just almost arbitrarily threw half out, and then he would go back and pound on the desk of the Chief of Bureau Personnel and say you didn't give me the top. You gave me a bunch of guys that I didn't take. They weren't any good. And the BUPERS would come back and say, well, wait a minute, now, Admiral. You know, we gave you the top based upon—he says, I don't care. I've interviewed them and I know which ones are going to make good ones and which ones are not, and I've picked the good ones. You give me the top. So they'd give him another half a dozen names. At that level the top are all good. Now, when I went in for my interview with Rickover on a Saturday, I guess this was about August of 1958. I went in with one other officer. He had also had command. He was a year senior to me, in fact. And he was in command of a diesel submarine at the same time that I was. And we both went in and we both were interviewed. We were both shouted at, we were both thrown into the penalty box, we were both told that we were lying, we were both told that we were no goddamn good, we could not enter his program, and we were sent home and the next day I was called, I'd been selected and the other guy had not been.

Each of us was interviewed separately the same day, and we were also interviewed by about three or four guys that Rickover had on his staff. For instance, his Chief of Staff at that time was a Navy captain who was an EDO (Engineering Duty Only) brilliant guy out of the class of thirty-nine, I think, and he interviewed me as well as two other civilians that were on his staff that were technical people. What books had I read? Why did I want this program? What did I think about the leadership of the Navy? What did I think about, you know, my ability to lead? All these questions. And then we were handed over to Rickover and then he was the final arbiter of who was in and who was out. But this is the way he selected his officers, and he kept stating all this time, I cannot wait until I get my force up to such a level that I don't have to go to the fleet anymore. I can take new guys in from the ROTC units and the Naval Academy, which he was able to do in about ten years, maybe less.

DG: But in the initial stages he had to dip into the diesel boat officers.

CG: Oh, he had to, yeah. Oh, yeah. All of us.

DG: Did you detect an idea that he didn't want to contaminate his nuclear power Navy with people with a diesel mentality?

CG: I don't know that it was the diesel mentality or whether it was a mentality of people who had already formed their opinions and ideas and so forth. Rickover was a rare man. First of all, the schism that came about between diesels and nuclear was caused directly by him. He was the wedge. And the poor guys that were not selected, those guys felt inferior because they were not selected. Those who were selected all felt like we were goddamn lucky to get selected and that the guy that wasn't selected was just as good as we were, and that Rickover had no ability to be able to select leaders better than anybody else, and that he would have done just as well had he taken the ones that he didn't take as he did with the ones he did take. That's my opinion. That's my real honest-to-God belief, and I know there are some guys who were selected in the nuclear power program who didn't necessarily agree with that. They merely thought that maybe Rickover had done a good job. It was all done on the interview—and the reason I know all of this is that after I was selected. I was there for my year. On Saturdays I would have to go in and sit in all day for about eight, nine, ten hours while Rickover interviewed new nuclear power officer candidates. He interviewed every nuclear officer that was ever in the nuclear power program. And I sat in on maybe fifty of those, and at the end he would ask, 'What do you think about him?' Well, I think he, you know, he answered your questions well, Admiral. I think he'd be a good man. Rickover would respond, "Well, I think he was evasive. I don't think he's going to do it." Or, he might say, "Well, yeah, I think so, too."

In my interview, for instance, his approach to me was, you know, you stood at the middle of your class. That's not very high. Why didn't you stand higher? And I said, "I didn't stand higher probably because I didn't apply myself as much as I probably should have. I also found it difficult to compete in the Naval Academy system of memorization. I used to have to derive formulas, whereas the guys with great memories could go up and just write them from memory. It took me more time, and I'm more of a logical thinker than I am a rote thinker. And, therefore, the Naval Academy system favored those who could do the most in the shortest period of time. And I never thought that was the best way to teach." Well, I think he liked what I said, but he said, "Well, you know, you're pretty arrogant. I don't know what gives you such a high opinion of yourself. You know, it isn't because you look smart. If I were picking people on their looks, you'd be the last one. You're not very smart-looking, you know." And I said, "Well, Admiral"—if you remember what Admiral Rickover looked like—he was a little short, squat, ugly bastard—and I said, "Well, Admiral, as you and I know, we didn't have a lot of choice in our looks." I felt I'd probably said as much as I could get away with when I made that comment, you know. I stood up to Rickover on several occasions, even after I was in the nuclear power program, oftentimes to my detriment. But he always, I think, respected the fact that I took him on.

DG: So that says something for him. You don't think he punished you for that?

CG: No. No, he admired it. That was good, that was very good. The worst thing about Rickover was that it was so blatant that one guy is okay and you're not. And the guys that were not were outstanding officers and had proven themselves to be outstanding officers. Now, later, when Rickover was able to only take his input from the Naval Academy and from the ROTC units, he selected a lot of people and he did a much poorer job of selecting because he did it mostly on their academic performance because they had not had a leadership judgment made on them. And I know I had serving with me some of these guys, and they were brilliant. They stood one, two, three, and four in their class. But, they had not proven themselves in the fleet to be good leaders. And the correlation—and I was at the Naval Academy as an officer for two years, and one of my jobs was to see if there was a correlation in aptitude and in academic standing and in success in the fleet. Very little. Very little. I mean, guys like Halsey stood way low, you know, or Nimitz was top third. Or maybe higher than that, a little higher than that, maybe the top 20 percent. But the guys that stand two, three, four in their class oftentimes make outstanding engineers but are not good leaders. And Rickover had no insights or prescient ability to determine that leader by interviewing, particularly, and so he took a lot of men later on that were standing high and I served with them and they were brilliant, and they were absolutely total flops. I had to kick them out. I went back to Rickover, of course, you don't kick them out yourself. When I went back to Rickover saying that this officer had to go and Rickover said, Oh, no, no. That guy's a good man. And I said, Well, Admiral, you know he is going to get into trouble, he said, I'm going to send him back to school for retraining. So they send him back to school, then sent him back to me in two months and said, He's fine, he's a wonderful guy. And three weeks later he'd done some of the same damn things, and I called Rickover and I said, Either he goes or I go. So, Rickover said Okay, I'll send him to an operating submarine. He sent him to an operating submarine and eighteen months later he had a collision while he was officer of the deck. That same guy. So, you know, I knew that I was right.

DG: Why would Rickover have resisted?

CG: Because he was bright. He stood number three in his class. Brilliant guy. Rickover's obsession with academic excellence overshadowed his ability oftentimes to select operators. Rickover knew nothing, really, about being a good operator. You know, he never had a driver's license. He couldn't operate an automobile. That's right.

DG: Had he had experience in submarines though?

CG: Yes, when he graduated from the Naval Academy he went into submarines. But his penchant for the technical end of things, the engineering part of it, overshadowed all of his other skills. I think—I'm not certain about this, you'd have to do some research on it—I think he got his dolphins but I'm not certain of it. But, anyway, he did not stay. He went to EDO. (Engineering Duty Only)

DG: Did he wear dolphins on his uniform?

CG: No. You never saw him wear them, so that makes me feel as if he probably did not get qualified. And I'm not so sure but what he may have gotten partly qualified and then I've heard mixed stories on it and I've never researched it myself. But, for instance, when I had command of the Barb, it was after we'd lost the Thresher. And a lot of the questions that came out of the Thresher was how'd it go bad? And a lot of it centered around the hydraulic systems, and there was speculation that maybe the hydraulic system had gone bad. I guess not so much on the Thresher as it was on the Scorpion. And so he came on board—he rode me on my first sea trials. He always rode the ship when a nuclear ship went to sea for the first time. Always. Always.

Okay, to give you an example of what I'm talking about as far as an operator goes, he came on board my ship and decided, "You guys in the submarine force, you don't know how to control your depth. You're always trying to maintain depth. Why don't you give them a range of fifty feet and say maintain your depth between 300 and 350 feet? That way we don't have to move the planes so much." I said, "No, Admiral, you know, the problem is it's like driving an automobile. I mean, if you drive an automobile you're always going back and forth to maintain course. If you were to have a real long, wide highway, and you went this way and you went from one extreme, one side to the other, you're still operating that hydraulic system and also, there are other things that are wearing out." So he said, "Now, let this thing go. You listen to me, Grojean! You tell your guy to—just because he's off depth by two feet, let it ride." So, of course, what happens is that the submarine is—first of all, it's off two feet, then it's off eight feet, and then it starts to get worse. And the next thing you know, you have to go throw it hard over—your diving plane's—hard over in order to bring it back down to depth. And it would have been a lot easier if he'd just made minor corrections and stay right on the depth. But Rickover couldn't understand that. He just did not understand operating. He would come on board and insist that you cut off the 1MC system. You remember the 1MC system? Because it was keeping him awake. Or he would insist that there be no coffee at watch stations when he was onboard. I mean, when he left I did what I wanted to do, but when he was onboard—no coffee.

DG: What was his rationale?

CG: Well, coffee is interfering with your job. He didn't understand that standing on watch for four hours, that nobody can stand and give the attention that you can give something for thirty seconds or a minute, for four hours. But four hours is a different kind of attention. Your brain absorbs what's necessary and it lets the junk go away. Whereas, if you're thirty seconds, you can concentrate on everything that's happening. And he didn't understand that. And so he could never have flown an airplane. And, you know, Rickover was a—I have a close friend of mine who is a Vice Admiral in the Nuclear Submarine Force, who was selected by Rickover three or four months before me. And I said, "You know, George, you really did know this guy probably better than anybody because there were fewer people here when you went through. Why haven't you written a book about him?" He said, "I can't. He had so many flaws in his personality that I would never want to publicize them and detract from his greatness." Because he was the guy that built the Nuclear Submarine Force. He was the father. No question about it. He, alone. He was responsible for it. He was responsible for the safety of it, and he did it. And most of us who were in Nuclear Submarines feel very beholding to him and don't want to see him pilloried or we don't want to see his reputation dragged down, but the cold hard facts of life are he was a genius. He was a wonderful, great man, but he had some serious flaws. He was the kind of man that wouldn't hesitate to order you to pick up your family on Christmas Eve and go to another ship. On the other hand, if you lost your child—I know of one officer who lost his child in a drowning incident on a beach, and he called the man that night and said he'd like to read to him some passages from the Bible. He was a mixed bag of greatness and horribleness. In his later years when he was finally fired by President Reagan, he was at his worst. I mean, he had become terrible. I didn't serve with him then, I just heard rumors, so I don't really know. But he had outlived his usefulness by that time. But prior to that time he created this Submarine Force. He made every submarine officer and most of the submarine enlisted men want to go into the nuclear power force, and he did that by making it very desirable.

DG: How did he attract people with a personality like that? It seems like that would be a turn off.

CG: Well, he created such an incredible weapons system that people wanted to be on. And he saw to it that if you were serving on that thing that he was going to see to it that you got rewarded. Later on, you know, I watched him as I progressed from 1958 and all during the early sixties, and I saw that he was despised by a lot of the high-ranking Navy. The admirals in the Navy did not like him at all, as a group. And, of course, the diesel submarine people didn't like him at all. And those that served with him didn't like him but they respected him. He maintained an engineering excellence onboard his ships that was impeccable. What was I getting ready to say about the way he did things is that he made this ship and this whole Nuclear Submarine Force the kind of thing that you really wanted to go into. In 1961 he went to sea with me—I went in the nuclear power program and then I went back to being an executive officer of the Patrick Henry, the second nuclear missile submarine. The executive officers on the first three or four had already had command of a diesel submarine, but we were executive officers on these missile submarines because they had their own problems, which were different. He took the two execs; he took Harvey Lyon, who was the gold exec and I was the blue exec on the Patrick Henry, and he said, Now, I know you guys are going to be the new leaders of this Navy, and I want you to understand one thing, above all else, and that is you must maintain your integrity. If you believe in something, I don't care what, you fight for it and don't give in. Don't let the hide-bound Navy rules and things change your integrity. You understand? And we said, Yes, sir. Well, both Harvey and I made admiral. In fact, all four of us, the two skippers and us made admiral, and the early nuclear submariners certainly had their share, much larger than their numerical share, of flag officers. And, you know, Rickover was insistent that these people become flag officers, and he was insistent upon saying okay or not okay to become a flag officer, if you were in the nuclear power program.

When I was first eligible to come up for flag officer, I didn't make it. And the four-star admiral who was in charge of the thing saw me at a cocktail party a few weeks later and said, "Chuck, I'll tell you something. I'm awful sorry that you didn't make admiral. You were supposed to make admiral this time. All of us on the board except for the one nuclear guy that was on the board said yes, but the one nuclear guy on the board said that Admiral Rickover had not approved of you." And I said, "Well, I'd kind of maintained my distance from Rickover. I didn't think it was necessary." He said, "Well, it is." After that a friend of mine came around and visited with me. He said, "I need to talk with you. Your spear with Rickover is crooked. You need to straighten it out. You need to maintain your contact with him. You haven't written him in a year and a half. And you are just acting like he had nothing to do with where you are. And he is maintaining that admirals who were submariners are going to have to be guys that can get along with him or he doesn't want them to be admirals." I gave a cheery aye-aye, I wrote the admiral a letter, and I went back to Washington—I was in Naples at the time—and visited him. The next time I made admiral. Rickover maintained total autocratic control over the Nuclear Submarine Force. It was all his. And so the Diesel Submarine Force was not his. There's your schism. Rickover was always at battle stations with COMSUBLANT and COMSUBPAC until those guys became nuclear admirals. And he was—when I first went to sea as commanding officer of the new Barb, and this was in 1963, it was right after the Thresher, and the operating forces, SUBLANT, had said, "You can't go below 400 feet until we have your ship inspected thoroughly and we've conducted 'sub-safe' modifications on it; you're limited to 400 feet." So Rickover came onboard the day he was going to ride us and says, "Do you have orders from your bosses as to limiting your depth?" And I said, "Yes, sir." He said, "Well, you've all become cowards. Ever since the Thresher, all of you have become cowards. No reason for this." He said, "Are you restricted in what speeds you can make?" And I said, "No, sir, I can make any speed I want. I was just not going deeper than four." He said, "Well, we'll see."

So we got underway, and the first thing we did was do our deep dive. Test depth was over 1000 feet, we went to 400 feet, and this really ticked him off. And so then we did our full power run (one thing that he really is in charge of) and you do that for twelve hours. You have to build up to full power and maintain that for twelve hours, part of the acceptance things. When we went down to 400 feet we had a tremendous leak in the auxiliary diesel exhaust system. Yeah, in the cooling system for the exhaust. It was such a big leak that it was going to eventually flood the engine if we stayed down there very long because the pumps wouldn't keep up with it. So when we came back up he said, "Well, at what depth are you going to run your full power run?" I said, "Well, I thought I'd run it about 150 to 200 feet" and he said, "You coward." I said, "No, Admiral, we've got this big leak in the diesel exhaust system." "No, (he says) you're scared to run at 400 feet, and that's the reason you're not running the full power run at that depth."

DG: And this was in front of everybody!? This was in the control room? *In front of everybody!?*

CG: No, this is just between him and me.

DG: Oh, okay. Well, that's good.

CG: The first part when he came onboard was just to me; the second time—I've got to get my facts straightened out. The second time, I was in the control room. I was right at the periscope when he said, "You're a coward." And I said, "Admiral, COMSUBLANT's rep is onboard and he feels that we ought not flood out the engine because this is a big, costly overhaul." He says, "You're a coward. That's the reason you're all not doing it. You're all cowards." And he walked away and he went down to my stateroom, and he sat in my stateroom. He takes over your stateroom when he goes to sea, you know. The only one that does. The president doesn't, nobody else does, but Rickover did. So I got to thinking about this thing and I got very angry and I went down to him and I said, "Admiral, I've been thinking it over, and I said, you know, I think that it's going to flood out the diesel but I'm going to prove to you that we're not cowards. I'll run it at 400 feet." He said, "No, no, no, he said, I think you're all cowards." And he said, "It'll depend—I'll tell you what depth you can run it at, depending upon how you handle your ship." So he was sitting at my desk, he was facing the bow and he had a cup of coffee, a steaming hot cup of coffee was brought to him, so I went back up to the control room and I said, "Build up your speed to, I don't know, 15 knots, 20 knots", and I said, "Okay, give me a 20 degree up angle."

DG: You did this purposely? Good for you!

CG: Spilled his whole coffee in his lap. He sent the word up by the steward to tell Grojean to not take high angles without notifying me first; the Admiral spilled the coffee in his lap. So, you know, we went on then and we ran it at 400 feet and we flooded out the diesel engine, you know. It cost the taxpayers seven or eight thousand dollars. That's one of Rickover's flaws. And when you try to point out to him that the reason that we were doing these things was caution, and that he was very cautious as an engineer. As a matter of fact, after we did our sea trials and everything, we went in for a post-shakedown availability at Mare Island, and when we took the lagging off one of the five-inch seawater lines, we found that the shipbuilders in Pascagoola on a five-inch line which carried seawater at test depth pressure, the wall of the pipe was about an inch thick, and they had ground out a bad weld three-quarters of the inch and had never filled it in. So had we gone to test depth, that would have unquestionably given way—failed, and we could have gone the way of the *Thresher*. So, you know, these were the perils of early nuclear submarining, and the engineering principles that Rickover insisted upon were not being followed by the rest of the Navy, and that's the reason we lost the *Thresher*, that's the reason we probably lost the *Scorpion* because we knew that—I don't know, but I think that was a bad torpedo battery and we'd had previous indications that that was a bad problem. They'd had explosions on it and they didn't take care of it. But Rickover insisted upon extremely severe—rigorous, I should say—engineering practices. Everything was done right. You did not accept anything that did not pass a very stringent criteria.

DG: But his judgment and leadership ability?

CG: He oftentimes exercised poor judgment. If you want evidence of that, one of the best stories is Secretary Lehman's. He was present with President Reagan when President Reagan told him he had to retire. I don't know if you've read that book or not, but it's a great story of how Rickover was fired. But I had heard from friends of mine who were still serving that Rickover had outlasted his usefulness. And those of us who served with him find that to be very sad because he really had a lot of great qualities about him. But he was caught in that business that, you know, he would—this thing right here (points to a plaque on his desk). All of us got one of those. Let's look on the back. Yeah, turn it over, let me just read what it says. "Oh, God, thy sea is so great and my boat is so small". And on the back it says, "Presented—Lieutenant Commander Charles Grojean, from Vice Admiral H. G. Rickover."

CG: Now, he made a number of casts of those and gave them to us. Now, that's illegal expenditure of government funds, you see. This is part of his leadership. This is the reason that he did get people in there. He did things like this. And, you know, in that sense of the word he was really great. But he drove a wedge in the Submarine Force and he separated the sheep from the goats. I had a number of friends who were not selected and who felt bad about it, and they should have been selected. And I think that permeated the whole force.

DG: How did the nuclear power program get chiefs of the boat?

CG: I think that he went to BUPERS and found out which enlisted men had high ratings, and he brought them into the submarine force. I think a lot of them he brought into the nuclear force. I think he brought a lot of them in when they didn't necessarily want to go. But he didn't interview them.

DG: Did all rates go through the enlisted nuclear power school? Did they all have to go?

CG: Everybody in the engineering spaces had to go. Everyone had to go through nuclear power school. The fact that one enlisted man was selected and one was not was troubling.

DG: That was not in the best interests of the nuclear power program.

CG: No. Nor the submarine Navy. The enlisted people that we had on those first nuclear submarines—brilliant. I mean, some of the IQs of some of those guys was bordering on genius. I had a Chief of the Boat that was on the Patrick Henry that although not well-educated had a brilliant mind and was able to assimilate anything you taught him. He learned everything. And there was no question but what the nuclear-power enlisted personnel were very, very, very bright and capable. Was the level there a little higher than the new diesels? Probably so because they took them based more upon their technical ability.

DG: Could he or his subordinates examining those records, would they know intelligence level? Didn't we take a bunch of tests?

CG: I think you took a bunch of aptitude tests of some sort or another. Yeah, I think so.

DG: So he tended to do the same thing as he did with the commissioned officers?

CG: Yeah. But he didn't select out half of them—no, as at the interview. You see, that's where the mistake was probably made. He was not able to be God in terms of being able to select a good leader or a good officer, which he thought he was.

Bob Gautier also mentioned the relationship Chuck Grojean had with Rickover;

BG: Oh, yeah, he's a hell of a good guy. *Meaning Chuck Grojean*

DG: And he gave a very, very frank, no bologna, interview. And I sent him the transcript, which is what I will do with you. I was hoping he wouldn't change anything. And all he did was pencil in a few grammatical changes and sent it back to me. He was impressive. I really liked him immediately.

BG: Well, I'll tell you about Chuck. When he was over in Naples, he was a four-striper, and the word went to him, You'd better get your act squared away or you're not going to make it. And I don't know what that meant, but evidently he had done something that Rickover didn't like. And I guess Dennis Wilkinson was the guy that was given the task to tell Chuck to get his act in order.

DG: He said that in the interview, now that you mention it. And what he said was, whoever the messenger was—he didn't identify him. You said it's Wilkinson? The message was, You should communicate with Rickover...because he didn't like Rickover. And he also wasn't some pushover. He's a tough guy. That's the impression I've gotten. But the advice was, I think you should sort of kiss the ring once in a while, go and write him a letter, visit him or something. And he did it, and [snaps fingers] he got his stars.

BG: But you know, another thing, now, when the selection board would meet, usually they would get about four submarine admirals selected, and Rickover always would pick one. So this guy, Yogi Kaufman—Yogi's a classmate of mine. And he was the senior member of the selection board. And he didn't go see Rickover before the board met. And so after the board met, he got a phone call because the old man really didn't approve of who was selected. So Yogi went to see him, and he said, basically, what do you want to talk about? And the old man said, I want to talk about the selection board. Yogi said, The selection board is over. We don't have anything to talk about. That's right, and he literally walked out on him. He sure did.

Mike McLane, like those I interviewed, had the distinction of having served both on diesel boats and nuks, capped off as CO of Daniel Webster SSBN 626 Gold (1973–1974).

During my four years on USS Wahoo (SS-565)—a diesel boat—I had qualified in submarines and qualified for command of subs. Near the end of my tour, my C.O. said that I should "volunteer" for the nuclear power program. I did so and went back to see Rickover, got the standard humiliation treatment and was sent back to my boat on the "study program".

About 4 months later I returned to Rickover's office and took some tests. I got something like a 3.8 (out of 4.0) on one test and 2.49 on the math one. After getting a bunch of run-around from Rickover about my "miserable failure" I had had just about enough so I said, "Admiral, may I say something?" He stopped short and said "Yes". I said "I'm Engineer on a boat that is getting ready for a WestPac deployment and if you are going to accept me, please do so, otherwise I'd like to get back to Pearl Harbor".

Rickover GLARED at me and said "Get out, I never want to see you again". I got up and left. My "handler" (a submarine commander in PCO "charm school") went into Rickover's office for a moment and came out. He then said "You are back on the study program". I replied, "No, he doesn't want to see me again and I don't want to see him". The commander said "Well, just take your books back to the boat and if you find you don't have time to study, just send them back to me"

Returning to Pearl with my books, I put them in a locker where they stayed for two months and, in the middle of our deployment, I sent them back to Rickover's office. Several weeks later, I received a phone call from BUPERS saying "What are you doing, returning your books to Naval Reactors? We put you on the study program." Annoyed, I responded, "Commander X told me to return the books to him, I'm just following my last valid order" (and, besides, I knew who REALLY put people on the study program and it wasn't BUPERS.)

Imagine my surprise when, about a month later, I received orders to PG school at Monterey to get my Master's Degree in Nuclear Physics. We moved to Monterey, bought a house, and started in school. Several months later they announced a luncheon for "all submariners" in the school. I went, and the guest speaker was a submarine commander from Washington. He told of the great need for nuclear trained submarine officers and announced that some of those in PG school were being called back to Washington for interviews with Adm. Rickover. I leaned back in my chair and smiled, thinking to myself "Been there, done that! Have fun, you who are called"

Imagine my surprise when my name was the third one on the list. In shock, I returned to Washington, reporting first to BUPERS where we all had a talk with a senior submariner (captain) who said, in effect, "We need people, and here is the deal. You go over to Admiral Rickover's office and volunteer for the nuclear power program. If he doesn't accept you, you go back to PG school. If he does accept you, you go immediately into nuclear power school."

The captain continued "If you DON'T volunteer, and he doesn't accept you, we'll send you to some place like Adak (the Aleutian Islands) or Midway (no more PG school). If he accepts you, you will go to nuclear power school immediately. Now, how many of you volunteer?" Only one of the 10 submarine qualified lieutenants held up his hand.

Off we marched to Naval Reactors. With one preliminary interview by a civilian, we entered the admiral's office (one at a time) and were asked maybe two very innocuous questions, then dismissed. As I walked out of his office I was immediately greeted by my handler (who did NOT consult with the admiral) who said "Congratulations, you made it". I realized it was a foregone conclusion and the interviews were a sham. I thought if the navy was so hard up for nuclear trained officers that they went through all this, I'd do it. As my mother always said, "things work out the way they are supposed to."

One funny postscript. Shortly after entering nuclear power school in Vallejo, California, I receive a letter from BUPERS saying, "When your services are no longer required in the nuclear power program, and provided you are still of proper seniority, you will be returned to Post Graduate School, Monterey". I laughed at the mutually exclusive statements. Upon completing my Polaris command with about 18 years of service, I was still laughing.

Pat Hannifin had a softer view of Rickover with not much else to say about him than the following:

DG: How was the recruiting of officers for the nuclear program approached?

PH: The way that worked, Rickover had absolute control of it. As you know, he not only was the Assistant Bureau of Ships for Nuclear Power, but he was also the head of Naval Nuclear Power for the Atomic Energy Commission, so with the Atomic Energy Commission hat he was responsible for training, of all operators in nuclear reactors, officers and men.

DG: Ashore or at sea.

PH: Didn't matter. But you couldn't go to nuclear power training without going through Rickover, the officers couldn't. So the submarine detailing officer and bureau personnel was pretty damn careful to send people over there that he thought would make it, I'm talking about older officers. I went in as a Lieutenant Commander having already had command. I went in as the first executive officer of the first Polaris submarine, the George Washington. Grojean was on the second one, the Patrick Henry, as XO. So I was the first XO assigned, and the guys out of class of '42 were commanding officers of the first Polaris submarines. But BUPERS, the detailing officer, was very careful to send an officer over there that had good operating experience and also had fairly good academic credentials, too, because Rickover was concerned about that also. A quick anecdote here.

When I went in for my interview, I'd left the *Diodon* and I was back in the Bureau of Ships—in the Submarine Type desk in the Bureau of Ships—and was sent over to Rickover's to be interviewed to be the exec on *George Washington*. And I got in there for the interview, and Rickover said, Alright, Hannifin, what have you done to pay the Navy back the money that you defrauded them during the three months you were at submarine school? We're talking 1944, and here it is 1957, and I said, I don't understand what you mean. He said, Where did you stand at submarine school? And I said, Oh. I stood about four or five from the bottom in submarine school, and he said, You didn't earn your pay there, did you? And I said, Well, I guess not. He said, Why didn't you? I said, I was just married. I guess I was more interested in being a good husband and not that much interested in the academics. And he said, Okay, what are you going to do to pay that money back to them? And I said, I don't think there's any way I could—Well, you'd better figure out a way. Get out of here. [Laughter] He knew where I stood in every class at the Naval Academy. He had the complete background, and I told him, You know, I did some post-graduate work at UCLA, I went to the Armed Forces Guided Missile School in Fort Bliss where I stood two out of a group of 55. He said, That doesn't make any difference. So, Ned Beach was the inside man when I got this interview. And so I went on back home and I told Mary, I said, Well, so much for that. And Ned called me and he said, Well, the Admiral decided to take you anyway.

And the reason why he usually had one of the other commanding officers sit in is because of the stories that come out of there, he wanted to have somebody on the inside to make sure that it wasn't stretched too far. But they're still stretched a lot.

DG: Admiral Grojean told me that instead of sending people like you, who had been commanding officers of diesel boats, to Nuclear Power School, they trained them right there. He was with four or five former diesel COs.

PH: Well, that's where I got all of my nuclear training was right there in the Admiral's office. Rather than going off to Idaho or someplace like that, where the junior officers were sent, all of the first commanding officers and execs did their training right there.

Now, we had to go out to the reactor site to get our practical training, but all of our academic work was there. And he had the best people in the world, you know, all of his vice presidents who were doing the teaching on it, and they were damn good. And I think he wanted to make sure that we got absolutely the best, and it worked; it worked well. And so we went out to the reactor site, and Oz—Jim Osborn, who was CO, and I were out there for about six weeks, I guess, and then took our reactor exam, both practical and a written exam of about eight hours. There was no guided missile school for Polaris at that time, so we went to the various companies—contractors and finally ended up in New London to do the commissioning.

DG: I hear that there were lots of really good people who were not chosen, and that sort of was a career ruining thing.

PH: Well, not necessarily. Here's my impression of what Rickover was trying to do. One, if he needed a lot of people, he took a lot of people. If he didn't need very many, he got much tighter. That was one of the things. The other thing is that I think that what he really wanted to find out when guys came in there, the younger officers, is whether they really wanted to be commanding officer of a nuclear submarine or a nuclear surface ship, whether that was a real goal or whether our goal was just to get a good education in nuclear engineering. And so he probed them pretty heavily to find out what their motivation was and also what their motivation had been before in the Navy, whether they had really worked at being the best that they could, not so much on the operational side, but what have you read lately? You know, what kind of books do you read? A consistent question, to get the feel for what they were. That was just his way of trying to sort people out. He did, he turned down some awfully good people, and I sat in on some when I was there.

Bob Gautier was not selected for nuclear power and had a great career nevertheless.

DG: At what point did you get involved in the nuclear program?

BG: I didn't. Well, when it came—Rickover picked two guys in my class, Les Kelly and I forget who the other guy was.

DG: You said Chuck Grojean was in your class?

BG: Chuck came later. But Rickover picked Les Kelly and another classmate, and so they started off short. Dean Axene was one of the first. Well, what happened was the submarine detailer, when Rickover needed some skippers, he'd call over to the detailer and said, I need two skippers or three skippers or something. So they'd send him six names or whatever. Hell, he could have picked them with a dartboard, because they'd only send six good guys. And so Rickover—all he had to do was take what was sent over there to him. Because they'd already gone and made the cuts, and they were all good guys.

DG: But he would reject some of them.

BG: Oh, yeah.

DG: So what happened to them—were their careers ruined?

BG: Well, as a matter of fact, one of my bosses, Mike Moore—Mike's about the class of '43 or something, and he had gotten a Legion of Merit during peacetime for his work on nuclear power or something. Rickover would not pick him for the nuclear program. He said, 'That guy is too smart for the program. He's a detriment.' And so Mike Moore was never picked for the program.

DG: I thought that his whole point of view was how smart you were, and he picked just only the smartest.

BG: Mike was never picked, which is kind of strange. But I was right at that cutoff point, and so when I came along, they really didn't need anymore of my classmates. And, you know, I stood about the middle of my class, anyway. So I wasn't a brilliant star student. And so I didn't have to go through that thing.

DG: So the result for you in your career was not detrimental.

BG: No, I went on and put the *Blueback* in commission. As a matter of fact, I ended up, out of 30 years I had command for 13 and a half years. I had an amphibious squadron, amphibious ship, submarine squadrons, had the laboratory. As a matter of fact, Hal Scherer, who was vice chief, asked me, he said, How'd you get two major commands? And I said, We don't talk about that. We don't even discuss it. So then I went on and got an amphibious squadron, and I told Jim Watkins, who was the detailer, I said, Don't punch my ticket. Just give me that squadron. Then I went to the squadron and then I came back to the laboratory. So those were all major commands. And, so, really it was not a detriment that I didn't serve in nuclear submarines. It wasn't to me.

DG: That has been mentioned to me by later people. I mean, you had enough time left to continue. The diesel submarine force lasted another decade probably. Wouldn't you think?

BG: Oh, yeah. Sure.

Note; I was once told by someone that Rickover wanted to eliminate the diesel boat's independent, swashbuckling culture from the US Submarine Force—that he did not want to contaminate—perhaps infect is a better word—his nuclear power submarine forces. I asked each of those interviewed if that was the case and interestingly all answered negatively. In fact, several said, as you can read below, that that had nothing to do with it.

I asked Dave Oliver about this.

DO: No, I don't think so. I was part of that group, in that I was either the first or second year he took the guys directly in. And he knew, as did everybody else, that that wasn't as good. It'd be much better to have a guy who'd been seasoned in the rest of the Navy and who the rest of the Navy had evaluated for two years, the way it used to be.

He knew that. Everybody knew it was not as good. The problem was this—you needed submariners. Remember, you've just got to go back and look at the building rate that happened when the President decided to build submarines to counter the Soviets. So the reason they started picking officers directly from college was just a warm body thing. It was driven by the need to get officers.

There was also another reason to get the new officers immediately. You need to catch these kids when they're young and they don't know anything different in order to have them work the hours they need to do to become good. On my first ship, when I had the day shift, I came in at 4:00 a.m. The day shift was over at 11:00 p.m. At 4:00 a.m. we had a written test for half an hour and then we worked all day. At 10:30 we had a written test for half an hour. We worked these hours seven days a week for two years. It was easier for me than for someone who knew the rest of the Navy didn't work like this.

Chuck Griffiths' comments on the subject:

DG: I've gotten the impression that Admiral Rickover couldn't wait until he could take people from scratch out of the Academy or OCS and bring them into the program.

CG: That's true.

DG: Was he trying to eliminate the diesel culture?

CG: No, I don't think that had anything to do with it. I think he was just trying to get enough better people. He was just trying to get smarter people. I think he absolutely—from an officer's standpoint—he absolutely worked his way through the whole diesel officer community and milked it and took the guys he wanted from it. They were the guys, at least, his interview team thought could pass the course. They were all middle, upper third of their class. The main thing he was looking for were people that were—he hated the attrition, and he was looking for people that could pass the course, and the course was tough. Most of the officers, other than COs, that went in from diesel submarines did not go through PCO school, but instead went to the regular nuclear power school.

DG: I heard when I was a young man that his personality could be abrasive and difficult.

CG: Oh, no question.

DG: Was he ever a CO?

CG: No.

DG: It seems like I've seen pictures of him and he didn't have dolphins.

CG: Yeah, he did. He did. He was not a CO, though. He was known throughout his whole career as being a brusk, difficult person to get along with. On the other hand, he also had a real genuine concern for people, and he looked after his people, up to a point. He looked after them as long as they were working for him. When they wanted to quit, he all of a sudden took a different view of them, and so there was really nobody—not many people that quit him that ended up friends with him. But let me say this, of course there were a lot of naval officers that worked for him, but they were there for a specified period, so they weren't leaving him. Jim Watkins worked for him.

DG: Didn't Lehman write a book about Rickover?

CG: Oh, Lehman hated him, hated him. And eventually he was the guy that fired him. And, certainly, for all of the people and the people relationship problems that Rickover had, he had a tremendous amount of integrity, and Lehman had almost none [laughs]. So there was a big difference there in the two guys. And, obviously, Lehman couldn't push him around. And Lehman did push people around. Rickover probably stayed 10 or 15 years longer than he should have. It was a horrible mistake. He began to believe he was omnipotent, and when he got to that point he became irrational and he only did himself a lot of harm.

DG: So do you think his reputation would have been different had he left 10 years prior to when they kicked him out?

CG: Oh, I think so. No question. Well, he'd been looked upon as absolutely one of the greatest naval officers that we ever had. He changed the culture of the whole Navy, not just the submarine community, you know. They introduced his techniques into the surface ship program and then the aviation programs, and so he really influenced the whole Navy and in a positive way. But he stayed too long.

At the end of that interview Chuck Griffiths mentioned Rickover's 'charm.'

CG: Incidentally, I can say this about Rickover. Rickover could be charming if he wanted to be. He was almost always charming to women. None of the women could figure out what the problem was with that guy. What's your problem, you know, because every time that he would get around them he would charm them. And he used to enjoy talking to my wife on the phone. He used to talk to her all the time, for example. And I would say, "Tell him I'm not here, tell him I'm not here", you know. [Laughter] Because our contact was frequent, both while I was a submarine detailer and while I was the Deputy CNO. And sometimes it was bloody, but there were also times that it went very well. He came to dinner at my house twice, he and his new wife. We had charming dinner parties. As I say, my wife thought he was great because she only saw one side of him. And he was always so nice to her. He could just be absolutely charming if he wanted to be. He was a very interesting guy.

DG: But he had to be charming on the Hill, too, didn't he?

CG: Oh! He was unbelievably charming and smart, and he had the Hill in his hand.

DG: It seems that if he had had that attitude, that abrasiveness, and went to the Hill, they'd have run him right out of town.

CG: Absolutely. He knew where to turn that abrasion. When he lost that power on the Hill—which he did in his last, say, 10 years—it slowly petered away as his old friends died or got replaced. And it was relatively easy, therefore, in effect, for Lehman to get rid of him.

Dave Oliver is an admirer of Rickover which is obvious in the following. With his permission I am including a portion from his excellent book, "Lead On!"—Chapter 17 is named Location and it is about the admiral. First his interview segment on Rickover:

DO: Now, I happen to think Rickover was absolutely right to personally screen officers. The worse kind of officer is the one who works his ass off, has a gorgeous wife, wonderful children, wonderful personality, and he can't keep up with the work. One sub-par officer in a small submarine wardroom is just a tremendous burden on everybody else. He needs to go somewhere out of the submarine force where he can perform adequately. The only administrative way for this to happen is for you to fire him. But most people find firing someone hard. And they'll pass him on and he'll do a below average or mediocre job at his next submarine.

The problem is the sub-par officer is dragging down the standards, and he's making other people think less of themselves. And I've watched this. He'll make other guys work less because they get irritated. I don't care how good they are, they'll slack off because they're tired of carrying him. And a peer can't say to him "I'm tired of carrying you," because the kid's doing the best he can. In fact, he'll try until he kills himself. And I think Rickover understood that. And what he did was he cut guys out that he didn't think could do it.

Now, the bad part is the guys who can do it are not necessarily straight-arrow people. Because the perfect officer for nuclear power is a student who got straight B's and never studied and drank a lot in college. Because you can take somebody like that and you can motivate him and you can raise his performance.

On the other hand, the student who sudied his ass off and got straight A's is frequently not going to make it in nuclear submarines because he can't take his effort up another notch. I believe Rickover understood this. There are all kinds of great officers that he turned down who later became very successful in the Navy and other places. At the same time, there were several men that he should have screened out but he didn't, and I watched how badly they would hurt until you finally took them out. And it wasn't that they were bad people, they were doing the best they could. They just couldn't keep up.

I'll tell you what I was astounded by. Rickover's a four-star admiral that's spending I guess he spent an hour—an hour and twenty minutes with me when I was 20 years old. There's no four-star admiral that spends an hour with 20-year-olds. There's no CEO in any business that does it. It was extraordinary what Rickover was doing. Here's a four-star admiral spending an hour with 20-year-olds. I care a great deal about the people that work for me. But, I couldn't have cared less about 20-year-olds when I was an admiral. And the other thing is, Rickover gave you his home telephone number, and if you had a problem you could call him at home. Now, when I was 28 years old and I'm a lieutenant and I have a problem, and I call him. And, actually, over the next couple of years I personally called him several times and Rickover answers the phone. Some 28-year-old is calling a four-star admiral and saying, I need help. Here's my problem. Well, a normal 28-year-old officer has to go through seven layers to get up to the four-star, right? Now, what happens is when I called him I had already done a lot of homework. It was a question that was relatively difficult to solve. I called him because I didn't know what to do. And he would get his staff to work on it. They couldn't go home until they called me back and told me, okay?

Let me give you another feel for Rickover. When I was a commanding officer—I heard about guys being killed aboard two different ships doing some evolution. And I thought about it and decided that I didn't know what had caused the problem.

It was a nuclear procedure which supposedly Rickover had written himself, but it had killed two sailors. So I did it myself one night, and then I thought about it later, and after awhile I said to myself, you know, I almost killed myself at this point right here. And so I thought about that. And I figured I was smarter than the average kid, and if I'd almost killed myself, I understood what those sailors had done wrong.

So I rewrote the procedure and changed it and rewired some things, etc. Then I did it on my ship to test my procedure. And then I wired my ship back the way it was supposed to be.

And I wrote all this up and I sent it through my squadron commander to send on to Rickover, and the Squadron Command comes down and he says, "This is not your role. Rickover knows what he's doing, etc., etc. I'm going to return it to you."

I go home and I wrap that procedure up and I send it to Rickover at his apartment and stick a note with it saying, "Dear Admiral Rickover. If you want to kill somebody else you just keep doing it the same way, but if you don't, do it this way. Dave Oliver.

Now, what does Rickover do when he gets that at his house? He takes that package in to work the next morning and he says to his staff, I want this reviewed today. I want to know the answer. And he didn't have just the guy who was in charge of the electrical area do that, which is one of his vice presidents, he has his deputy and the vice president do it. And they get through with it and they say, Dave's right. And Rickover says, Right, fire the vice president in charge of electricity. And Rickover puts out my procedure, word for word, by message to the entire fleet and says do it this way now.

Now, see, I like that kind of performance. That's the kind of guy I like. But he was not perfect. What he then did was he called up my boss and he said, I understand you turned this thing down, so I want you to go down and call Oliver and his wardroom together and his crew, and then I want you to apologize in front of the crew to him. Now, it was a neat thought, but it showed a slight lack of understanding. Because my squadron commander was not nearly as forgiving as Rickover was, okay? And he came down and did what he was ordered, but I'm not sure the Squadron Commander was fond of me.

Let me give you another example, I once called Rickover because I didn't like what some other admiral's command was doing, I was lieutenant commander, I said, "relieve him or me." Rickover had an investigation done; the admiral got relieved.

Rickover was an extraordinary guy if you were willing to put your butt on the line and if you were right. Candidly that's not the way most people saw him, but most people don't truly put their butt on the line. We weren't buddy-buddies. But I loved him. I thought he was funny, I thought he was fascinating, and I liked his standards.

DG: Wasn't he the man for the hour? Do you think somebody else could have pulled it off, in other words made the transition to the nuclear submarines?

DO: No. No, because of his political understanding. I'll tell you a story you don't know. Wilkinson was the first CO on the Nautilus. I knew Wilkinson. He's since retired in San Diego. And I took him out on a 688 once when I was the admiral there because I wanted him to see what submarines had become. You want me to tell you a story about him?

DG: Absolutely. I want you to say whatever you want to say. This is your 15 minutes of fame.

DO: This is a feel for how smart Rickover was. Rickover went through the files to find all these brilliant kids and guys. A guy named Hans Mark, who was head of Livermore, later became Secretary of the Air Force and the head of Science and Technology, Deputy Director at NASA, is now down as Regent of the University of Texas. He recruited Hans in 1948 when Hans was a 22-year-old kid and sends him off to MIT to pay for him to get a Ph.D. He went around the country and picked these kids up who were just brilliant, okay? But who does that? Who goes around and recruits brilliant kids? And one of the guys he recruits is a man named Wilkinson. Wilkinson was a diesel submariner in World War II, had gotten out as a lieutenant commander and is happily teaching mathematics at San Diego State. In the evenings, Wilkinson's driving up to Berkeley and he's taking courses in nuclear physics because he thinks—this is '47—he thinks nuclear physics is sort of interesting. Wilkinson's an odd guy.

So Rickover comes to him at San Diego State and says I really need you, etc., etc. Why don't you come work for me. And the guy says, Well, I'm not sure. And Rickover says, Well, come and take a trip.

So they get on a train and they go up to Chicago and they walk down to see Fermi, and they're talking to Fermi across a desk and Fermi is writing while he's talking because he hasn't yet got his critical mass assembled and he is in a hurry. Wilkinson's sitting across the desk from Fermi, watching him write upside down, and he says, You just made a mistake, sir. And Fermi says, What? And Wilkinson says, you calculated it wrong. And Fermi says, What the hell do you know? So Wilkinson gets up, goes over and shows Fermi he's made some miscalculations.

So they walk out of the room and Rickover says, Come with me. And they go down to the Salvation Army. Now, Wilkinson is a tall, lanky sonofabitch. He's about 6 ft. 2 or –3 and he probably weighs 170 pounds. Rickover buys him a brown suit, one of those ugly brown suits, two sizes too big, and he says, Wear this. Then they take the train to Washington, and they go up to Senator Pastori's office, and Rickover says to Wilkinson, When we get there you sit in the corner.

They get to Pastori's office and Rickover makes his pitch for the fact that he has to be in charge of both sides, the AEC side and the Navy side, in order to maintain nuclear safety for the country. And Pastori says, give me a break. That's not the way this country works, etc. Rickover says, But I've got the best guys in the country working on this, and nobody else has the talent I do, and I can maintain safety. (Truly, Rickover was prescient about reactor safety). And Pastori looks at Wilkinson and Rickover says, Look, you see that kid over in the corner? That's one of the dumber ones I've got. Look at him. I mean, is that not a stupid-looking bastard? Now, he's smarter than Fermi. Call Fermi. Call Fermi and Fermi will tell you that Wilkinson's smarter than any of us. So Pastori dials Fermi in Chicago, talks to him, and Fermi says, Yeah, I think he is smarter than I am. And Pastori writes in the law that the senior nuclear-trained officer in the Navy should be double-hatted and be in charge of reactor safety.

DG: That's how that happened?

DO: That's exactly how that happened. That's how Wilkinson related it to me.

Excerpted from Dave Oliver's book, "Lead On!"

I once watched Admiral Rickover on the initial sea trials of a new submarine. (As I have said, he rode each and every one.) We made our first dive. On the way to test depth, the after escape trunk began leaking. Water was spraying into the small enclosed chamber from which we would have to escape if the submarine went down. We immediately surfaced and talked about what we should do.

It surely was a problem. The leak was inside the trunk, but with the ship on the surface there wasn't enough pressure to cause visible leakage. We thus couldn't see the problem unless we submerged again. Someone would have to get in the trunk to fix it, closing the hatch behind him. The hatch to the escape trunk opened into the trunk. If the submarine submerged and the leak got larger than the drain line would handle, the person in the trunk was going to be in the deep weeds. Once water was in the trunk the hatch could not be opened. It would be like trying to push open a door against a leaning elephant.

A half hour went by. Everyone stood around.

Suddenly Admiral Rickover's voice came over the speaker from the escape trunk, "Tell the conn to take the ship down to test depth. The engineering officer and I are in here and we'll fix whatever leaks."

So we did. And they did.

The sea trials did not drag. We got back on schedule. Every event was accomplished successfully. Another fine ship delivered to the nation. No stories about a bad luck ship or questions about whether the submarine had been built too quickly. Just another little problem solved. We continued training. Admiral Rickover went back to Washington, D.C. and his uncarpeted little office.

None of us recognized it as bravery at the time. Once you think about it all that could happen would be that the escape trunk would fill up and pressurize the men inside. A small bubble would remain near the top. Which is exactly what would happen if you deliberately used the trunk for an escape. Worst thing that could happen to the people inside would be their eardrums might get broken. Maybe a little bends.

Heck that was a good engineering decision that Rickover made. Getting into the trunk himself was the right thing. Would have done it myself if I had thought of it. Not really bravery.

I would follow that man though.

Jim Watkins knew Rickover better than most. In fact he gave the eulogy at Rickover's funeral.

JW: I no sooner got to the coast of Japan on *Barbero*, than I flew back for an interview. And while I got beaten over the head and shoulders by Rickover about how stupid I was and dumb I was and just like all the other Naval officers and couldn't hack it, he not only picked me to go in to fill the executive officer of the new commissioning submarine Snook—USS *Snook* down at Pascagoula, and they needed it urgently, needed somebody to go in there right away because they'd pulled the XO out and they needed a new XO but unknown to me until my family got all moved, moving towards nuclear power school at Mare Island, I got a change of orders and no longer had to go to nuclear power school.

DG: Oh, you dodged the school?

JW: I'm one of the few. I don't even know anybody else who ever bypassed nuclear power school. But I did. So go right to Schenectady, don't stop in Mare Island. Leave your family there. We'll see you later.

DG: That's amazing. I'll bet you're the only one.

JW: I don't think there are many. Because he (Rickover) detested any thought of avoiding the full year of education and training.

DG: Were you just a natural for nuclear physics?

JW: Well, you know, I always was good in mathematics, but in physics I loved the science, I loved that kind of thing and I just thrived on my work at post-graduate school. And I knew I was a dummy out of the Naval Academy with the then by-rote learning process there, you know. You'd memorize more stuff than you'd learn, and for the first time I was now using my brain. I'd always been good at math and science in high school, but I didn't dedicate myself that much at the Naval Academy except the last two years. I finally stood about where Rickover did when he graduated, so he couldn't bitch at me too much about my standing (about 135 out of 800).

DG: He was really a stickler on that, wasn't he?

JW: Oh, yeah, an absolute stickler on it. Well, anyway, so that was my genesis in the nuclear power business. A new construction ship at Pascagoula, went from there to post shake-down availability at Mare Island Naval Shipyard, through the Canal. But no sooner got to Mare Island Naval Shipyard, where I'd hoped I'd stay on the Snook at least another year, because I was only there about a year and a half as a commissioning exec, I got ordered back to Rickover's office to work for him. I worked for him for almost three years down in the old "N" building on Constitution Avenue, and I was his Assistant for Selection, Education, and Training of Naval Officers, and enlisted to that extent, too, i.e. on the personnel side of his work. So that was my baptism in his own office, which was really incredible. But I learned a lot about him. I've given many speeches on my interaction with him and if there's any interest I can give you copies of a couple of speeches. One was at his funeral in 1986 at The National Cathedral.

DG: Someone told me that you'd given the eulogy. That's extraordinary. Were you asked by his wife?

JW: Yes. Well, I was one of the few in the inner sanctum, and that doesn't mean a friend. That means you're in the inner sanctum and he still yells and bitches at you, which was the sign that you were still on his team. If he ever said to you, Dan, you've really done a nice job and thanks very much for your help, you knew you were finished. When he said, Goddamn you Watkins, you're just like all those other naval officers. You don't know what the hell you're doing, and da-da-da, you knew you were still on the team. Yeah, right, everything was backwards.

DG: I was also told that he could just turn on the charm. I just somehow couldn't imagine that.

JW: He could woo the women, you couldn't believe. He was so smooth and pleasant at times and then he could go right through another door and just hammer the hell out of you. But I learned this technique after a year and a half of spending a plebe year with him down on Constitution Avenue in the old "N" building, and then the light came on about what he was interested in. He was interested in converting the officer corps of the Navy to be professional and engineering oriented. The Navy had been during World War II. He felt we should not forget the lesson and know how to fight your ship when it's under attack or it's under fire. Keep it going, keep the weapon systems going, and it takes a lot of discipline, it takes a lot of understanding of engineering. It isn't all just white collar stuff high up on the bridge. A lot of tough stuff has to be done yet he saw the WWII standards going down the tubes, in the Navy as a whole. He was also criticized because it would cost too much to incorporate some of his standards. For example one standard set was that we were not going to impose on the environment a greater hazard than nature does, in terms of the radioactive material. Well, when you tell the engineers that, you now double the cost of a ship. But history has proven that it was the right decision. His decisions were good decisions. His tactics in some cases were atrocious, but that was never his intent. His intent was good. It was a better Navy, it was a more professional Navy, it was a better educated Navy because of him. The Navy he wanted was going to stay in tune with technology, which, I think if he hadn't come along, it would not have been as strong a Navy as it is today. And I'll have to say for Zumwalt, Zumwalt triggered off the new relationship in engineering for all non-nuclear ships because of this. In fact, he started the Operational Propulsion Plant examinations for all non-nuclear ships and their related engineering schools and so forth. So he used Rickover as a model, even though they didn't like each other. They were at odds with each other on so many other issues but on this one they weren't. So it was interesting to watch that evolve. Now, I don't know that the impetus for change was all Zumwalt, because he had a lot of nuclear trained officers beginning to come up the line from the nuclear business. But it was very important, so the impact on the Navy as a whole by Rickover was significant, not just on the nuclear side.

Rickover also won the battle of a smooth, seamless transition from his reign to his successors. There wasn't a ripple on the water, no standards changed, nothing changed. I was called once by the Secretary of Defense ten years ago, either when I was Secretary of Energy or maybe shortly thereafter. They wanted to downgrade the four star position of the Director of Naval Reactors. At that point it was…it wasn't Bowman yet, it was his predecessor, a wonderful guy, Bruce Demars. They wanted to downgrade it from four-star to a couple stars, put it back in the Navy chain of command. I said, You do that and you will bring the wrath of Jehovah down on you from Congress. I said, You'd better not do that. I said, This nuclear Navy has never had an accident. If it has one accident anywhere in the world, you'll be not only out of those ports in foreign countries, we'll be out of our own ports. And you'll destroy a great thing. Leave the standards alone and pay for it. It's worth it. Well, they didn't downgrade it. They couldn't have anyway. Congress would never have put up with it. It's one program that has been professionally run in a solid fashion. The top technical people did not leave naval reactors. They continue to stay with it, which we were all worried about when Rickover left. And McKee, Demars, Bowman have done a superb job over the past twenty years since Rickover was forced to retire.

DG: Weren't you the one who forced that tenure to be a lengthy one for continuity purposes?

JW: Here's the fascinating thing about working around Rickover. He was so disliked by people like John Lehman, Weinberger and even Reagan because they were convinced it was time for him to go. These D.O.D. leaders were totally, anthetical to Rickover's approach. On the other hand, I don't think Rickover would ever have been on President Reagan's screen if it hadn't been brought up by others who said, Let's get rid of Rickover. Which they finally did in '82, and I was called back by Tom Hayward then CNO—I was CINCPAC Fleet at the time—to come back and draft up the necessary documents for a smooth transition to the post-Rickover leadership in Naval Reactors, which I did. I worked with Bill Wagner from Naval Reactors. I worked with Frank Kelso, who was later CNO, but at the time Frank was Director of Submarine Warfare and was nuclear trained. We put together a hell of a package that turned into Presidential executive orders, and they went through the bureaucracy like greased lightning. And why? Because they wanted to get Rickover out of there, and they would sign anything. These Executive orders took the best of Rickover and cemented them into executive orders turned by McKee two years later into law. These directives are on the books, so no one can screw up the nuclear Navy. It's the law. And that is good. That law requires an eight year tour of service as Director, Naval Reactors.

It's a great idea. It's very unusual in the Navy or anywhere else to have something like that, but it's very critically important that you have that continuity. In the first place, you've got to pick the right person and they have to pick the right person.

Mike Barr was the latest serving officer I interviewed for this project, retiring in the mid 90s, so I was uncertain whether he had a Rickover story. I asked him the same question I had asked the others. His gets "the funniest" award.

MB: Well, my first interaction was my interview for acceptance into the Nuclear Power Program. In the interview process, you had interviews with three of Admiral Rickover's staff people before you went in to see him. So I suspect that the decision as to whether you were going to be accepted or not was pretty well made before you saw Rickover, unless he saw something that he just didn't like. But he would make things very uncomfortable for you, and so I went in there for the interview scared stiff. There's always a CDR, somebody who's in the PCO training pipeline, who would bring you in. I now know they were as much on the spot as I was, but I didn't know that then. And so Rickover said to me, "I understand you don't push yourself." This was about two-thirds the way into the interview. And I said, "Well, no, sir, I think I try to let my record speak for itself." The Admiral replies "That's not what I meant! I meant that you don't work very hard." I said, "Well, Admiral, I try to work hard." He said, "Well, what do you do to waste time?" And I knew, because a couple of my classmates who had completed the interview with him had told me, that he was very hard on Midshipmen with fiancés. One of them had said he (Rickover) pushed the phone across to him and said, "Call your fiancé and tell her you won't see her until you graduate." And this was four or five months before graduation. I was engaged, so I absolutely did not want that to happen. So what was I going to say? It was wintertime, it was January, and we had been, in my little room—you know, midshipman being young guys—we'd been seeing how close to shut could we get the window and still throw a snowball through it. So I told him that. That was the wrong thing to say [laughs]. So after I got chewed on for about two minutes, he said, "Now, tell me what else you do to waste time." And I said, "Well, I go to too many movies." And he said, "I don't want you to go to another movie until you graduate." I replied "Yes, sir." And I didn't. But I could see my fiancé. So, that was my first interaction.

Then I worked for him as the Commanding Officer, Nuclear Power School. You know there is only one Admiral Rickover. There will never be another. His abilities were unbelievable. He had a lot of people that reported directly to him. For example, as the Commanding Officer of Nuclear Power School, I called him twice a week and I wrote him a letter once a week. This was a three-year tour. He never called you by name; at least he never called me by name. I think the reason he did this was so the line of communications between, in this case, him and me, was always open. If I ever had a problem that he didn't know about, I would have absolutely no excuse for not having briefed him on it because I had that opportunity. For the phone calls, the officer I'd relieved had said for the first half of his tour most of the time when he called the Admiral he'd said, "Admiral, I have nothing to report." About halfway through his tour Rickover chewed him out for not telling him anything. So from then on he'd told him things and he suggested that I do that, too. So I start out doing that. And I'd say

DG: Stuff you would not have naturally chosen.

MB: No, because it was so far down in the grass. It wasn't that it wasn't important, but it didn't rise to the level where I needed him to do anything or I thought he'd want to do anything. So I'd tell him things like—well, first of all, his secretary would pick up the phone and I'd say, "This is Lieutenant Commander Barr calling for Admiral Rickover from Nuclear Power School, Bainbridge." She'd transfer me to the Admiral and I'd hear "Go ahead." I'd say things like "Admiral, the Senior Officer Class completed the first Power Plant Characteristics examination with a 3.26 average and two failures." He'd respond with something like "Is that good?" I'd say "Admiral, it's average." He'd say "Okay, thank you." Then I'd hear the click as the phone was hung up. If you told him something, he was very polite. I got halfway through my tour and I thought this is nuts. I'm wasting the Admiral's time. There were a couple of things that *were* important and, of course, I did tell him. But he usually knew the important things already because I'd tell the staff first, and they'd run down and get to him before I could! So I decided to see what happened if I didn't tell him anything during most calls. I started saying, "Admiral, I have nothing to report." Not a word from him, just click. I would always keep the phone up because I knew sooner or later the Admiral was going to get that phone halfway down and he'd pick it up again and want to talk. Sure enough it happened. He said "You know you could save us both a lot of time if you don't have anything to report, just say no!" So from then on if I had nothing to report, the phone calls went: "Go ahead", "No", click. And that was not the shortest one because I learned later he'd done the same thing to another training activity CO, and his conversations went: "Go", "No", click. [Laughs] And that was it.

DG: So he must have had a sense of humor, don't you think?

MB: Yes, he did. There is no question that he had a sense of humor.

DG: But he would not let you know he thought that was fun or funny.

MB: He wouldn't share with you, that's for sure. [Laughs] What to me was most amazing about Admiral Rickover was that he had the vision—and I know he got lots of staff input—he had the vision to see what was needed to prepare for the future. I mean, the nuclear power Navy was so far ahead in all areas, such as radiological controls, formality of operations, safe operations—so far ahead of everybody else that—when, for example, people came to the conclusion that the nuclear industry ought to reduce radiological exposures, the submarine and nuclear surface Navy were already there. Of course, the Admiral may have had a part in pushing higher standards for the entire industry.

DG: Were you on any boats with him for sea trials?

MB: Yes. The only one that I went on with him was my second command, which was Los Angeles class submarine USS BOSTON (SSN-703). I went out with him in 1982—excuse me, that's not correct, in December of '81 on the ship's first sea trial—and it was quite an experience. You had a list to prepare for his arrival, and this was about a four-page list. (see *Rickover Package at the end of this chapter*). Some people would get upset at the length and complexity of some of the list. I suspect at least half the stuff, if not more, were things that people thought he wanted as opposed to anything he had ever said. One of the things he did want was a light tight stateroom to stay in. He would normally stay in the XO's stateroom. It's not easy to make it totally light tight. And, of course, he had to have his own phone line, and he did like to have fruit, so we'd give him fresh fruit. And he did like to have books, so I went out and personally selected three or four books for him to read. At the end of the sea trials, he asked if he could take them, so I guess I must have selected ones he liked. The Admiral also brought several members of his staff to ride—they were primarily interested in checking out the propulsion plant. The night before sea trials, when you're getting ready to go to sea for the first time, it seems unusual problems crop up. In this case we were having a lot of trouble with the sonar. There was a corrupted disk or something, and we had to reload the software. We did that three or four times and finally my weapons officer (the sonar fell under him) came to me and said, "Captain, I don't think the sonar is going to work." Well, you couldn't go to sea without the sonar operating. So I told Admiral Rickover's senior staff rider. They were back checking out the propulsion plant. I mean, those guys did a very thorough job—they were superb professionals, as you've been told before. And they were right in there looking at things, checking them, making sure they were right, making sure the government was getting a good product. The crew knew what they were doing. They were fixing some problems as well. So I went to the senior rider and told him about the sonar problem. I said we'd fixed it about three times; it was still not working correctly and I was not sure we would be able to go to sea the next day.

DG: Was it one of the civilians aboard?

MB: Yes, a civilian. Except for the Admiral, they were all civilians. And so he thanked me and he obviously went and told Rickover. About half an hour later I was summoned to the XOs stateroom where the Admiral was staying. In addition to me, my squadron commander was there, the senior representative from the shipyard was there, and the Navy Supervisor of Shipbuilding was there. The Admiral was yelling about the non-working sonar. As fate would have it, we'd managed to fix the sonar again, and this time it stayed fixed. And he was going on about he wanted every single spare part for this sonar that's in the shipyard. He wanted them down on this ship. And then I made a mistake. I told the Admiral we'd fixed it. He said "I don't care!!", or words to that effect. We got so many repair parts for that sonar that I think the ship lived off them for the next two or three years, and the sonar worked fine! The actual sea trials were absolutely 100 percent great. No problems. When we got underway, the Admiral came up to the bridge. He was very pleasant, very nice. We went through all the paces for the submarine and it worked just great.

DG: How long did the sea trials normally take?

MB: It was two days, as I recall. We got underway one morning and came in the next evening.

DG: So you had a lot to do. I mean, it was like nonstop, it was a marathon.

MB: Oh yes, you're testing, you're doing this, that, and the other, particularly in the propulsion plant. You did a series of reactor scrams, and Admiral Rickover was back watching those from the maneuvering area. After the last one, we were walking forward and he said to me, "Captain, how do you keep your boat so clean?" Well one of the things he was really into was clean ships, so I just about fell over. And I said, "Admiral, we work at it." He said "Oh, okay, thank you." When we got back to port, he was finished, he left, and it was just fine. I think he rode one more boat on sea trials and then he retired, or re-retired!

DG: So I wonder if he had mellowed. Well, it doesn't sound like he'd mellowed because he raised hell with you guys.

MB: Oh, I don't think he mellowed. I think he was the absolute 100 percent professional until the minute he left. I'm sure, I mean at his age he couldn't be quite as mentally sharp as he had been, but he was *so* mentally sharp that even if it was a little less than it had been it was still about ten times that of most people.

He was truly, in my opinion, a great man. Of course, he wouldn't know me from Adam, and wouldn't care. One of the great qualities that Admiral Rickover had was that he made you feel—at least he made me feel—as a Commanding Officer of a nuclear submarine, that he had a direct interest in what I was doing. He didn't have a direct interest in me, at least I don't think he did, but he was very interested in what I was doing. I think it was an important facet of his ability to make sure things went well.

Chuck Griffiths brought up the idea of Rickover succession for the stability and continuity of the nuclear Navy. Director of Naval Nuclear Propulsion.

CG: That's Linda Bowman. (*she walked past us during the interview at the Army Navy Country Club*) Her husband is the Rickover of today. But at any rate, he (Rickover) and those individuals on his staff that interviewed people were looking really for people that they thought could take responsibility. At first, in the early days when there was only one or two submarines, they were looking for brilliant guys, in the top one or two percent of their class. But they obviously had to give up on that or they would never have been able to man the submarines.

DG: Do you imagine that was a difficult thing for Rickover?

CG: I'm sure it was hard.

DG: It was like changing your philosophy.

CG: Oh, it was. It was hard. And he did reach down for guys like Grojean and me, but I do know of instances where I think he made mistakes. And he made plenty of mistakes, I'm sure, in his choosing people. But I've known some instances where he was right on, and he spotted people that could have been a disaster and could have caused an accident. He spotted some flaw in the guy in that battle that goes on during the selection process.

DG: So it wasn't all brilliance. I sort of got the idea that if you were just really, really smart then he wanted you. But that would not necessarily make a good operator.

CG: Not at all. Not at all. And he finally came around to recognize that, but I think he realized by the law of averages, smart people were more likely to work out better. For the work that he was doing, for the system he was setting up he needed people who were smart enough to understand their ships and understand even the theory of nuclear power and that it was important that people were smart enough to graduate from his course, which was a tough course, really tough. Certainly I'm sure it was the equivalent of a post-graduate course. No question that he was an important guy and that his system was important and it still goes on and it's important that it does. Bowman, her husband—you just met her—is the guy that interviews every guy that goes in today. He's got his job for eight years—four-star admiral for eight years—because of procedures that Rickover set up with the help of guys like Watkins. At the time that he left, Jim was a very important guy in setting up that long tenure because it is extremely important that the guy who has that job be there long enough so the industry knows he's going to be there for eight years, so that the Navy knows he's going to be there for eight years and they can't mess with him. And that he's got the confidence that he doesn't have to try and become CNO. He just needs to do his job and do it well. And, fortunately, they picked wonderful people, since Rickover, and the three guys that have had it: Kenny McKee and then Bruce Demars and currently Skip Bowman. Now Bowman has had that job for about five or six years.

DG: And what, exactly, is this job, Admiral?

CG: Director of Naval Nuclear Propulsion—Navy Nuclear Power. So he is the boss of the whole industry-wide effort.

DG: And that's a peculiar thing to be someplace eight years, right? Unique.

CG: Nowhere else. Nowhere else. Not even in industry you don't find many cases where you're going to have a guy who is in a responsible position like that for eight years. But the reason for it is to make sure that the procedures don't get changed and make sure that the importance of the thing is understood and that the money comes in to make it possible and that you've got a guy who is really sharp that oversees it all and all three of the guys that have replaced Rickover have been spectacularly sharp people.

DG: Now is that a job where he has, built in, implicit in the design of the job, no further aspirations?

CG: Oh, absolutely.

DG: That's it. It's the best job. He's not going to be CNO, he's not going to be bucking for anything.

CG: Nothing. He's got four stars. You know, there have been plenty of attempts made to try and knock that down by people, but nobody has been able to get it because it's law.

DG: That was pretty smart design. You think Watkins had something to do with that?

CG: Oh, yeah. I think Jim was directly behind it.

Mike McLane sent me the following item just prior to printing this book. I include it because it says something about Rickover which will probably surprise many submariners.

13 October 1965
About 10 miles west of Barber's Point, Oahu, Hawaii

While conducting exercises, USS Sargo and USS Barb had a submerged collision, causing extensive damage to Sargo's (ice penetrating) sail. No periscopes worked and the upper bridge hatch was missing. The bridge access trunk was flooded and would not drain due to debris in the drain system. Gaining access to what was once the bridge, via the torpedo room topside hatch, the ship was conned into Pearl Harbor by use of a sound-powered phone from the conning officer on the bridge. (No compass repeater, rudder angle repeater or MC systems remained functional on the bridge. Harbor entry was made several hours after sunset. Upon tying up at the pier, the shore telephone was rigged to the wardroom. It was now about 10 p.m. (Hawaii time) when the captain placed a phone call to Admiral Rickover at his home. It was about 3 a.m. in Washington.

The conversation went like this. "Admiral, this is George Vahsen, C.O. of the Sargo. We have had an underwater collision with the USS Barb. There were no deaths or serious injuries on either boat. Both boats are safely in harbor. I'm calling to tell you that the nuclear plant performed flawlessly. There was no abnormal operation. No relief valves lifted and there was no release of radioactive material from the ship." (condition and operation of the nuclear plant was the only area in which Admiral Rickover had any jurisdiction).

As we watched, the captain, obviously under a lot of stress stood silent for a few seconds, then his jaw literally dropped. Several more seconds passed and he said, "Thank you, admiral. I'll let you know" and he hung up the phone.

He turned to some of the officers sitting in the wardroom and one asked "What did he say?" to which the captain replied, "What can I do to help you, George". Like the captain, we were all stunned, having expected he would get chewed out royally. The lesson we all took away from that evening was that NOBODY was going to screw around with one of Rickover's captains.

Footnote. The result of the collision investigation exonerated the captain. He had taken all prudent and necessary precautions to prevent the collision but the existence of a previously unknown submerged current, counter to all charted surface currents, had caused the Sargo to be out of position. The performance of the rudimentary SINS systems at the time could not have detected this.

Now, if by this time you have not yet seen Rickover's sense of humor sprinkled throughout the preceding interviews, just read the following memorandum. My over Xeroxed copy was given to me by my brother Paul who was a Rear Admiral and who's service career overlapped that of Rickover's. It seems authentic.

United States Government
Memorandum

To: NAVSHIPS—PMS 81   Date: 6 August 1968

From: NAVSHIPS   08

Subject: SPECIAL AUDIT REVIEW OF THE NUCLEAR POWER DEEP SUBMER-
GENCE RESEARCH AND ENGINEERING VEHICLE,

NR-1 PROJECT, AUDIT NO. S00388

1. On 23 July 1968 you requested my comments on the draft NR 1 audit report.

2. The subject report puts me in mind of the review of D.H. Lawrence's <u>Lady
Chatterley's Lover</u> which appeared in the November 1959 issue of "Field and
Stream":

"This fictional account of the day by day life of an English gamekeeper is still of
considerable interest to outdoor minded readers, as it contains many passages
on pheasant raising, the apprehending of poachers, ways to control vermin,
and other chores and duties of the professional gamekeeper. Unfortunately one
is obliged to wade through many pages of extraneous material in order to discover and savor the sidelights on the management of a Midlands shooting
estate, and in this reviewer's opinion this book can not take the place of J.R.
Miller's <u>Practical Gamekeeping</u>."

It is evident to me that the reviewer lacked comprehension of the <u>primary occu-
pation</u> of the gamekeeper as described in <u>Lady Chatterley's Lover.</u>

3. A cursory review of the subject report leads me to conclude that its authors,
likewise, lack comprehension in the manner of accomplishing Research and
Development. Therefore, I believe no useful purpose would be served by
detailed comments on my part.

(Signed)
H. G. Rickover

The Rickover Package

*It is probably not uncommon for a writer of non-fiction to come across sur-
prises—something unexpected. Toward the end of this project someone mentioned
"The Rickover Package". Only hints of the subject come up in all the prior interviews.
When I inquired I was informed that when Rickover rode the submarines for their sea
trials or for some follow-up trip, certain articles were expected to be aboard for his
comfort and convenience. Under the circumstance that seemed to me to be understandable for a Vice Admiral's visit. I can't imagine some submarine base PIO (Pub-*

lic Information Officer) failing to provide some visiting member of Congress or other big shot, some goodies such as a foul weather jacket and a ship's ball cap to make him happy. If the CO found out this person liked chocolate pudding, I am sure it would magically appear at the evening meal. It is just what is done.

I have not been able to determine just where the admiral's requirements and needs end and Navy lore begins on the subject. Ric Turner, a Stewards mate, mentioned the famous grapes, adding that it was in his mind possible that Rickover may have once mentioned, "...grapes are good for you", which may later have been interpreted by those most interested in his approval as, "ALWAYS HAVE GRAPES". For this reason I find no particular fault with Rickover's desires to be comfortable while aboard.

Remember that a short sea trial cruise was the culmination of several years of very hard work on the part of the officers and crew. The 'finals' were administered and witnessed by none other than Admiral Rickover. You wanted everything to work and you wanted to 'pass', get it all behind you and go to sea and operate your brand new submarine. If providing grapes or a foul weather jacket made the 'proctor' of the exam a bit more comfortable, it was a small price to pay indeed and it appears that they were utterly willing and anxious to accommodate.

At first I thought that 'the package' was material things—grapes, khakis and the rest. I was really not surprised, however, when Chuck Grojean sent me his list, seen just below this. This list appears to me to be empirical. After some number of sea trial cruises I am certain Rickover commented on the evils of coffee on the watch stations, or how lousy ball point pens are, facts rapidly communicated to the next submarine's CO. That 'list' just grew by two items. I can only imagine how much conversation must have taken place between those who just went through the Admiral's last visit and those about to be visited by him. The 'traffic' must have been substantial.

Dan, here is my Rickover information:

<u>Rickover Check-Off:</u>
1. System for keeping track of deficiencies.
2. System for keeping track of rejections.
3. Logs and reports up to date.
4. Plant grooming (explain why temps hotter on one side than other, gage which are supposed to read same are the same.)
5. Initial and Deep Dive Stations assigned by name.
6. Do not rig for red on initial or deep dive at night.
7. Get permission to dump steam to 100% for Fast Cruise.
8. Check location of wrenches for all valves.

When Rickover rides check:
1. Supply of library books.
2. Check on food for his tastes and diet (lots of fruit).
3. Underway on time, no excuses.
4. No Mc's (i.e., chow, sea store cigarettes, anything but emerg.)
5. No 7 Mc's to maneuvering
6. Keep excess people out of maneuvering and Control Room.
7. No trainees around
8. Use last names only
9. Orders repeated back word for word.
10. No count down for back emerg or scram
11. Answer throttle before 1MB on back emergency
12. Don't use garbage ejector until after he leaves
13. Report all problems to his assistant and big problems to Adm. and assistant.
14. Adm. will initiate scrams and back emerg
15. On building up to full power and once there, don't slow unless Adm says OK.
16. SPCP and EOOW look at gages and not at just RPM
17. MWS relieves only after all other watches under him have relieved. EOOW after MWS
18. Coffee—not at watch stations
19. Unofficial conversation—no
20. No ball point pens
21. When in port he wants the New York Times in the morning
22. Adm sleeps in CO stateroom
23. No clocks are to sound the hours

Oh yes, I forgot, the Admiral always required the ship to provide him with khakis whenever he rode a submarine, so the smallest officer or chief would have to provide the trousers and shirt. More often than not he walked off the ship in them and failed to return them. Cheers.
Chuck

Responses from several submariners on the subject.

Well Dan, when he came on board for sea trials in about 15 minutes the XO would come to the Goat Locker looking for me as I was about the same size, only taller. He always expected a set of clean working khaki's. Shirt fit and he roll up

the pant legs. He had about 3 sets of mine when he died because they were never returned! I did corner his Steward one time at the brow in Holy Lock and demanded my foul weather jacket (New) back and there it was on the top in his suitcase. I got it after a couple threats! Also, he always wanted grapes on the Wardroom table. Don't know what else but I'm sure others can tell you.
"Spider"

While on SSN-592, SSBN-624 and SSBN-599. He didn't bother with DBF's. I watched EB shipyard workers making sure no "LIGHT LEAKS" in the stateroom he would use. Grapes Seedless, two sets of Khaki's, a haircut and a foul weather jacket.
Jim (Red) Lawton

We had grapes for him but I never saw him eat any. He never looked at them. Seems I heard that he commented one time that the grapes were good so everyone carried them after that. He probably thought it was funny and was waiting to see who would not have some for him.

He used the XO's stateroom on Flasher. We installed a button and bell for him straight to the panty so he could summon the duty steward. Only happened to me once. We came in from patrol and Capt Carr was on the phone to him. I was trying to ready the wardroom for the afternoon meal. stepped behind the Capt. and then back. tripped on the phone cord and pulled right out of the jack. Capt looked at me and asked me to get a ICman to repair the connection. ICman was pissed. Capt. never said a word. He just explained to Rickover that the cord had torn loose.
Ric Turner Stewardsmate

When he rode the Nathanael Greene for sea trials, he got a couple of sets of new work khakis, a box of seedless grapes, and a copy of the Sunday New York Times. Our yeomen also had to prepare nearly 600 personal letters, one to each U.S. Senator, and each U.S. Representative, announcing the successful sea trials. They had some kind of automatic tape-driven typewriter that did the letters from a furnished script. I believe that they were signed with some kind of facsimile signature stamp. Those are the only things that I remember, but there may have been others.
Tom Curtis

I think some specific type of lemon drops were on his list, as well.
John Bay

I answered the phone in the Crew's Mess on FLASHER one day, when ADM Rickover called after he received one of our incident reports. I never saw the XO move so fast when I came to tell him who was on the line. Also, the ADM rode us when I was on LAJOLLA, and visited us on SALT LAKE CITY. Both times I remember the Supply Officers sweating over the grapes. Over the course of his life, Rickover must have seen more grapes than any man alive other than farm pickers. When he rode LAJOLLA, he kicked the XO out of his stateroom for the two day underway.

Gene Brockingham ETCS (SS/SW)

Well, I have heard that a lot of stuff was provided to Adm. Rickover by various commands because they thought he wanted certain things. Maybe he did and maybe he didn't. Some of the stories may be legitimate, but I think the rest of them were started because some CO thought he could curry favor with him and the "success" traveled by word of mouth and eventually became "fact".

Long before I went in the Navy, Rickover had published numerous reports that the American school system was not nearly as good or demanding as the Germans or other Europeans systems. Rickover was concerned with results and competence and would tolerate nothing less than the best efforts of the top candidates. Don't believe me? Talk to Jim Flanders or any nuke officer that had to interview him. I was always amazed though, that some commands did not fully comprehend this. I know that Rickover would have nailed the CO of A1W if he had known that the students had to forego studies to clean up the plant in anticipation of a visit! I was fortunate (or unfortunate) enough to not have met the admiral, but I have the utmost respect for him, his ability, his courage, and his foresight and what he gave to the US NAVY and to the United States. Thank God for H. G. Rickover! This nation was blessed to have him on our side!

Dave Stoops

A strange but dedicated man. Stories about clothing are true as I remember; Fritz Kent ICC on *Kamehameha* provided khakis when Rickover came. Slept in the XO's Stateroom on 602 and 642. I remember having to disconnect phones and MC systems in the stateroom because true or not someone said he did not want to be disturbed. I believe that without him our Nuke Navy would not have been as safe and effective as it was. He demanded excellence and as a result Nuke boats achieved excellence. Our country will always owe him a debt of gratitude. (I was a non-nuke.)

Ray Turner

Mike Barr's response:

Yes there was a Rickover preparation list. However, I don't know how much of it he asked for and how much was generated by well meaning (?) others and just stuck. Lists like that are passed down and tend to grow without reason sometimes! He did expect:

To have a private stateroom with a phone line (while in port) to which no one else had access

That the stateroom would be light tight

A selection of books to read (choosing what would satisfy him was a challenge!) and current newspapers

Someone available who could give him a haircut

Suitable uniform to wear (wash khakis)

A selection of available fresh fruit

There are more, but these are the only ones I remember that I think he really asked for. Not unreasonable for a 4-star Admiral—and part of the mystique! He never, to my knowledge, groused about any of these things when he was aboard.

Mike

Transition

*"Harder, Darter, Trigger and Trout
Never come in because they never go out."*

The transition from diesel to nuclear power submarines took considerable time. Depending on how you measure such a period it was about twenty years. That number could be stretched out as a technicality if you measure from the Nautilus SSN 571 September 1954, as the first and only nuclear ship, to the very last and only diesel in commission—Blueback SS 581 in December 1990, a period of some 36 years (I have omitted Dolphin AGSS 555). But the bulk of it happened in a shorter period. One could make the case that considering the massive amount of sub building which occurred during this period, that it was actually rapid.

Several of those interviewed stated that Nautilus was really a diesel boat with a reactor. One look at the hull design confirms that. It was equipped with basically the same weapons, navigation and other equipment as the latest state of the art diesel boat. However, it was the beginning of an evolutionary and developmental process both for the ships and the weapons they carried.

There was a hyperactive building period in the decade of the 60s where all of the Permit, Tullibee, George Washington, Ethan Allen, Lafayette, Benjamin Franklin and nearly all of the Sturgeon class submarines were built. This totaled a staggering 72 nuclear powered submarines!

Quite often we see references to "nuclear powered submarines" as if it was an era begun abruptly—we had diesel boats, and then we had nuclear powered submarines. The fact is that the developmental process contained many experiments using both diesel and nuclear power. The Navy was looking for the best hull and power plant designs at the same time it was developing missiles and other weapons systems in a race with the Soviet Union. There were a number of single class submarines for instance. Here is a list from Nautilus through the first class with a significant number of ships—Lafayette Class: (*Note the continuation of building new diesel submarines. The letter N designated ships powered by nuclear reactors—G for those carrying nuclear guided missiles—SSBN designates Fleet Ballistic Missile Nuclear—SSNs are attack submarines)*

Nautilus Class—one ship, SSN-571

Sailfish Class—two ships, SSR-572

Grayback Class—one ship, SSG-574

Seawolf Class—one ship, SSN-575

Darter Class—one ship, SS-576

Growler Class—one ship, SSG-577

Skate Class—four ships, SSN-578

Barbel Class—three ships, SS-580

Skipjack Class—six ships, SSN-585

(Includes the USS Scorpion SSN-589 lost May 1968)

Triton Class—one ship, SSN-586

Halibut Class—one ship, SSN-587

Permit Class (Short)—ten ships, SSN-594

(The first of the class was actually USS Thresher SSN-593. Lost April 1963)

NR-1 Class—one ship

Tulibee Class—one ship, SSN-597

George Washington Class—five ships, SSBN-598

Permit Class (Long)—four ships, Jack, Flasher, Greenling and Gato

Ethen Allen Class—five ships, SSBN-608

Lafyette Class—nineteen ships, SSBN-616 through 636 (USS Nathanial Greene)

(Note my source for this list was a chart assembled by BAE Systems 12–01–1999)

By contrast to the limited number of boats per class above, there were well over two hundred fleet boats built in the WWII period if you combine the Gato and Balao classes. The first and most notable example of the Navy getting it all together was the building of the first Fleet Ballistic Missile (SSBN) submarines—the Polaris submarines. They are often referred to as "41 For Freedom." These began with the George Washington Class SSBN-598 in December 1959 through the last of the Benjamin Franklin Class, the Will Rogers SSBN-659, in April 1967. Everyone interviewed for this project commented on the really amazing accomplishment of building the ships, training of the crews (two crews per ship! Blue and Gold) and going to sea, the majority in under four years! On one memorable day—June 22, 1963—four nuclear power submarines were launched! Two at Electric Boat—Tecumseh SSBN-628 and Flasher SSN-613. Daniel

Boone SSBN-629 at Newport News and John C. Calhoun SSBN-630 at Mare Island.

Guppy

The Guppy conversions were truly transitional, but they had nothing to do with nuclear power submarines. I mention this because it illustrates, visually with the pictures below, the never ending effort on the part of the U.S. Submarine Service to improve their submarines. Even today I believe that if the original CO of U.S.S. Santa Fe SSN–763 were to go to sea on her he would agree that they have made considerable improvements. Status quo *is simply not in the vocabulary of the U.S. Submarine Service.*

WWII 'fleet boats' were very good and did the job. Through three classes, Gato, Balao and Tench, they went from hull number 212 to 525. The Cold War demands on submarines were considerable and prompted conversions of existing submarines. The new version was called "Guppy"(Greater Underwater Propulsion). The main improvements included a sleek, more hydrodynamic sail and superstructure, a snorkel mast, bigger and better batteries along with many other additions. Once a fleet boat was 'guppied' that was not the end. I chose U.S.S. Blenny SS-324 as an example of the continuing changes to the same boat.

August 1955....Just outside Portsmouth NH after overhaul

USS BLENNY (SS-324) 1968
Headed for the Med

While this book is about the transition to nuclear power in submarines, Don Walsh makes the case that the diesel boat community was, certainly since the end of WWII, constantly in transition as well. Here he gives a good tour of that era and its many experiments and attempts to debunk the notion that diesel boat submariners resisted change.

Sure people don't like change and when you collect them into organizations it seems to heighten the collective sense of unease. This is normal in any evolutionary process where people are affected. It is perhaps more intense in military organizations where tradition and stability are some of the primary institutional attributes.

But to say that the diesel submarine community resisted change is simply not correct. We all recognized the tremendous operational advantage that nuclear power would bring to the Submarine Force. Most of us of us wanted to be part of it. But not all were chosen and the way in which the 'people change' was being made did make a lot of us uneasy.

In fact, the submarine navy was an organization that was constantly changing in the post WWII years before the advent of nuclear power. Captured German and Japanese submarines along with the creativity of US submarine designers led to the very successful "Greater Underwater Propulsion Project", the "Guppy" conversions of fleet boats. Meanwhile, two new classes of diesel attack subs were designed and built. Special purpose submarines for missions such as the SSK's antisubmarine boats; the SSR radar pickets, troop carrying subs for special warfare support, missile subs carrying nuclear warhead weapons. There was even a brief operational test of a submarine 'tanker' to support naval seaplanes in forward areas. In addition to these 'fleet assets', there were several experimental submarines which explorer advanced hull shapes, deep diving capabilities and acoustic measurements. There was even one boat that for many years was a oceanographic research 'ship'. No, this was not a submarine force that was living off its past glory of WWII. It was a dynamic organization that was trying to find the best ways to do its missions. It was this spirit of change that set the scene for rapid acceptance of the ultimate technology, nuclear power.

It is too bad that some people have equated the slogan, "diesel boats forever" (DBF) with a resistance to change within parts of the submarine community. What DBF was then and remains today, is a state of mind. A way of life and an outlook that reflected the great traditions of the submarine navy that were forged during WWII. This culture fueled the very successful evolution of the Force after WWII and while change was somewhat forced at times, I believe that this general outlook is alive and well in the submarine force today.

Chuck Griffiths made the transition from Cochino which sunk off Norway

CG: I waved goodbye to them as it headed out on that trip. So I wasn't with them for that disaster.

DG: That was hair-raising. Do you think that spirit changed in any way during the transition? What was that process like?

CG: Very clearly there was a transition. I think it would be wrong to say that the sense of élan was lost, because it wasn't. But very clearly, the transition to nuclear power was such a huge transition from a standpoint of responsibility, and we were forced into accepting and being a part of that sense of responsibility by Rickover and his policies. And, frankly, there was a sense of fear in the whole community because of the concern that one of us was going to create a nuclear accident. So we changed the way we operated. We started following the check lists, everything we did, following procedures; which we hadn't done to a great extent before. On diesels, each ship was run its own way and without really detailed sets of procedures for operation. Each ship had a set of ships binders we call ship's procedures, we all had procedures, each ship did, but it was an entirely different type of procedures, and not anywhere near the number of procedures that were required with nuclear power. Now, you might question, could we have gotten there without that old man and without that set of procedures and without that understanding of the extreme importance of responsibility. Or that we could have gotten there without the old man. I don't know, I kind of doubt it. I think it took *him* to change the way we operated, to change the way we looked at responsibility, to change the way that we looked at procedures. Now, all of this did have an effect on morale, in that we had people that were working far harder than anybody worked on diesel submarines. They really worked hard. We would take these kids and shove so much at them—they had to learn so much, and their hours were unbelievable. And, of course, the ships operated a lot more than the diesels did, and they operated for much longer periods away from care, refit facilities, tenders, and that sort of thing. So there was definitely a huge change that came with the transition and you could say that I don't believe it could have happened without having the fear of God forced on us. I don't think it could have happened.

Now, on the other hand, just like diesel submarines, nuclear submarines all were very much influenced by the CO. And in your diesel submarine Carlos Dew was a tough task master and it was very hard, I think, to have had a real great morale on that ship, I would guess. And there were other diesel submarines that were like that. There are lots of nuclear submarines that were like that also, and so the CO was the critically important guy. And I think we had our share of poor COs in the nuclear submarines just like we had them in diesel submarines. We had our share of great COs in both, and with a great CO you had a great ship. That's what it really boiled down to, and even when you worked hard you had morale, and had fun.

Thomas John Bachman—Albacore AGSS 569

Wow, where to begin. Albacore was and remains a one of a kind boat. We were the last of a few diesel boats. A high speed test platform used by our Navy in conjunction with places such as the David Taylor Model Basin and the Scripps Institute in San Diego.

Often we thought of ourselves as a training platform for future nukes, as they came to us from nuke school at that time for qualification in submarines and thence to a new boat.

As one might expect I noticed that the new arrivals were very technically orientated. They, for the most part, learned quickly and earned Silver Dolphins. It was evident that the non-rated and lower Petty Officers did very well. We had a few PO 1 Class that did not make it. They sometime came from a carrier or large vessel and could not shake the big ship mindset. For example not being allowed to watch a movie if they were behind in quals. We all noticed that in the shipyard in Portsmouth, the nukes in the barracks waiting for new boat completion thought they were "better" than us. We seldom if ever had any liberty time with them. We used to call them bubble heads.

I later returned to the Naval Reserve after a long absence (earning a degree and raising my family). I had the good fortune to serve in SubGroup 8 and worked with many damn good officers and enlisted members. Here I continued to see that yes, they all are sharp and like us old Diesel Boat Sailors, not afraid of hard work.

Mike McLane
CDR USN
Wahoo (SS-565) Sargo (SSN-583) Roosevelt (B) SSBN-600, Webster (G) SSBN-626
1960–1980 (in subs)

I think one of the greatest "cultural" changes between my diesel days and my nuke ones, was the age spread in the wardroom. On my first boat, the CO was a LCDR and the most junior officer (due to the requirement to be a surface OOD before going to sub school) was a LTjg. Our families and social lives were much more congruent. When I went to my first FBM, the C.O was a Captain in his 4th command and the most junior officer was an Ensign. There was just NO WAY the wardroom could be as "close".

Note: Two years after Mike submitted this entry I asked him for some of his ideas on a subtitle for this book. This was his amusing response:
"Diesel sailors, dragged kicking and screaming into the nuclear era."

Robert P Kail
LCDR. USNR (ret)
USS Sea Owl SS-405
Jan 64-Jan 65

I enlisted in the Navy in 1962 under a Nuclear Program. My induction physical indicated a vision acuity that did not meet submarine service requirements so was dropped from the nuclear program. I did go to ET school and while there continued to pursue submarine service. I subsequently passed the physical and was selected for Sub School. I made it very clear that I no longer had any interest in serving in the Nuclear Navy. From Sub School I went to the USS *Sea Owl* where I fully expected to spend my career. After approximately 11 months I was notified that I must immediately "volunteer" for either Nuclear Power or Polaris training or I would be transferred out of submarines. I refused and within a couple of weeks had a set of orders to a reserve destroyer. It had become very clear that the diesel submarine fleet had become a holding pen for warm bodies for the nuclear navy! Oh, there was another ET that came aboard with me and he suffered the same fate at the same time. My "experience" with the Nuclear Navy took another turn. While on the *Sea Owl* I applied for NECP (Navy Enlisted Commission Program) and was accepted. During my junior year a representative of Mr. Rickover's Navy visited the campus and a "special" recruiting session was conducted. Each of us was interviewed and asked about volunteering for Nuclear Power. A couple of years prior I had received advice from a rather senior officer in Nuclear Power Sub Service not to go that way. His observation was that the service had so changed, and not for the better, that he would not recommend it to friends. Needless to say this did not go over well with the officer interviewing! His general attitude certainly reinforced my decision.

A second thought from Robert Krail a day after the above submission.

I believe that what would emerge if "people who were there" really opened up was that there was a clear cut "Sub Service" up to the nuclear introduction. Then there was this "transitional" era where the Nukes were ascending and the fleet boat era was literally withering on the vine. Finally there was the all Nuke SS. The fierce pride of riding the sewer pipes certainly existed(s) for all three. Culture is much more encompassing. The "culture" is quite similar (parallel is probably a better word) for the strictly fleet and strictly nuke eras. That for the "transition" fleet boat service was different. For starters you had a boat composed of three "classes" of sailor. One was people who came from fleet boats and knew they would only be on fleet boats, probably the one they were on, for their term of service. Another group, and a progressively larger proportion, were on the fleet boat waiting to go to school for serving on a nuke (I can remember on the Owl the snipes referring to the engine rooms as "reactors forward and reactors aft). The third group, particularly interesting, were those that for one reason or another did not make the grade either at school or after going on a nuke and were sent back to fleet boats.

John E. (Jack) Bennett
CAPT USN (Ret)
XO Queenfish SS-393, XO Tilefish SS-307, CO Caiman SS-323
August 1943–August 1966

While riding SSNs, I first observed the lack of seagoing experience of the officers, including COs, due to time spent ashore in nuclear training. They also appeared to lack the aggressiveness which marked the successful wartime skippers. This was caused by the fierce competition with their peers as the Navy became more cautious in peacetime and the personal demands made on them by "the Admiral" (Rickover). They didn't seem to be having any fun submarining. In time SSN skippers began to more fully exploit the tremendous capabilities of their ships and excel in Cold War SpecOps. Finally, the nuclear submarine Navy reached a state of readiness and aggressive attitude well beyond the scope of the valiant diesel boats before them. With more operating experience over time and spectacular technical improvements these boats and the men who man them now give our country an ever-increasing, unique capability not imagined just a few years ago. During the period diesel boats and nukes co-existed there was a healthy rivalry, seldom bitter, and I observed little or no arrogance on the part of the far superior nukes, who seemed anxious to learn from the WWII experience of the diesel boats which accomplished so much with so comparatively little. So I would rate the transition smooth and very successful.

Don Walsh, no doubt along with many DBF'rs, feels that the traditions of the diesel boat predecessors were not conveyed to the nuclear power sailors. He is probably right at least for some of the transition period. However, as Dave Marquet's article which winds up the final chapter—Full Circle—says, that has all changed. Our present submariners most certainly respect and admire their predecessors.

I believe that the 'human costs' were high during the transition from the diesel to the nuclear submarines. That is, some very good people did not get selected for the program and those that were chosen were subject to incredible work pressures. In the early years most of the nuclear submarine crews and wardrooms were made up of people who had served and qualified in diesel boats. I think the 'DBF culture' moved on board with them. But as it became increasingly difficult to find personnel to man the rapidly growing nuclear submarine fleet, the old culture gradually went away. Some might say that there was no room for the old attitudes in the new submarine navy. My view is that these great numbers of new people were never exposed to the past as we learned it and their work loads were so overwhelming that there was little time to care much about heritage.

So I believe that one of the disservices during this time was a failure to impart to these new people, who had never served in diesel boats, the traditions and culture of that era. I suppose that a lot of less experienced nuclear people didn't feel that it was necessary. It did not make their ship run any better. They had gone to nuclear power school and knew that plant backwards and forwards. The 'old way' was not pertinent to the present. Yet on board each of the subs were enlisted personnel who did not need to be nuclear trained. Also on the FBM subs you also had some officers in navigation and weapons billets who were not 'nukes'. If not carefully monitored, these divisions could lead to a 'them and us' way of life. In a small unit elite organization, this was not a good situation. The diesel boat heritage was not about how to do your job but how to think about your job. That is, attitude.

A lot of WWII tradition and operational know-how was not made part of the formal training of the new submarine Navy. Not a lot of tactical doctrine was written down. We got a lot of it by being exposed to those warriors who were then flotilla commodores, squadron commanders, division commanders, men with the patrol badge and combat decorations.

I had skippers who made a point of inviting these people down to have lunch in the ward room so the officers could learn firsthand from these people. When I was in *Rasher,* we were visiting Hong Kong and had invited the senior Royal Navy officer to dine in the wardroom. It turned out that he was a submariner and had won the Victoria Cross as commander of one of the 'X craft' that successfully attacked the German battleship Tirpitz. It was an interesting lunch.

I did the same thing when I had command. Occasionally it had its humorous moments. During a visit to Sub Base Pearl Harbor I invited Admiral McCain to lunch on a Saturday. During WWII, he made several war patrols, five as captain of *Gunnel.* I had known him in Washington when he was a captain in OPNAV. At Hawaii he was CINCPAC but had to virtually sneak into the base. Problem was that as soon as CINCPAC's car shows up on base, he's being trailed by ODs and probably the base commanding officer. As I recall he borrowed a car that had an innocuous bumper sticker and came through the gate in an aloha shirt. My wardroom was all at the table waiting when the topside watch called. "Captain there's some guy up here in an aloha shirt saying he's McClain, or something like that, and he has an appointment to see you. Is he an insurance salesman or something? I said, "No, I'll be right up." The admiral looked triumphant and in his usual gravelly voice, waving an unlit cigar, he greeted me with, "Goddamnit, Don, I had a hell of a time getting here. Christ, they never leave me alone. It's the dammed weekend, can't we all just take some time off? Now where's that lunch?" We went and we had a grand lunch. One that none of my officers would ever forget. And for a few hours in that wardroom Admiral John S. McCain Jr. was a young submariner again.

It was not only the 'old timers'. We also learned a lot from our contemporary seniors in our own wardrooms. A lot of it was oral history; how to do things by watching and listening. An 'apprenticeship' in the most classical sense.

All of us in the diesel Navy would have loved to have that 'infinite battery' back there in the new power plant. But in the very early days we 'outsiders' had the impression that everyone was facing aft towards the reactor rather than forward to what new capabilities it could provide. Now, many years later I am prepared to concede that this was probably more 'reactor envy' than a correct assessment. Clearly the submarine navy of today has its own great traditions and culture honed over nearly a half century of spectacular operations since *Nautilus* first went into service. To put this time line in perspective, when I joined the submarine service in 1956, if you counted back a half century from that time would have been only six years after the Navy's very first submarine, *Holland*, was commissioned.

DG: I'm concluding that we're in great shape now. But the transition was a painful adolescence, really.

POLARIS

Chuck Griffiths.(He gives an excellent, meaty snapshot of the early program).

CG: The Polaris submarines were built faster than any submarines except the diesel boats in World War II. Of course, the first five started out as SSNs and they cut them in two and inserted the missile section in the middle.

DG: Did they keep the names?

CG: No. They changed the names. I was the commissioning XO of the Robert E. Lee, which was the third Polaris, and we were built at Newport News. We were the first submarine they ever built. Interesting. But at any rate, those ships were remarkable—we built 41 of those in a little over five years. It's unbelievable. Now, they had to do it in completely new places. They did some, as you know, at Mare Island. Newport News, which was a new place for submarines. So, Electric Boat did most of them. And Portsmouth Naval Shipyard. And the only way they could do it was that they marshaled the whole nation to the task. It was the number one priority project and it was certainly the number one priority project in the Navy. Arleigh Burke ran it personally and made sure that it stayed on track, that nothing got in its way, it was an unbelievable feat. I don't believe the nation could duplicate it. It was really something.

DG: This is significant to me because I was on *Barbero*, and it along with *Tunny, Growler* and *Grayback* existed to simply buy time for Polaris—fill in the gap.

CG: Yes, that's right. Of course, the whole missile development was a crash program, if you will remember, and, of course, they developed along with the boats. And the Regulus missiles that you guys carried were air breathers, very primitive, but they were something.

Started out as SSNs. The *Robert E. Lee* was to be the *Shark*. They just cut her in two, split her open—same engineering plant as the *Shark*—and put the missile section in there and then it became a strategic submarine. Interesting. Well, the progress that was made on the shipbuilding side was matched by the progress made on the missile side, and that Polaris missile was an unbelievable achievement, to squeeze in that huge Jupiter—the Army Jupiter is what we were going to use and take to sea. Jupiter's, at least five times the size, I think, of a Polaris missile, and if you can realize what it would have taken to have put that thing which was liquid fueled then in a submarine. And, of course, one of the first things they went after was to try to make a solid fuel rocket, and that was Levering Smith's field of expertise. It's really an unbelievable achievement. (To say nothing about the engineering which allowed for underwater launches!)

THE PRESS

I have always assumed that all submariners were volunteers. This is true of the enlisted men but there was a short period where, "due to needs of the Navy", officers in other Navy communities were given the choice of the Nuclear Power program or resign. Two hundred years ago the British Navy, for lack of crews, would board any ship at sea and "press" its seaman.
Chuck Griffiths mentioned this:

CG: Now, you know, I was a submarine detailer for a period back in the late '60s, and so I had a real good look at what the difference was between the two submarine communities. I had them both.

DG: You had new ensigns by then who had been through nuclear power school?

CG: Oh, yes.

DG: And then you still had guys off the diesel boats.

CG: Oh, yeah. Now, you have to understand that to go from zero nuclear submarines to 50, 55 or 60, really, in a period of about seven or eight years required an unbelievable buildup of people, both officer and enlisted. And that had to be forced because they weren't there. Actually, we were drafting surface guys out of grad school into submarines. Those who didn't put in for it or didn't want any part of it, we were drafting them. We had to, in order to fill the billets.

DG: That produced people who didn't want to be there. I've always associated submariners with volunteering.

CG: For a very short time. Almost every one of those guys turned out to be real successes. And they, of course, changed their minds. But in some cases and for awhile they carried a real grudge about that, but several of them became admirals and several of them became wonderful skippers. So it turned out to have been a necessary and a positive thing to be able to build that large number of nuclear submarines in such a hurry and, of course, Rickover is famous for having his control over selection of personnel. And I can tell you that he had tremendous control over BUPERS (Bureau of Personnel) and over what BUPERS did.

Mike Barr said this about "The Fabulous 500"

MB: In '64 or '65, I think it was, there was a one-time input of sea-experienced officers (I think they were called the "Fabulous 500"). The nuclear Navy was growing so fast this one-time input was a necessity. Many of these officers were in graduate school, particularly at the Post-Graduate School in Monterey. After that, almost all nuclear trained officers were direct inputs and it's worked very well. Direct inputs are volunteers, but the "Fabulous 500" were drafted. People told me—I obviously wasn't there—that they were called to Washington and the Chief of Naval Personnel basically told them you've got two choices: you can resign or you can go to nuclear power training. We got many very high-quality officers. It was absolutely necessary. I mean, the submarine program, particularly the SSBN program, was a major national priority and we could not grow officers within the existing nuclear surface and submarine force fast enough to man the ships. On SNOOK, for example, at one time we got down to eight officers, and most of the time we were running with nine or ten. Today, the same basic ship has 15 or 16 officers, so the workload was very high for the wardroom. As soon as people got qualified, they were being sent off to go man new ships, SSBNs in particular. We commissioned 41 SSBNs from 1960 to 1966—six years. That's incredible. At the same time we were building a lot of SSNs, so you're looking at the need for about ten new crews every year, and you just couldn't home-grow that many fast enough. So that input of the "Fabulous 500" was vital, I think. Some were very unhappy for a while, but they did the job and most did it very well.

DG: Watkins said they were angry, like you said, but some of them turned out to be splendid.

MB: Oh, they were great.

DG: And they loved it which sort of surprises me.

MB: And a number of flag officers came out of that group. I remember just the quality of the people. When Admiral Watkins was the CO of SNOOK, I was the officer of the deck on a special operation; I think I was still a JG at that time. My junior officer of the deck was one of the "Fabulous 500" that had just reported to the ship. He was a LCDR. You'd think there might be some friction with the OOD being a JG, and the JOOD being a LCDR. There was none. That was the quality of the guy.

This portion of the Chuck Griffiths interview is the most thorough and insightful assessment of the transition period covering, in particular, the problem and solution of the retention rate and the bonus program.

CG: I think it covers a period of time that doesn't exist any longer, and your study can help describe what that change in culture was and why it was and why it occurred, and that's good. And it was a necessary change, clearly a necessary change. And the Navy is better off for it. But I've got some very good diesel boat friends, close friends, that didn't get selected. And I'm sure they would have been superb had they been selected. They just weren't selected, and that was unfortunate.

DG: Well, was that a career ender, a non-selection? Because they still had diesel boats to deal with and operate.

CG: No, it was not normally a career ender at all. In those days, if you'll remember, both COMSUBPAC and COMSUBLANT were diesel guys. All the DIVCOMs and the squadron commanders were diesel guys. The superstructure yet had not been integrated. It was still a diesel boat Navy, which led to some of the problems. For example, I was a detailer and, of course, I had a diesel boat guy as COMSUBPAC and a diesel boat guy as COMSUBLANT, and I dealt very closely with those guys on everything. We had a terrible problem in retention of young nuclear trained officers, as we were building this force up, which was blamed totally on Rickover by everybody. That problem, though, was created by the unbelievable working hours that we had, the tough conditions that we had for these young kids. We were taking them right out of the Naval Academy or wherever, and we were sending them to a year's nuclear power school immediately. Then we were sending them to six months of submarine school. Then we were sending them to a submarine. Now, in the first place, having just come out of an academic environment for at least four years, to go through a very much tougher academic environment like Nuclear Power School which was tougher than most of the college courses they were in. And then to have the prototype and things to qualify. Then to have to go to submarine school for six months immediately after that. And we saw a letdown in submarine school. As a result of this, these guys were just tired of school by the time they got there. And then they got into these submarines and all of a sudden they were working 12-hour days, and we were building a lot of them at the time and that shipyard time is very hard. They were working night and day and living on bennies and greenies and whities, the pills to keep them awake during the day and then the pills that would make them sleep in the few hours they'd get in the pad; because that was the life. Well, it took pretty strong young men to want to put up with that, and so our attrition rate was horrendous. This was in the late 60s.

DG: How was that situation mitigated?

CG: What we did was, with a lot of effort, we got a huge bonus paid to these young nukes right as they came up to their point of deciding whether they were going to stay or not. Big bonus. That wasn't easy to get. The people that fought it the toughest were the diesel community. And they had a lot of friends in Congress. We put it through the Army, the Marine Corps, the Navy, the Defense Department with a lot of work and a lot of briefings.

DG: What do you mean you put it through?

CG: We got the approval. I was the guy giving the briefings, and this was my project.

DG: And you were selling them—the other services—on the idea that this wouldn't apply to their people. You were going to pay your guys to stay.

CG: We're going to keep these guys in the Navy, and we've got to. That was the whole rationale. So amongst the things that we did at that time was we changed the submarine school from a six-month school down to a three-month school, and put in a second submarine school at the department head level, after they had had their first sea tour, which we called the Advanced Submarine course, and this was essentially a department head course, where we took the stuff that was department-head related out of what we were giving the fresh-caught guys out of nuclear power school. So we got them to the ships three months quicker. We also instituted a pin—a Polaris Patrol pin—which gave recognition to these kids. Most of them had zero ribbons, and their contemporaries in other areas of the Navy were picking up ribbons right and left, and they all had none.

The non-nukes got to be involved in campaigns, in things that were going on around the world, while these guys were in school. And so they got some recognition. That was tough to put through, but we got that done. We made several other changes in there that made life a little better for these guys. And, incidentally, the money did it. Everybody said, that money will never do it, you know. The money did it. And all of a sudden the people stayed in much larger numbers. Now, that bonus has been refined many times over the years. It's much bigger and it goes to many more people now than it did at that time; it only went to those young guys—not to the skippers, not the execs, not the department heads, not the people that were putting in the hours—it went to those young kids. And it was a big bonus, several thousand dollars.

DG: You said it didn't go to the XOs. Did it cause a little resentment? Were they a little resentful of it?

CG: A little bit, but they all understood. The people that didn't know, really, or understand it were the diesel guys. And for good reason. So that created probably as much hate and discontent as almost any thing at that particular time. So you have to throw that one in as being part of the problem. That's an important one to kick in. Jim Watkins would understand it very well because Jim then improved the bonus significantly during his period as a detailer, so that it went to other submariners as well. And, eventually, it went to everybody that was on a submarine, in one way or another. The enlisted guys got their bonuses, different, a selective re-enlistment bonus, where they got highest amounts of bonus to keep them in. But we've been paying people for a long time to keep them in. The only people that got a bonus before that were doctors. We copied the doctor bonus. We were the first to come in with a bonus, for retention purposes, in the Navy. The doctors had come in before. So I think that's a piece of history that you should understand, and I think it had a lot to do with the jealousy that existed between the nukes and the non-nukes.

The Navy News, on 3–15–05 had a story about bonuses headlined "Submariner Gets $100,000 Reenlistment Bonus"

DG: Enlisted guys in particular, have sent e-mails, and they talk about the nuclear power crews and how, at least in their period, there was more of a distinction between the guys forward—they call them nose-coners—and the guys aft.

CG: Oh, big difference. Big distinction.

DG: Is that still the case, do you think? Was this peculiar to the transition?

CG: That was a transition. I don't think it exists that way today. I think there may be some, but it's a fun thing today rather than an actual problem. And it definitely did exist, but the reason it existed again was the highest re-enlistment bonuses went to those guys. More of them got selected for the various officer programs. For example the NECP program. The most selected for this program were nuclear trained guys. They got it. So all those things created it. There was no question that the people back aft felt that they were superior, and in some cases acted like it. In fact, in most cases they were sharper people, smarter people, but I don't believe—because they pay now re-enlistment bonuses to people wherever they're needed. And there are lots of guys that are needed that aren't nuclear-trained, and so I don't believe that that's creating the differential that it did during the transition. There was a transition, and certainly in the earliest days we took our new construction crews, for example, for the *Robert E. Lee,*—the electricians and the machinists mates that were nuclear-trained, went with the CO and XO and the officers to school together at Bettis, which was the laboratory for the Navy nuclear power industry. It's in Pittsburgh. And we all went to a school where we studied that plant under the designers of the plant. And we all took exams together and we were all treated exactly the same, no matter what rank or rate we were, we took the same exams. And so there was a natural tendency for that group to feel like they were special, and when they went to the ship, you know, and started right in working very hard and got there always right before reactor fill and were there for all of the operations to the reactor plant from that day on. The shipyard never operated the reactor stuff. It was all done by the ship's crew. And it was, perhaps, a reason for having a feeling that you sort of owned the ship and were very special. Now, the missile guys went to school in their areas. The missile fire control guys went to GE, to school. Of course, the skipper and XO went with them. We did that, too, and so they felt they were special—but that initial cadre of individuals, whether they were the nukes or whether they were the missile guys felt they were special. So I think there was a feeling of sort of owning the ship that went with all of the guys, not only the nukes. I think the guys that were the initial weapons guys felt the same way, and for the same reasons. And, of course, they all ended up getting pretty much bonuses as well; from a money standpoint, less of a differential.

I had difficulty deciding where to put this portion of my interview with Jeff Van-Blaracum since much of this part is really about submarine culture. That is, the differences between diesel boat sailors and their nuclear counterparts. It is difficult to separate the cultural shifts from the technological advances in submarines. They are embedded in one another.

JV: Well, I think the other thing that made it easier for the diesel boat guys to transition to fast-attack is the fact that they, especially the guys that were in the Pacific fleet, were constantly on WestPac. They were out there seeing the world. And you take a guy like that who's been doing that his whole life, and doing things a certain way, and now you put him on a nuclear boomer, and everything's different. You've got all these procedures now for everything. 'Training? You have to do training? What? What is training?' Now, you have to *do* training and document it. Oh, well, that's something new, too. But I don't get to see anything, other than the boat. I don't get to go anywhere.

DG: Because they come back into their homeport.

JV: Right. They go to sea and they come home. And sometimes they go to Pearl Harbor, but they never go anywhere outside of the country; very seldom. And, whereas, you know, the fast-attacks, they're out there running around, making port calls, around the world. And so that's another thing that tied the diesel boat guys in with the fast-attacks. Master Chief Doug Coffman, was a torpedoman on three diesel boats and then went to 637's—or served on 594's, 637's and 688's. He served just about on every single one there ever was. Just about every type. And he's a crusty old master chief.

DG: But he made the transition.

JV: He made the transition. He was the chief of the boat of one of the newest SSNs He never went to a boomer. He dodged that bullet. He said he'd never, ever, set foot on one. He said I'm afraid I might catch something if I walk onboard. [Laughter] So those guys were very colorful, and they had many, many stories about diesel boats.

DG: So do you think they were any more colorful than you guys?

JV: I think that they probably were, in that as we got more nuclear submarines and fewer diesels, there weren't that many of them around. They'd been around for a long time and so there were a lot of material problems on them. Little leaks here on valves. So you have more material problems and things where they'd say—'oh, yeah, well, whatever.' And it's not like that on a nuclear submarine. If you have a leaking valve then you're going to fix it; you're going to do something about it. They did that, too, but it was harder for them because there just weren't parts available, coming towards the end of the diesel boat era.

DG: So the Navy let that deteriorate a little bit?

JV: Right, because it was harder to get them. Because "we weren't buying that anymore". And it was actually like that when I was on *Kamehameha,*—same thing. Because we're getting rid of those ships, so we're not buying this equipment anymore. Unless it was something that would happen to spill over into 637's and 688's. But even at that time there weren't a lot of them around.

DG: So I guess that's an age-old problem. If you're phasing something out and you're the last guy, and you've got to contend with stuff that the first guys didn't have to.

JV: Right. The biggest difference—diesel vs. nukes—is that they did more, and they did more as a crew. There weren't as many of them, number one, on the crew, and they did more. Spent a lot of time in foreign ports on liberty, and that in itself right there will make a person more colorful. Because he has lots of sea stories, and he has lots of knowledge, too. I mean, they were good submariners. There's no doubt. And there were a lot of them that made the transition. Some of them more easily than others, but they made it. They didn't like it, but they did it.

DG: It's clear to me that I, as a second-class torpedoman, didn't have to know much, honestly. I mean, we just had—I think it was the Mk18—an old electric torpedo. Then we had the Mark 14 and we just kind of installed gyros and worked in the shop on the sub base a little bit, and then that was it. We didn't have to know anything really sophisticated. But you guys had the Mk 48.

JV: And the ADCAP, which is the advanced capability Mark 48 and we got Tomahawk missiles and the Harpoon.

DG: So you don't have as much time to be colorful as the old guys because we really played a lot of cribbage and stuff.

JV: Sure, sure. I remember it on my first boat, a lot of that stuff went on. You know, we spent hours after watch playing cribbage, playing spades. And there's not as much of that goes on nowadays because quite honestly there's too much work. I mean, it does go on. Don't get me wrong, but not as much. And that, too, takes away from the color of the crew because they don't sit and do that as much. These guys nowadays—I'll try to put it in perspective from a torpedoman aspect nowadays. There are literally so many man-hours of PMs (Preventive Maintainance) that you cannot complete it all. It's physically impossible. Preventative maintenance that is due on the vertical launch system, the weapons, the torpedo tubes, the handling system. There are literally so many man hours of that type of maintenance that has to go on, and you don't have the personnel. You physically can't do it all in a year.

DG: Because the platform is just vastly more sophisticated and complex.

JV: Yes. Absolutely.

DG: That makes sense. One thing I keep coming back to is I remember some really, really bright people back then on the diesel boats, and so I have a feeling that probably, just on an I.Q. level, maybe it isn't that far advanced on the nuclear power boats, except that we just didn't have to learn much. I mean, we were plenty smart, we coped with situations and things, but you guys have to learn, six times as much as we had to learn, maybe. And so it appears that your guys were basically smarter, and I think that smart isn't a good word for them. They're just more educated.

JV: Right. Because we have to be. And that's the point that probably should come out of that is that we have to know more about it because we're made to. There's more requirements on us now. The requirements, even since I was first in the Navy, are ten times what they were. It's a good thing because what you get is a better, well-rounded sailor at the end. But you don't get the expert torpedoman, maybe. He doesn't know quite as much about his space as the old guys did. They don't know how to fix as many things as the old guys did. And that's one of the things that we're losing throughout the Navy.

DG: So do you think that your guys are resourceful? I'll give you a good example. We went to sea and we used to distill our own water, as you know. And we had evaporators. And then above the evaporator, was a big direct current motor—a powerful motor with a bunch of pulleys and a bunch of belts that would connect to this evaporator, and we'd run that, and that's how we got our water, which was vital, of course, since we were battery powered. So we go to sea and somebody had ordered the wrong belts. We're out in the middle of the Pacific and our belts don't fit.

JV: That's a bad thing.

DG: They're too long. Like you said, that's bad, because we're a long way from anything and we've got some mission to do, by the way, and we just have no means of making water. So a couple of guys, I'm sure Machinist's mates or Auxil-iarymen—they just said, 'Well, let's just make the distance between the pulleys the right distance for the wrong belts.' So they just unbolted everything, got a bunch of plates, drilled holes in the plates, stacked the plates up and extended the distance between the pulleys until it was the right distance, bolted it all back together and we just went about our way. And so, that was like four hours and somebody figured that out. I was always impressed with the ability to kind of deal with problems out of the blue.

JV: Exactly right, and I remember my first chief was like that. You know, we'd have a problem and we're all standing there looking at it like, Oh, my God, what are we going to do? And he'd sit back and he'd think about it and he'd come up with a solution. And over the years, because that's the way they were—the diesel boat sailors were—as we got more maintenance facilities and more support from shore and this, that, and the other, the guys on the boats didn't do as much because they let the maintenance facility do it. So I think I would call that pride in ownership, that if the diesel boat guy could fix it himself, no matter how big the job was, he was going to fix it.

DG: He'd prefer to fix it.

JV: That's right. He prefers to do that. Whereas, over the years we've lost that in that if the job—even if our own guys could probably do it, if it's too big or too time-consuming for the division, they let the shipyard do it.

DG: Well, you don't have time. In fairness to you guys, you don't have the time. You have more ship to fix and less time to do it in.

JV: Right.

DG: And isn't there also kind of a bolt-on thing going on here? I mean, now, you know, if this tape recorder craps out—it cost me 29 bucks. I'm going to just chuck it. I'm not going to take it down like it was 1942 and try and get some-body to fix it. And so can that be said about the equipment in the modern sub-marines?

JV: Modular. Yeah, we're heading that way. You see it more and more. But it's that mentality is what I was talking about. That mentality says, Oh, I can have the shipyard fix that. Even if it's a small thing. So that used to be just the big item. Now it's just about everything. We don't want to fix anything. We'll fix as little as we have to. And that would never have been on a diesel submarine. I used to sit with my friend, and he'd talk about it all the time. That our guys don't know how to do shit anymore because we let someone else take care of our sub-marine.

DG: It's the same today though when you're out by yourself. Something happens, you just say how are we going to overcome this?

JV: I think the other thing is that there's a lot of things we're not allowed to work on anymore. There are things we have no training to fix onboard the ship, which to me doesn't make any sense. That would never have happened on a diesel boat.

DG: So is there some device aboard, they don't want you working on it because they're not confident that you can?

JV: Well, it's because it costs so much money, and the manufacturer says if something goes wrong with that—you take that thing, unbolt it, take it out and send it back to us.

DG: But in the final analysis, if your tasks are overwhelming, then you just don't have time to fix everything. But on the other hand, if you're at sea and you don't have a spare for something. What do you do?

JV: Exactly. And we have been losing that over the years. I guess because the way I was trained, I didn't allow my division to do that. We did things that were still in the books but nobody did it because we didn't have to anymore. But my guys do it. I made them learn how. And that's the bottom line—that we *should* know how to do those things. And that's what made the diesel boat sailors great submariners because they figured out a way to make it work. And our guys are losing that. I think the biggest difference, pride in ownership. They're a little bit more colorful because they've seen and done a lot more things. But other than that, submarines are submarines and we still have in place submarine qualification, which is the same as it was back then. I have a lot of respect for those guys. Anytime I meet them, especially being in Pearl Harbor, I meet a lot of them, it's a pleasure and an honor.

Paul Crooks
ET1 (SS)
SSN-618 Thomas Jefferson
1977–1984

As a Nuke RO (Reactor Operator) it appeared to me that there were two crews on my boat. There were the Nukes and then there was everyone else. What caused this was the big difference in the way we were treated.

The difference in treatment started before we even reported to the boat, Nukes didn't go to Sub School so we lost out on an opportunity to be instilled with the history and traditions of the Submarine Service. The best in-port watch rotation I ever saw was 3 section duty the worst rotation that the non nukes saw was three section duty. When preparing to go to sea Nukes had to be on the boat midnight the night before to do a pre-critical check of the reactor plant, then early in the morning we would do a reactor start up and be prepared to be underway at 0800. In Contrast the non nukes would show up at about 0700 drink a cup of coffee, suck a butt and what do you know they're ready to go to sea. Of course on the maneuvering watch as we left port all the damage control parties were under Nukes and all critical phone talkers were Nukes. Then when at sea the Fire Control Tracking Party was manned only by Nukes, we would actually have to adjust the Nuke watch bill to be able to support the Fire Control Tracking Party. Another BIG thing to do at sea was drills and at least 90% of them were Engineering related, now for some reason this used to bother a few of the non nukes "seems like we came to sea just to do your drills." I think they were jealous they didn't get the same attention we did. Well now they have stationed the maneuvering watch again to pull back into port, then over the 1MC came 'MOORED" within about 10 minutes every non-nuke that didn't have duty was gone. Meanwhile all the Nukes were bringing on shore power and then shutting down the reactor. Even the slowest non nuke could be pretty well tanked by the time the Nukes dragged their tired butts off the boat. And finally if a nuke did reenlist the Sea Shore rotation was 5 years at sea for only 2 years ashore.

To sum it all up the Nukes had more responsibility and work load then the rest of the boat and very little respect or reward for the extra work. Maybe that is why the reenlistment rate for Nukes while I was in was less then 10%.

I know the last couple of paragraphs may sound kind of like sniveling, but I was trying to give you an idea of how we perceived the differences between people on the boat in just a few sentences and snivel at the same time.

Because of these perceived inequities we often felt it was great sport to "mess" with non-nukes whenever they came aft. For some reason you almost needed a pack of wild horses to drag a non-nuke aft of the tunnel. One of our favorites was to convince a non-nuke (usually some poor nub) that there was some kind of reactor problem. It started with the RO turning on an alarm over the after tunnel hatch in Mach. 2 UL that was for a low level in the Shield water tank around the reactor. Then the Mach. 2 UL watch, EWS and ERS would convince this guy that he needed, in order to save the boat, to get a portable air sample to Control. So we would dress our friend up in anti contamination clothing and give him a garbage bag that had been swished thru the air and tied off with a knot. Then we would send him off as fast as he could go to report to the OOD with an inflated garbage bag that he thought was a portable air sample. It may not sound like much now but we thought it was the funniest thing in the world at the time.

Another big difference between the Nukes and non-nukes was phone talking skill; nukes conducted a lot of evolutions over the phones with direction coming from Maneuvering and consequently were comfortable talking on the sound-powered phones. Every so often the Chief of the Watch would get a wild hair..... to have the JA phone circuit manned so that we could practice phone talking. Well the only JA phone in the Engineering spaces that we manned was in Maneuvering and the RO (that would be me) had to man it. After listening to the non-nuks stumble through their communications and wearing the headset for 20–30 minutes I would be tired of playing. The best thing I found to do was send Primary chemistry results to the Control Room via the phone talker. After the C.O.W. (Chief of the Watch) and O.O.D. listened to the poor phone talker being corrected on saying "micromicrocuries" for a while they would call back and tell us that we could secure the phones which oddly enough was exactly what we wanted.

Well this is a little of what it was like to be a Nuke. I think that there was probably a better sense of being part of one crew on the Diesel boats and I envy them for that reason.

This was a submission which I had a hard time assigning to any particular chapter. Don's first few paragraphs are about flooding—a sensitive topic for submariners to be sure—while the rest is about the transition and the feelings I believe to be shared by many of the older diesel boat sailors. It is my hope that after reading this entire book they will soften their feelings on the subject. Actually he conveys better than any other submission that "DBF" gripe about nuclear power submarines completely replacing the old diesels. I hope Don et al will come to see that the transition, while painful, no longer exists and accept today's submariners as the outstanding sailors they truly are.

Don Ennis
ETCS(SS)
Boats Served: Carp SS-338, George C. Marshall SSBN-654 (precom) Stonwall Jackson SSBN-634, Daniel Webster SSBN-626
January 1960—August 1987

I never saw real flooding on a submarine. I mean I never saw "holy shit" real flooding: the kind that bounces off of walls and equipment and finds you before you find it. I loved the submarine service's "there is no such thing as a drill" attitude. When you heard the collision alarm you reacted as if it were flooding. One mid watch on the *Daniel Webster* I had the dive and we were doing a sound cut off of Andros Island back in 1983 or 1984. We were at test depth making a standard bell when I heard a voice on the 7MC say "Hey guys there's a lot of water coming in back here." Was that the 7 MC? Who is that? Why isn't he reporting on the 4MC? I knew who it was and I was surprised at the quality of his report, but I am the guy who once passed the word "fire in the kitchen" so I let it go. Flooding in the engine room is not a situation for equivocation. It's damned serious. So I responded on the 7MC "How much water is coming in?" I could almost hear a nuclear trained brain flipping through a quals manual. "118 gallons per minute." One GPM short of the official definition of flooding. Damn! I've waited my whole career to do something heroic and that f___ing nuke ruins it with his accuracy. I let my hand slip from the emergency blow valve handles just as the OOD said "Chief, take her up 300 feet." Sir, said I, Sir I recommend periscope depth where we can sort this out. Truth is I was going there anyway. When we got to PD the water coming in through our shaft seal was just a trickle. The oncoming watch wanted to know what the fuss was all about and why was I acting like a guy with a combination white knuckle syndrome and pucker factor. No harm done. Still we had to run at PD for a couple of days to Kings Bay where we got the shaft seal replaced and we replace the paint in the engine rooms after bilge bay. The incoming water had stripped the frame bay cleaner than a chipping hammer could. No harm done. So what?

Well this exercise in journalism isn't about water tight integrity. It's about the integrity of the submarine community that has been leaking long before captain Anderson passed the word on the 1MC "Underway on Nuclear power." It's about what happens when one cultural community displaces another. No it's worse than that it's what happens when looking back on it's past and evolution people fail to recognize and acknowledge the virtues of the parent. The displaced community is not only set aside it is dumped into what a submarine sailor might call the shit can of time. It is what Dex Armstrong meant when he wrote: "Today diesel boat sailors have been relegated to a place on the chart of the development of man, down around the point previously occupied by Cro-Magnon primates. The Requin is a Neanderthal now, a living naval fossil. Time moves on. Technology renders perfectly serviceable things obsolete. Obsolescence takes hold and you are history.

How did this happen? How did the naval force that made such an overwhelming contribution to sinking the rising sun come to be thought of in such terms? Think of the implication of this statement. It is the opinion of what a patriotic American who volunteered to serve his country thinks that his service and his country thinks of him. This is a travesty. It should read "Diesel boat sailors are the icons of our military. With less than 2% of the Navy's resources they sank

50% of all Japanese Warships and 75 % of the Japanese merchant ships. The Requin stands as a monument to what brave men on ships they love can do. It was placed on this site to remind a grateful nation of the sacrifice these silent warriors made in defeating an evil enemy. The people of the United States of America acknowledge that during World War II the submarine service of the US Navy suffered greater losses and casualities per capita than any other branch of the armed forces. As Sir Winston Churchill said: "Of all the branches of men in the forces there is none which shows more devotion and faces grimmer perils than the submariners." Bear in mind that when Winnie said this he was talking about smoke boats. No one told me about any of the above. Oh I knew about Morton and Dealy and Gilmore. I knew Harder, Darter, Trigger, Trout when I went to Submarine School in 1964. No one told me that the submarine force had all but cleared the Pacific of Japanese and had them confined to the islands they had conquered and had them starving on their homeland. The US Submarine Service did to the Japanese what the Germans failed to do to England. With this kind of record you would think that the submarine force would be turning recruits away by the boat load. Truth is the submarine force at its best had to beat the bushes to send the boats to sea fully manned. Back in 1963 a detachment from BUPERS made a world wide trip to entice surface sailors enrolled in advanced electronics service schools to volunteer for duty on board the brand new Polaris submarines which our ship yards were turning out at a boat a month. At the same time qualified submariners were bailing out of the navy in droves. I volunteered for Submarine duty the day after the Thresher sank and I don't remember a long line behind me. By 1963 the word was out on Admiral Rickover and his crew. It's probably not fair to put the blame on the Admiral for all of the ills of the sub navy. He should be immortalized for the engineering and development work he did in merging the submarine and the nuclear reactor. He should get credit for his courage for presenting his case before Congress despite the misgivings of the Navy brass. One only has to search the literature of the day to verify his accolades in these areas. However, I never heard nor have I ever read a word that indicates he had any leadership qualities or that he was a nice helpful person to deal with. Words like pump handle obnoxious and irritating are among the most charitable I can remember. Who was it that said "There's a part about Rickover that is good. There's a part that is bad and there's a part of him you just won't believe. When Rickover came on board a submarine, the request for leave rose dramatically. It would be almost impossible to quantify Rickover's contribution to the schism between the front end and the rear end of the Nuclear Navy's submarines, but most sub sailors will tell you he was better suited to the rear end. Before Rickover submariners had developed a society where each man depended on the other and everyone was expected to know the other man's job. It seemed to the Admiral, I think, that this would cause him to lose control of his precious reactors and control was a major issue with him. He hand picked all of the officers who served on nuclear submarines using a Machiavellian interview.

Admiral Rickover maintained this kind of control over the nuclear power program even after his naval career and well into his retirement. Any one who didn't agree with the admiral found employment elsewhere. That the nuclear power program performed as well as it did during the early years is a tribute to the men who rode those boats. Thankfully there was only one of him and he couldn't go to sea on all of the boats all of the time. I always got the feeling that the officers in the nuclear powered navy were slightly embarrassed with Rickover's leadership mode and I wonder if Whitey Mack on the *Lapoon* would have been as successful as he was with Rickover onboard. My experience on nuclear powered submarines came in three separate time frames sufficiently separated to give a view of the program. Rather than seeing gradual changes and effects I saw discreet changes. Early in my career and association with nuclear power, when Admiral Rickover was in his hay day, there were lots of diesel boats still around and there were sufficient combat experienced submariners to make a difference in submarine force. I only saw these men in the schools I attended but it was easy to pick them out with their "War patrol Dolphins" by the deference qualified submariners gave them.

I spent two months on the USS Carp in early 1965 with through orders to the USS *Geo C. Marshall* SSBN 654 (precom). Before I got to *Marshall* I had orders to the NECP summer school at Bainbridge Md. I worked hard on the Carp fixing equipment and supplementing the watch bill when the Carp was required to provide a petty officer for barracks or security duty on the shipyard. Everyone on the Carp had a nick name except the XO who everyone called Frank and the Commanding Officer who was respectfully referred to as Captain. More than the animosity I expected to experience for being transferred to a Nuclear Submarine I felt a sense of pity from the crew. When they found out that I was headed for 4 years of college and a commission the nuke/puke advisory relationship stopped altogether. I became a Nuke once again when I banged my head on the TBT and required stitches. Several of the guys in my division applied direct pressure to my wound while holding me up by my arm pits and all but carrying me to the shipyard dispensary. On the way to the first aid station one of the guys kept saying that they had better take Ennis to Doc Deprado the Carp's corpsman. I found out how jealously submarine Hospital Corpsmen watch over the men assigned to their boat. Deprado called me nothing but Nuke thereafter and my shot record did not make it to the Marshall with me. I went from hand shake and best wishes from the CO USS Carp to the handshake of the CO SSBN 654 with his welcome on board together with "What can we do for you for the next two months? and what can we do for Carol (my wife) and your children, what were their names? Oh yes Pamela and Jonathan." Commander Cobean was a nuclear trained officer with experience on diesel boats. He epitomized professional competent! He knew both men and machinery. I expected the kind of Officer my friend Bill Perry ET1 (SS) told me about when he describes CDR George P. Steele and I got what I expected. Most of the senior officers in Rickovers early navy were like Captains Steele and Cobean according to numerous submarine sailors I knew from those days. They were the kind of officers who maintained a professional aloofness but knew the names of your kids. I made it through Prep School and I made it through three years at the University of Washington before I flunked out and was sent back to sea on the USS Stonewall Jackson. Best command but the crack was showing. 15 bunks eight goats three years on 634, two years at BUPERS. Out of navy for 8 years. You won't believe what I came back to. Rickover was gone but the destruction he left behind

Bob Gautier was among several of those interviewed who thought some of the earlier nuclear power officers 'were looking aft too much' (paying all their attention to the reactor) and not enough attention to the operation of the ship.

BG: Diving a diesel boat and a SSN, is an entirely different evolution.

DG: Actually, you can effectively say they don't even do it.

BG: They don't even dive the boat. They just submerge. They go from surface to submerge, and that's it. And when they get there, it doesn't really make much difference. But that was interesting. When I had the division and I had this nuclear submarine in my division, I'd go out and I'd qualify these guys in the submarines, and that was a real experience because the knowledge of the people about the torpedoes, the torpedo rooms, diving a boat, and those kinds of things, they really were not too smart about that. But you could ask them about that nuclear power plant and the pressures and all that stuff, and they had that down right up the kilt, you know.

DG: I've noticed in all these interviews and the e-mails I'm getting, that there where people enamored of the power plant. That it was so dramatically different and it provided so much capability. Then if you jump ahead to today's guys, where the reactor is a given, that's just the power plant, that's the way we get around, and they seem to be way more aware of the front of the boat and missions—the weapons and stuff like that. That's just the power plant. It's how we get there. I'm noticing that. And I think that's a good thing.

BG: I think so, yeah. Well, as a matter of fact, I'm trying to think of the guy...oh, Creed Burlingame, during the war. Somebody asked Creed Burlingame, 'What kind of engines you have back there?' He said, 'I haven't the foggiest idea.' They said, 'You don't know?' He said, 'Hell, no. When I say, all ahead full, I want all ahead full.' And he was honest about it. That's Creed Burlingame. He could care less about that thing.

Chuck Groejean

DG: A former shipmate, a machinist mate sent me an email. He said there was sort of a separation or division in the crew. I guess his point was, that when we diesel guys got qualified, we had to know every inch of the boat. Every person had to know every inch of the boat, and that changed and he found that sort of objectionable.

CG: I don't know, you know, you're right to a degree on that. We would not permit that early on. On the Patrick Henry and on the Barb and the Thomas Edison there was—of course, the guys that were nuclear power trained had their own kind of club, so to speak, but the forward end of the ship people could go all through the ship. They were all given free access to everything. And we tried very much not to have the missile guys feel that they were better or worse or whether the navigators felt that they were better or worse or the enginemen felt that they were better or worse, and this was something that on a ship that I had command of or executive officer of, that we wouldn't permit.

Now, later on there may have been some more of this that degenerated I don't know about. There's no question but what the guys that were missile men didn't learn about all the nuclear power stuff. They didn't have to go through nuclear power school, that's right. The engineers went through nuclear power school.

DG: What about the torpedo men and the other non-nuke rates?

CG: No. The torpedomen and the quartermasters, no. The only rates that went through the program were electricians, electronic technicians, engine men. But they were the ones that had the nuclear power training and, you know, the missile men up here all had missile training, and the engineers didn't get any missile training. Now, when we went through submarine school, we all learned about torpedoes, whether you were an engine man or not. But once you started getting into inertial systems and the highly technical stuff, it became probably too much. And I don't know what it is now, Dan. I don't know to what degree that became a problem. A good commanding officer would never let that become a problem. But remember, early on, those of us who were commanding officers were very sensitive to the fact that we didn't want that to happen. We didn't want to have a feeling onboard our ship, the haves and have nots, and we didn't permit it.

DG: Is there anything that you can think of to add?

CG: I think that there's no question but what attacking this book is a big, big—a big subject. There's a lot to write about and a lot of it has got to do with Rickover. There was a tendency to find that some commanding officers, after they went through the nuclear power training, would become obsessed with the nuclear power end of things and sort of lose track of the importance of the forward end of the ship because of the fact that they did go through Rickover's training and that was deplorable, in my mind. But in the transition period there were a lot of commanding officers who became so focused upon the nuclear and the engineering aspects of it, that to my way of thinking they forgot that there was a periscope.

DG: Did they forget about the mission? I mean, after all, am I mistaken that the mission is paramount?

CG: The mission is paramount. No question about that. But at the same time, when something goes wrong back aft, does the commanding officer go back aft? I didn't go back aft. I sat there and conned my ship until I could get it to a position where there was time for me to say, okay, we're just resting now on our oars. I can go back and see what their problem is. But, you know, I always felt that there were some commanding officers who became overly nuked.

DG: Would they have been earlier in the program?

CG: Yeah, I think later on the guys who came up were probably not so enamored with the nuclear end of things. That was just another part of the ship. That's how the ship is run.

Dave Oliver's answer concerning diesel officers who had not been accepted into the nuclear power program.

DO: There were some guys who were not accepted into the nuclear power program that were extraordinarily able. It's just a fact. I mean, they were tactically able, they were well-spoken, they were extraordinarily capable. What I don't know is if they're academically bright enough to keep up, and unfortunately, you had to be able to do that.

I don't know if they could have performed. But I know in all other ways they were really good. And a whole bunch of those men who were not accepted for nuclear power were really hurt. And people didn't take the time to say, you're really a good person and we need you to do something else. Okay, there was some class consciousness, some snobbery, and all that. I'm not sure it could be done differently. See, when I was group commander, my operations officer, which was the key billet, was a diesel guy, and I recruited another diesel guy to be a captain—two of them—to run my diesel squadron. You know I was all over them but then I had a nuke run the nuke squadron and I was all over him.

Candidly, I thought I was better than all of them and I was senior. But those guys knew—in other words, I treated them, in my opinion, the way you ought to treat people. But then that has to do with my own style of leadership. And I would kill you if you screw up something on a diesel boat just as much as I'll kill you if you screw up something on a nuke. I'm even-handed. I mean, if you're going to threaten somebody's life, I'm going to take yours. Because that's what the business is all about. You don't want to kill kids.

But you're right. There's a whole emotion involved, and I think it's misplaced in many ways. But, you know, shoot, you're also all kids at the time. There's not a lot of mature thinking that goes into this when you're 19 to 20-something. There wasn't in mine. May have been in yours, but I wasn't.

Jim Watkins knows his history and really had a unique slant on the submarine forces.

DG: To make this transition comparison between diesels and nukes you know, the fact of the matter is it's a completely, utterly different job.

JW: It's a totally different job. And the trouble is that we don't convert fast in this country, in anything we do. I mean, I gave a speech at the University of Syracuse to Defense executives. And my speech was on the most difficult thing in Washington to effect i.e., change. And it's not just Washington but that was my focus at the time. What do you do to make a significant change in any approach traditionally taken by the nation, like SDI? Well, you know, that program was inaugurated in 1983, the white paper from the White House didn't come out till '84, and here we are 20 years later just struggling with one little demonstration project up in Alaska. And so the negative attitude coming from many scientists themselves, e.g. The Union of Concerned Scientists and others like that, said it was silly and couldn't be done. The "others" in this case included the Congress who couldn't get reelected by supporting research. So that's the issue, and to try to get change *then*, something like shifting to nuclear, it took an Eisenhower and it took.

DG: Rickover.

JW: It took Rickover, but it also took Admiral Arliegh Burke. It took Arliegh Burke and a big enough person like the President to say this is what we ought to be doing.

DG: To get people on the Hill onboard.

JW: Yeah. Had to get it. So some visionaries back in the fifties like Rickover went off on their own anyway. He'd lock up the members of the Joint Committee on Atomic Energy, Scoop Jackson and the other gang up there. But putting a ballistic missile in a submarine was another huge step change. You know, nothing quite like that had ever been done. To cut the George Washington in half and make it the first ballistic missile submarine was another huge technical feat and to make it successful from the outset. You have to give a lot of credit to those early guys. I mean, there's some real humdingers of guys that worked that program, both on the missile side and on the submarine side.

Frank Kelso's another guy you should talk to. Frank was in the effort with me in transitioning from Rickover to 'blue suit' management of the nuclear program, both carriers and submarines today. There are no more operating cruisers or destroyers with nuclear power plants. I was on the cruiser Long Beach, now shut down maybe six or seven years ago.

DG: Are the Nimitz class carriers the only ones that are nuclear power?

JW: No, Enterprise is nuclear powered. She's still operating after almost 50 years. Eight reactors. Unbelievable. The others have two. It's almost 50 years. I'm going to say about '58 or maybe '59. Well, she came out of that period, anyway. They were building her in '55, I think. Whenever the decision was made; it's in that time frame. But she's been around a long time. And that means that she has all of the new air wing on there, and she has all the new technology. So that gives you an idea—we asked the National Academy of Science when I was CNO. Much to John Lehman's dismay, I went over there to The Navy Studies Board and asked what the viability of an aircraft carrier would be 20 years from now, like 2003. Is there going to be a need for them? And they came back very strong, said, 'Yeah, we're going to need that platform.' You may have to have a different modular approach to the way you handle the upgrade of the technology of the air wings between now and then, but basically you're going to need that floating airport.

DG: Can you see that going away? I can't imagine that.

JW: No. Well, the anti-carrier crowd keeps talking about it, like they want to abolish the Service Academies about every 8 years. This crowd consists of a bunch of wandering minstrels who come to town and want to abolish something. Fortunately they seldom get anywhere because they don't know their ass from a hole in the ground. You know, there hasn't been one Secretary of State that I know of in the last 50 or 60 years that hasn't said, when he needs help, "Where the hell are the carriers?" But he doesn't have to go to any nation to get support for anything. He just sends them in to the 12-mile line and watches the aircraft bomb the hell out of something. It's a terrific mobile platform which the other services just drool over.

DG: It's funny the Navy has both of the best platforms—submarines and carriers.

JW: Yeah, you fly a tanker out of Montana or Wyoming or something, and you send them to the Middle East, you've got seven tanks en route—seven tanks. So you know as opposed to taking off like that, we get underway for seven years before the reactor gets refueled up again. Anyway, the good thing about submarines, I think, is they do play a large role in the total defense package because they go way beyond what you might say the conventional World War II thinking of shooting torpedoes at a ship. That's still okay, but that's a piece of cake compared to the other stuff.

DG: Someone told me, and he was very blunt, he said, you know, running a diesel sub was easy, was really easy. It was also fun.

JW: Well, it's a quasi-surface ship. You do a heck of a lot when you work on the surface, including firing torpedoes at ships at night. During the war we didn't have the radar sophisticated until later on. It then became a totally different ball game. There were a lot of opportunities for guys to get up on the bridge and have a cigarette or go swimming. I know.

Apples and Oranges

"An optimist sees a glass that is half full, a pessimist sees a glass as half empty, a submariner sees the glass as twice as big as it needs to be."
RADM Michael Tracy—Undersea Warfare magazine

In all the many interviews and submissions, opinions vary on almost every subject related to the transition. Diesels vs. Fast Attack boats—Boomers vs. Fast Attack boats—life on any of them vs. the other—Rickover and on and on. There is, however, one fact that I have found no disagreement about and which is simply irrefutable. There is a vast difference between diesel electric submarines and nuclear powered submarines.

Diesel submarines in all their variations, missions and evolutions were all really surface raiders which could dive for purposes of avoiding an enemy or for closing on a target. Their weapon systems were rudimentary, comprised of torpedoes, deck guns (on those in WWII) and basically small arms. My boat, U.S.S. Barbero SSG-317, along with U.S.S. Tunny SSG-282, was altered substantially to carry Regulus missiles with nuclear war heads. One other diesel boat—USS Grayback SSG-574—was made from the keel up to launch missiles as well. But the fact was that all of them had power plants which required air and were therefore relegated to the surface or to snorkeling.

Fast Attack (SSN) and Fleet Ballistic Missile (SSBN) submarines not only have completely revolutionary power systems, but their weapon systems represent an enormous leap from those on diesel boats. Even the early nuclear tipped Regulus missiles on Tunny, Barbero, Growler and Grayback were like comparing a catapult to a 105 MM Howitzer. Yes, current submarines still shoot torpedoes, but they bear little resemblance to the Mk14 and Mk18 torpedoes on the diesel boats.

Chuck Griffiths gave me the idea for the name of this chapter.

DG: The leap in the characteristics of a fast-attack boat, for instance, it was so enormous that it's hard to compare them to diesels.

CG: You can't. There's no comparison. There's no way to compare it. It's a different job. It's totally different and so really, I think, to try to compare—I think that your subject is a difficult subject, but it's a subject that to me has only one answer. Shifting to nuclear power made huge changes, and those changes created some bitterness, led to the 'diesel boats forever' syndrome. It's unfortunate because those problems were created by the fact that it was a different task, completely, and you were comparing <u>apples and oranges</u> to compare the two. Now, on the other hand, diesel boats were great, they were wonderful. You know, we enjoyed our lives in diesel boats very much. I spent over half of mine in diesel boats—half of my naval career—and I enjoyed it immensely. But it was a different life; you can't compare it. But let me say that I think your observation, from the Santa Fe, is right on the mark. *I had mentioned to him how impressive the COs of the Santa Fe were when I met them.*

DG: Yeah, I've been through two, and they're both absolutely topnotch.

CG: And the enlisted men are unbelievable. Unbelievable.

DG: Yeah, I got that, and this is not nostalgia. I mean, I've entertained these guys at my home for hours.

CG: Our biggest sales job in submarines is getting people onboard. If you can get people onboard, they can't help but be favorably impressed by the people, enlisted and officers, and by the ships, which are astounding.

Chuck Grojean, interestingly addressed both the transitional aspects as well as the mission changes between the two.

DG: Let me ask you this. Were the demands of command of a diesel boat vastly greater or just different than a nuclear powered sub?

CG: Of a diesel boat or the other? The same. The demands of command were essentially the same. I didn't find them that different. Oh, you had some problems in one that you didn't have in the other, and vice versa. The biggest problem that I had was early on my officers tended to be too technical and not human. You know, submariners of World War II, and diesel submariners in general, you experienced this common constant danger of being submerged and knowing the enemy is the sea, always. And when you go ashore you have a tendency to let go and the wardroom would go ashore as a group. The enlisted men would go ashore in groups; engine men would go ashore with engine men, so on, so forth. And you let off steam and sometimes you let off too much steam and got in trouble, but you always went ashore and had a good time, let your hair down, forgot about $e = mc^2$. Okay? And I had a problem with my officers. I felt that when we would go into port that there was all work and no play makes Jack a dull boy. And so I purposely said to my wardroom, Alright, we're going to go ashore and we're going to go out and have some fun tonight. And we did. And I felt that my ship was much better off for it. And I got my officers so that they would understand that life was not just all having to work out nuclear problems. No question but what the technical demands of nuclear power are much greater on enlisted and on officers. You had to learn a lot more and you had to—you know, one of the reasons that we had such an incredibly high safety record is because of the fact that we taught all of our people all of these things. What to do in these various emergencies, these hundreds of emergencies that you could have onboard ship. We trained for them and we had all these exams and these tests, and Rickover sent around his inspectors. The group goes out to test every nuclear submarine after so many months to find out if they're technically qualified to be able to handle the nuclear casualties that can occur. And all that's very important, but it's also very important not to be dull.

DG: I was wondering about Cold War missions, and you were on what I would call Cold War missions. With both diesel and nuclear power boats, probably. Were these missions any different in terms of risk?

CG: In a nuclear submarine your capabilities were so much greater that you took greater risks. For instance, never in a diesel submarine would you ever think of trying to go up and count the number of blades of a propeller of a ship you were trying to follow. But in a nuclear submarine you could do that. I was on West Pac, on patrol, on a diesel boat, as exec, and for six months we monitored Vladivostok and we listened for Russian submarines coming out of port, and we followed them, we tracked them at a very comfortable, reasonable distance. When I commanded the Barb, we built it and we got it all ready to do these things, and then I left and went to a boomer. Then I had command of the entire flotilla in Naples where the ships that were under me were all tracking and trailing Russian submarines habitually, constantly. And because you had a greater capability, you had a tendency to do more things that were risky. And as a result, we had all these collisions that nobody knew about until the last few years.

DG: *Blindman's Bluff.*

CG: Yeah, *Blindman's Bluff* and all of that.

DG: On *Barbero* we were there—we didn't want anybody to know of course.

CG: To know where you were? Just like we were. On a missile submarine, you're not ever doing anything risky. You're just out there and you're ready to go. Only when you were—of course, on the *Bream* we had only three engines because we had converted to an SSK, and so we had one of our engines removed.

DG: What's SSK?

CG: We took six submarines in the 320 area class, and we put big rubber hydrophone bow on them, bulbous bows, and our job was to listen and to monitor for Russian submarine activity. I was Exec on the *Bream* and then C.O. on the *Angler* which was also an SSK. The real risky stuff didn't occur and didn't much come about until later. There were some instances of diesel submarines trailing and doing some things that were really quite wonderful, but most of that stuff came about later on with the advent of nuclear power, where you could really control speed and stay down and everything.

My guess is that most civilians had never thought of Clifford's statement below concerning how seldom nuclear submarines go through the diving evolution as compared to diesel submarines. Diesel submarine crews practiced diving the boat all the time because it was vital to be able to quickly escape an attack or move undetected and necessary to approach a target. Diving a submarine is a dangerous few moments for a number of reasons. We know that a number of diesel boats went to the bottom as a result of a stuck open Main Induction. Who knows how many of the 52 boats lost in WWII failed to return to port for the same reason?

Clifford M Duncan
EN2 (SS)
Corsair SS-435
1957 to 1959

A few months ago while going through the Russian submarine in Seattle with my wife and grandsons I had an interesting chat, with a nuke sub vet who was a volunteer tour guide, that may be of interest to you.

My grandsons and I had got caught up in a long conversation with this young vet in the engine room of the Russian sub and the conversation finally got around to the amount of dives we had each made. I had been assigned to the fleet diesel Corsair 435 which in 1957 to 1959 was primarily a New London school training boat and we could easily make 15 dives a week while training, and I was aboard for her 5,000th dive. He then commented that he might have made 15 dives in 4 gold cruises on his nuke boat. We then discussed how the fleet submarines were primarily a surface attack ship submerging usually to hide, versus nuke boats surfacing usually to be seen. I have a screen saver on my computer of a fleet submarine and my secretary happened to notice it one day and asked what it was, when I told her she couldn't believe they used to look like that. It has been said that a diesel submariner never loses his smell but that's another story.

Brian's first paragraph describes almost identically an experience I had in a typhoon in almost the same place—except for the stitches. It must have happened many times on the diesel boats, partly because the deck of the bridge was so close to the water and the fact that we nearly always rode out storms on the surface.

Brian D. Turley
LCDR
USS Pomfret SS-391/USS Abraham Lincoln SSBN-602/USS Daniel Webster SSBN-626/USS Kamehameha SSBN-642
19 Oct 1954 TO 31 Oct 1979

I went aboard Pomfret a freshly busted TMSN in 1959 and almost immediately the boat went to WESTPAC. While on patrol in South China Sea we got run over by a typhoon and could not submerge. Rode it out on the surface, since I was very junior (even though I had four years in) I went topside as a lookout alone. Tied to the TBT with a safety line and wearing raingear all I could do was hang on. A big wave filled up the dog house (bridge) lifted me out of the sail and dropped me over the side. With the safety line I came up short and ended up banging my chin against the side of the boat knocking me out. Don't remember much after that but I did wake up on the mess hall table with the quack (Pharmacistmate) stitching my chin up and singing knit one pearl two!

I went on to put two SSBN in commission and make several patrols. The difference between the two types of boats is not even measurable. The nukes went places went to depths and made speeds that we could only have wished for on the diesel. However I did a patrol close ashore on a nuke and it was damn well a white knukekle trip. They were not suited for that kind of work. The diesel on the other hand could linger for days in shallow water and not make a sound even with a lot of traffic around. Good luck on the project.

This is a very long but worthwhile entry. Bobby Barbee spent a lot of time on it for good reason. He makes the point of this chapter—that diesel boats were vastly less complex than nuclear power submarines. He also wins the prize for the longest paragraphs. It is intended to instruct us—and it succeeds.

Not only do civilians know very little about submarines, but neither do the other communities of the Navy to say nothing of other branches of the services. Nuclear submarines are about the most complex machine of warfare that exists today. The submariners today know how to operate these extremely complex vessels under all sorts of conditions, doing all sorts of missions and are prepared to face all sorts of casualties (fire, flooding, gas, power loss etc.) Barbee below lists engineering systems, various drills and emergencies which every crew member must be familiar with. Some of his comments could easily be put into other, more appropriate chapters, but I thought it reads better as a whole here.

The notion that 130 men could, either individually or collectively, know about/deal with/operate/fix all the systems Bobby lists below staggers me!

Bobby Ray Barbee
MMCS (SS/SW)
Tirante SS-420, Thomas Edison SSBN/SSN-610 (Blue), Will Rogers SSBN-659 (Blue), Trepang SSN-674
May 1960-May 1981

To qualify or requalify in subs you had to know all the same systems that were on diesel boats, i.e., Trim & Drain, Fuel Oil & Compensating Water, Tanks & Compartment Arrangement, Steering & Diving, Potable Water, Main Ballast Tank Blow, Low Pressure Blow, Ship's Service Air, Hull & Battery Ventilation, Sanitary, Weapons & Fire Control, Electrical, Topside Arrangement, etc.

Plus all these Engineering and Nuclear systems:
Coolant Charging & Valve Operating
Coolant Discharge
Coolant Purification
Coolant Sampling
Reactor Plant Fresh Water Cooling
Emergency Cooling
Primary Shield
Secondary Shield
Reactor Instrumentation
Core construction
Rod Drive Mechanisms
Pressurizer
Main Coolant Pump construction
Primary Loop
Primary Coolant chemistry
Boiler Water chemistry
Radiological Controls theory
RADIAC instruments
Steam Generators
Main Steam
Auxiliary Steam

Gland Seal & Exhaust
Condensate
Main Feed
Main Condenser
Main Sea Water
Auxiliary Sea Water
Auxiliary Fresh Water
Lithium Bromide Air Conditioning
R-11Air Conditioning
R-12 Refrigeration
Main Lube Oil
Shaft Lube Oil
Diesel
CO-H2 Burners
CO2 Scrubbers
HPACs
HP Air
Main Hydraulics
Ship's Service Turbine Generators
Main Propulsion turbines
Main Reduction Gear
Shaft Clutch
Electric Propulsion Motor
Resonance Exchanger
Shaft Seal
Lube Oil Purifiers
8000 gal per day steam distilling plant
2000 gal per day electric distilling plant
Outboard Motor (no kidding)
Oxygen Generators
Electrical Distribution
After Escape Trunk
After Signal Ejector
(And a few others that I can't remember)

M-Div Watch Stations (since I was an MM):
Primary Plant Operator
Engine Room Lower Level

Engine Room Upper Level
Throttleman (Electricians also stood this)
Shutdown Roving Watch
Engine Room Supervisor
Engineering Laboratory Technician (ELT) (only 4 with the training on each boat; one stood the watch for whole patrol) Engineering Watch Supervisor (CPOs and PO1s who wanted to make Chief). Everyone had to requalify every couple of years on all watch stations

Major Nuke Drills (most of them got the rest of the ship involved, though): Primary Coolant leak; Primary Coolant spill; High Airborne Activity; Reactor Scram; Steam leak; Flooding; Fire; Loss of Electrical; Loss of Lube Oil; and then there was Battle Stations Missile on top of all this at any time of the day or night (self-initiated & initiated by higher authority). Had to know everything in a six-foot stack of Reactor Plant Manuals and keep up with all the changes to the changes to the changes to them. "Verbatim compliance" to all procedures in these manuals and in all tech manuals. When you performed a plant operation (or even maintenance on equipment) you had to have another person reading the step-by-step procedure to you.

No jury-rigging on any engineering systems. Every part had to be certified Level I, SUBSAFE, or nuclear-level. Valve lineups had to be done by two people independently of one another and then a senior enlisted watchstander and the Engineering Duty Officer had to double check the valve lineup forms. Could only use black ink ballpoints. CO had to inspect a section of one of the engineering spaces with the M-Div LCPO EVERY DAY. CO on USS WILL ROGERS (SSBN-659) had a thing for Engineering Laboratory Technicians (ELTs) and met with one of them (and the LELT) EVERY DAY for at least an hour. Daily lectures on some nuke system.

Practice interviews for ORSE (Operational Reactor Safeguards Exam) boards while on patrol. ORSE boards once a year upon return from a patrol. If you failed the crew had to stay aboard the boat until it passed. Boards by a CO, ENG, MPA from another off-crew boat while you were off-crew before a patrol before an ORSE. In port (for Fast Attacks), Naval Reactors reps (Rickover's boys) would come aboard every night and roam around the engineering spaces looking for problems they could report to Rickover. They were usually nukes who had made Warrant Officer.

Nukes also have to requalify on every boat they go aboard. It doesn't matter if you're an E-9 with 20 years in the Nuke Program, as soon as you walk aboard a new boat you can't turn a valve until some snot-nosed Second Class with a year or so under his belt (but who's qualified on a watchstation) signs you off. BUT, HEY, WE GOT PRO PAY FOR OUR TROUBLES.

CYCLE OF A TYPICAL PATROL AND OFF-CREW PERIOD FOR A PRE-TRIDENT FBM (From Sub Base, Groton, CT):

Took two Navy buses from Sub Base to NAS, Quonset Point, Rhode Island (went to Boston once because of fog in RI); boarded chartered plane (originally two Air Force transports, later one commercial plane) for flight to Prestwick, Scotland or Rota, Spain. In Scotland, boarded two double-decker "London" buses for an hour's ride to the boat landing in Gourock. There we loaded a large liberty boat for a 45-minute ride across the Firth of Clyde to the submarine tender anchored out in the Holy Loch (in Spain, the sub tender was right near the NAS where the plane landed). Stayed in tender's relief-crew berthing during a three-day turnover period. During this time we went over the boat's records and discussed equipment problems with our counterparts on the other crew. After the turnover period, a change of command ceremony was held and the other crew left for the States. We then moved from the tender to the boat. Underwent an approximate 25 days of upkeep on the boat on port and starboard duty days. Usually worked all night on duty days, but were still ready to go over on liberty nights. Liberty in Holy Loch and Rota was well worth it, even though you might be tired. After the upkeep period, we had a one-day "Fast Cruise" alongside the tender to check out the equipment after repairs. Then we went on two days of sea trials before leaving on patrol. On sea trials, we took the boat to test depth and performed "angles and dangles," i.e., put the boat through 30 degrees up and 30 degrees down angles to ensure everything was secure in place. Once the patrol started, all hands shifted to "poopie suits." These were blue coveralls used because of their low lint content (which helped to prevent spontaneous combustion fires in the laundry dryers, a problem which a few boats had prior to poopie suits being required), and they dried faster than dungarees. The laundry was kept going 24 hours a day. On patrol, the boat's mission, as it cruised along in Patrol Quiet conditions at a speed of 6 knots, was to man Battle Stations Missile (Condition 1SQ) within 5 minutes of receiving a verified message from higher authority, then launch all 16 missiles, one after the other, one minute apart (later boats could fire 4 per minute). Weapons Systems Readiness Tests (WSRTs), initiated by higher authority or the CO, were held unannounced at any time of the day or night. The boat received its communications via a floating wire antenna that was trailed behind the boat and floated just below the surface. In addition to Battle Stations Missile drills, the nukes constantly had emergency reactor shutdown, steam leak, flooding, radioactive water spill or leak drills, as well as other reactor—or steam plant-related casualty drills. And, the nukes had to attend lectures on the plant every day except Sunday. Watch standing consisted of 6 hours on and 12 or 18 hours off (depending on the availability of qualified watchstanders—my first few patrols we stood only 4 on and 8 off). We were given two patrols to qualify (or re-qualify) on the boat, while at the same time qualifying on our various watch stations (the number depended on which division you were in). It took several patrols to finish up on all your watch station quals. Even after we got qualified on everything, Admiral Rickover required his nukes to periodically requalify on all their watch stations. Admiral Rickover did not want his nuke Chiefs to qualify as Chief of the Watch or Diving Officer in Control because he felt it took away from their focus on the nuclear plant. Many Chiefs did it on their own, though. He also didn't allow his nuke Chiefs (even if one of them was the senior enlisted man on board) to be the Chief of the Boat (or COB) for the same reason. Entertainment on patrol consisted of half-way parties (where guys would put on skits or play instruments to entertain the crew), casino nights, raffles to raise funds for the Welfare and Recreations Committee, pinochle and cribbage tournaments, WSRT "anchor pools," and Plan of the Day Bingo. We also had movies every night that only qualified men (or those up on their quals) could attend. We had stationary bikes and weights in the Missile Compartment and guys could jog around the Upper Level Missile Compartment for exercise. For a sauna-like experience the forward guys could come back to the Engine Room and sit outboard a turbine. Occasionally, the officers, Chiefs, and each Department took a turn at cooking and serving a special meal, like "surf and turf," for example, to give the cooks and messcooks a break. A favorite pastime (as it was on Diesel boats) was to try to "get to" anyone you knew who could be bothered by something. Being on a nuke boat underwater is like being on a spaceship. You're always in a completely hostile environment. We made our own water and from that we made oxygen. Because of the long core life of the reactor (13 years without refueling on my last boat), but longer today, we weren't concerned with steam plant efficiency (which is all conventional steam-powered ships think about), so we didn't worry about being on water hours. Our 8000 gallon per day steam distilling plant ran most of the time. Patrol length was (and still is) limited by the amount of food the boat can carry and the crew's psychological endurance. To help psychologically, crews received "Family Grams." These were three (more these days) 20-word (also more these days) radio messages per patrol that could be sent by your loved ones back home. Guys really got upset if they didn't get a Family Gram when they were expecting one. Living conditions on an FBM weren't bad. Each man had his own bunk (no "hot-bunk-ing" as they do on Fast Attacks) with a pan locker under the bunk and a curtain for privacy. Also, each bunk had its own air-conditioning outlet. The heads were large, with four showers, about six sinks and mirrors, and four or five commodes. FBMs also had crew's lounge areas, the size depending on the class of boat. These areas were used for playing cards, telling sea stories, or for holding qualification boards. We had field day once a week and constantly performed preventive main-tenance on the equipment. With Admiral Rickover, there was no such thing as "if it ain't broke don't fix it." COs were required to spend at least one hour a day conducting materiel inspection on some part of the engineering plant. Admiral Rickover didn't want his COs to be like the COs on surface craft who knew very little about the engineering spaces (his ways for Engineering Departments later spread to the surface Navy). Once a year, the nukes had an Operational Reactors Safeguards Exam (ORSE) by Admiral Rickover's boys from Washington. This was usually held at the end of a patrol and if the nukes failed this exam, the entire crew had to stay aboard until they passed. The other crew could not take over the boat. No wonder everyone loved the nukes. FBMs at first had a regular Medical Doctor aboard during patrols. He was aided by two Hospital Corpsmen, who also performed the twice-daily atmospheric surveys to ensure that the oxygen was high enough and gases such as hydrogen, carbon dioxide, carbon monoxide, and Freon were low. Upon completion of patrol, the boat returned to its advanced base and reversed the process with the crews swapping places. It was like getting transferred every three months. Pack your seabag and take off. After returning to the States, the crew was given a 30-day R&R period. If you didn't want to take leave you only had to come in to the off-crew office once a week during this time to let the command know you were still alive (sometimes you could just call in). There was no duty except for an occasional turn by junior Petty Officers at answering the phone in the office or making mail runs. Once the R&R period was over we attended equipment operation—and maintenance-related schools at the Sub Base. We were also required to periodically attend damage control refresher training. And, during the six-month interim before the next ORSE, the nukes were given oral boards by a CO, an XO, an Engineer, and a Main Propul-sion Assistant from an off-crew of another boat. During the three months in the States we still got sub pay and Pro-Pay, but we lost sea pay. The married guys made up for that by getting Commuted Rations (ComRats—which was tax-free) and the single guys who lived in the barracks usually saved money by eating in the base chow hall. In the early 1970s, an FBM CO figured out that when a crew was in the States it was away from its "tax home," i.e., the boat itself. He argued, successfully, that a percentage of the money a crew member spent on food, lodging, clothing, and transportation should be tax deductible. This became known as the "FBM tax break" and it's probably still in force. Once again, the crew members on Fast Attacks did not have such a tax break. Two weeks before a crew was due to go back to the boat another R&R period was granted. Just prior to this time (for a while) everyone self-addressed envelopes to be used by the other crew for mailing paychecks to wherever a person wanted them to go. A few years later (after single guys complained that they didn't have wives to take care of their bills), the policy was instituted to give everyone three months advanced pay (including sub pay and Pro-Pay) so that bills could be paid three months in advance. Or, we could take the money and blow it all in Scotland or Spain. In summary, duty on a FBM was (and probably still is) the best sea duty in the Navy. For an excellent visual insight into what it's like to be on a nuclear submarine, watch the series NOVA's episode entitled "Submarine!" and the series "Sharks of Steel" that show up on cable or PBS.

Jeff VanBlaracum is COB aboard USS SANTA FE brought up the requirements for in port watches on nuclear powered submarines.

JV: Some of the old guys, they hated the reactor, in a sense, in that it caused more personnel to have to stay onboard because you had to have armed guards to guard the reactor. While the diesel boat Navy, they did have a duty section, but it wasn't near what it was on a nuke.

DG: It was a belowdecks watch and a topside watch. Unless you had a battery charge going. Then the O.D. So there were three actual people on watch on a diesel boat. So what would it be on the *Santa Fe* if you were tied up for a week? Do you have shore power or do you just always run the reactor?

JV: We do have shore power, but you still have personnel. There are three watches back aft, and three foreword, so now you have six watches and you have to have security forces, and that has to consist of non-watch standers.

DG: So you have guys topside all the time?

JV: They have a guy top-side all the time, most of the time two, and what really matters is the security forces that have to be there that are non-watch standers, which is eight people—a minimum of eight people.

DG: And that's crew. That's not somebody from ashore.

JV: And you have to have a supervisory watch, which is always an E6 or above in the engine room, and then you have your duty chief up foreword, the requirement now, and then you have your duty officer and an engineering duty officer.

DG: So you're up to 20 people or something.

JV: At least. Yes.

DG: Well, that's a big difference. And that irritated these guys?

JV: Sure.

DG: But young people today are accustomed to that, and they just are raised that way—they didn't know any other way.

JV: They know no other way. In fact, I don't know of any guys left that served on diesel boats that are still actively serving on our submarines. I know a couple of my friends that are more senior command master chiefs that have done their COB tour and they're gone off of submarines now. But as I was coming up through, I met a lot of them and they did business a lot different than the way our personnel are trained today.

By contrast, as I stated above there were two watches on a diesel boat—Topside and Below Decks. I wrote the following some time ago describing Below Decks watch:

The other evening I did my usual walk through the house just before retiring for the night. We all do this, checking doors locked, lights in their night mode, everything turned off and secured. All of a sudden I heard an unfamiliar sound and in a flash I recalled standing below decks watchs on *Barbero*.

Below decks on a sub there were a lot of things which could (and often did) go wrong. The man on watch had to be "qualified." He'd wander completely through the boat every half hour or so, simply letting his senses take over. Stepping into a compartment, he would first listen for a sound which did not belong. It could be a very noisy compartment, but we knew all the "right noises" and could distinguish them from the ones that would indicate trouble. He would smell for trouble as well. An overheated electric motor has a smell we all probably recognize; chlorine, fuel oil, etc., each have a signature odor. There were many odors in every compartment, and the trick was knowing which ones belonged and which did not. We were also aware of what I'll call "attitude." If the boat was a bit down by the bow or had a little list to port, we had to find out why. We were always alert and took this watch quite seriously.

Bob Roos
ETCS(SS)
Toro SS-422, Triton SSN-586, Henry L Stimson SSBN-655, Batfish SSN-681, Sand Lance SSN-660
1958–1977

You have picked quite a topic for investigation. I am of that period you are interested in. My first boat was the USS Toro SS422 1960–61, an old fleet boat with no modifications other than removal of the topside gun mounts. After a year on board the Toro I saw the handwriting on the wall, diesel boats would not be forever and saw I had two choices, become a SINS Tech (Navigation ET) or go to Nuclear Power school. I choose Nuclear Power school. At about that time 1960–61 there were a lot of people headed to Nuclear Power school that stopped off on a diesel boat to get qualified, I guess the theory was—wash out a few who could not make it on the boats prior to them going to Nuclear Power school. Their tour, which was usually about 9 months, also gave them some practical experience.

My first Nuke boat was the USS Triton, SSN586 1962–1966. It was in the yards at EB undergoing refueling and modifications from her former life as an SSRN. While on the Toro I had spent some time in the yards getting a new battery so at first things were about the same except there were a lot more senior people on board. The yard period was lengthy and the Triton was used as a receiving station for people needing a home that did not get underway due to family illness, personal issues or whatever. Eventually M Div, with 45 people in it, had 22 E-7's, one E-8, 21 E-6's and one E-5. After we got out of the yards we became less top heavy but still many more senior people than the old diesel boat. Many of these people were like me who had some time in the navy and wanted to be in on this new Nuclear Power stuff. Having all that experience meant we could get a lot done and solve difficult situations. There were surprisingly few problems with senior people having to do the menial tasks like cleanup, everybody just pitched in. Another reason there were a lot of senior people is that everyone had been screened for superior intelligence and skills by virtue of having been accepted for Nuclear Power school, so almost everyone passed their rating exams the first or second time.

The Triton was one of the early nuke boats and one of a kind, clear difference from my next boat or boats, the USS Henry L Stimson, SSBN655 1969–71, USS Batfish, SSN681 1971, USS Sand Lance, SSN660 1972–75.

To illustrate the differences, consider how we learned systems. On the Toro you had to trace everything out by hand and draw your own diagrams. There were no manuals to read, you just talked to people to find out how things worked. And there certainly were no written procedures readily available. The Triton had a piping book but it did not have all the systems. There were tech manuals available to look up some things and procedures were sketchy at best. By the time of the later boats there were diagrams for everything and you best look at them, making your own diagrams just wasn't done. There were procedures for everything and you best follow them. Gradually thinking for yourself was done less and less. The successful people were the ones who could find the right procedure to use and interpret ambiguous language.

A classic difference between the Triton and the later boats was how the engine room was started up. On the Triton after the reactor was up critical and hot, the order was given for the ERS to startup the engine room, he would do so directing the watch standers to do certain things and he would stop by the maneuvering room once in a while to update us. On the Stimson and later boats, every order had to come from the maneuvering room which came from a detailed procedure, no deviation was allowed, the watch standers would follow each step as directed and wait for the next order. No thinking required. On the Toro guys would know what to do and orders from above were for the big things, dive, surface, start a charge etc. Nuclear Power was more complicated, at first there was a cadre of very capable people, very senior, go getters. Gradually that all changed.

Dave Oliver on the difference between diesels and nuclear power submarines and his theory on the loss of Thresher.

I'll give you an example how different it was. I had the advantage of going to *Trumpetfish*, then I went to *George Washington Carver*. We're at sea on Carver and we're doing a hand dive. You know what a hand dive is where you're pretending like you lost electricity and you go around and you locally operate all the valves?

You pretend like you've lost electricity but you have to dive because the supposition is that there's an airplane coming at you, and so you do it manually. Now, I'm sitting on my bunk afterwards thinking about this, and I say to myself, this is interesting. On a diesel boat, the reason you did that is the same reason you had to have 20–20 eye vision. Because you had to pick up that airplane that was coming low over the water, and you had to get below water or it was going to kill you. And a diesel boat spends all its time on the surface.

Now, aboard *Carver*, we're talking about an SSBN that submerges when it leaves port and doesn't come up again, that weighs 8,000 tons and is 500 feet long. This is 1967, and we're still doing "hand dives" aboard a nuclear submarines. We're doing hand dives to pass inspections.

I'm a lieutenant JG at the time, but, I write a letter up the chain of command, saying hand dives are dumb. And once I explain it everybody thinks, Right, this is dumb. Okay, three years goes by. I'm now on Nautilus; we're still diving from the bridge for the same sort of reasons—you know, you dove from the bridge because you wanted to survive the airplane attack. But there are all sorts of safety things that you sort of shortcut. When you dive from the bridge, you do it because the ship can survive. On a nuclear submarine that submerges when you leave and doesn't come up for three or four months, why are you diving from the bridge? So I stopped it. And I wrote this up and then it got changed.

Same thing. I'm going to give you another one. This is the reason I happen to think we lost Scorpion. Do you remember Condition Baker? Whenever you came to periscope depth you'd set Condition Baker on a diesel boat, and it was where you shut all the watertight doors and flappers? And you did that because when you come to periscope depth there's a risk factor, and if a ship hits you, if he's hit with Condition Baker set you're going to survive because the diesel boat is designed to survive with one flooded compartment.

A nuke can't survive with one flooded compartment. Any compartment that floods is going to kill you. Okay? Now, that's an acceptable risk because the nuclear hull is made of better steel. If a surface ship hits a nuclear submarine, the surface ship is going to sink, which we've demonstrated again and again.

Returning to Condition Baker, it is a routine on a diesel submarine. If you're out operating in a diesel boat, you come into periscope depth in one day, eight or ten times. I mean, it was just…everybody's good at it. In a nuke, you come to periscope depth once a day, once every two days.

I was out on Nautilus one day and we came to periscope depth and set Condition Baker while we're doing a battery charge. This is when I realized the other significant difference. You don't do a battery charge on a diesel boat when you are submerged because you have to be snorkeling to get the air to power the diesels. On a nuke you do battery charges any time. You come up to periscope depth in a nuke when you're doing a battery charge, and somebody sets Condition Baker, your battery lineup is all of a sudden screwed up and you had better get the charge cranked off immediately or your hydrogen level's screaming up to explosive levels.

But the supervisors hadn't thought through that. In other words, when we started building nuclear ships, they just took all the old diesel boat procedures, so we're still setting Condition Baker.

Let me think when this was. Fifteen years after the Nautilus was commissioned, and there's no rules about stopping a battery charge before you go to periscope depth. We're doing it just like a diesel boat except we've forgotten that diesel boats didn't battery charge because they didn't have power. We changed that.

Chuck's right. Nuclear boats were just completely different. But, since we started using the same procedures, most officers didn't realize how different the two platforms were. I think *Scorpion* went down for that reason.

DG: So it wasn't the torpedo

DO: The battery charge incident—my personal opinion. I really have a strong opinion about it, but there's a whole group of other officers who have investigated and written about it and they disagree. I don't believe it will ever be resolved.

DG: Would you enlighten me because I didn't know what you were just saying. They charge batterys. They can do them submerged because the power is from where?

DO: It's coming from the reactor. And a guy says, Go to periscope depth, set Condition Baker, and you screw up your ventilation line, right? And as soon as you screw up the ventilation lineup, particularly if you are on a finishing rate, right? If you're on a finishing rate, you're boiling hydrogen off. The only thing that's saving your ass is your exhaust line. On a nuke, what you're doing is you are recirculatin the air much faster than if you're on a diesel boat to dilute it, and you've got two burners onboard that are red hot burning that crap up. But what's really saving you is the ventilation scouring through the battery well. You set Condition Baker, you shut those flappers, all of a sudden you stop air circulating, and each one of those batteries is just generating pure hydrogen. If it gets to 8 percent, it's going to blow you up. And if the guy back aft isn't thinking—anyway, it's a terrible situation which people hadn't thought through. Fifteen years after Nautilus's commission guys are still setting Condition Baker throughout the fleet?

DG: That's very interesting.

DO: I thought it was interesting to change things so significantly (diesel to nuclear power) and not recognize what a big change it is. But, I mean, you're kids, you don't know any difference. And most of the guys don't think about the big picture because they're just working their asses off. They're trying their best to stay up. They don't have time to daydream.

You (Dan Gillcrist) wrote me a note and said, "You know, the guys aboard nukes couldn't fix any—didn't fix their equipment; whereas, the guys on diesel boats could fix their equipment." Bullshit. The reason you could fix everything aboard a diesel boat is it was so goddamn simple. I'm aboard a nuke and I am lapping valves, which I never would have done aboard a diesel boat—lapping chromium-plated valves which are contaminated and go inside the reactor, and I've got these guys beside me rewiring an entire cabinet of equipment. I mean, guys just busting their ass.

With 40 sailors onboard a diesel boat, you could keep up with anything. The 130 guys aboard a nuke were overwhelmed by work. There's no difference between the two sailors. They all just work their butts off. You're overwhelmed sometimes and you had to ask for help. There was just too much.

And every now and then you'd run against stuff that you couldn't solve aboard and you had to bring in specialists who are brilliant. I did more on a nuke than anybody ever did on a diesel boat. It was just an extraordinary amount of work. It's the 40 guys working on a relatively simple thing versus 120 guys working on ten times the amount of equipment.

Now, the diesel boat guy says, Hey, those nukes are candy asses. They weren't. I had both nukes and diesel sailors work for me; they're all the same.

A nuclear ship was just much more complicated. I did all the work necessary to qualify on a diesel boat in four months. With that experience and eighteen more months of training—it took me 18 months on a nuke to qualify. The nuclear and diesel problems were that dissimilar.

Mike Barr on the influences of the engineering formality of the Submarine Service on the rest of the Navy

MB: All the things that people talk about as to how to run organizations well were there. One of the most interesting, as I look back on it, was that in the early sixties there was formality in the nuclear engineering area, but not nearly as much in the rest of the ship.

This difference stemmed directly from the nuclear power "revolution." The legacy of the submarine force, particularly the war-fighting legacy of the submarine force, comes directly from diesel submariners. The way of running diesel submarines had evolved over many years and the approach was more than adequate. Admiral Rickover recognized nuclear propulsion required a very different approach than that which had served the diesel submarine fleet so well.

What I saw for the next 10 to 12 years was that the approach which started in the propulsion plant moved throughout the ship, so the whole ship was operated the same way. We could not operate sophisticated nuclear submarines without that methodology and formality. For example, consider sonar. In the early sixties, the primary sonar on most nuclear submarines was an AN/BQR2B passive sonar, which was basically a German World War II sonar. All you could do with it was to listen through headphones and get bearings. I mean, that was it. And there were tape recorders so you could play it back and forth, but there was very little technology past that.

Now, look at the complexity of today's sonar system. The sensors are orders of magnitude more complex; signal processing is done using computers with massive capability. You are able to analyze contacts analytically. And I'm not saying that the sonar technician's ear isn't still important; it is. But that was the only thing you had back then. There is no way you could efficiently and effectively operate a modern submarine sonar system without a great deal of formality. You can look at virtually every non-propulsion part of the ship and tell a similar story.

Another example: we had to learn how to talk. My second ship, USS TECUMSEH, (SSBN-628) was in overhaul in 1970. In comes this publication called the Submarine Interior Communications Manual. And, basically, it tells you how to talk. I thought to myself, this is nuts. I know how to talk. It required an eight-step process to start a feed pump. We're not talking about how to actually start the pump, just the communications to do it. But the more I thought about it, you really have to do it because there have been times an action has been ordered and you assume it's done, but it isn't done because of communications failure. So we had to learn how to talk. It's an important aspect of formality. For example, consider "close" and "blows." You don't ever say "close", and I think that came from the diesel boat days—I don't think that was new—because it sounds too much like "blows." If you ordered something to be closed and something blows instead—not good! So you always say "shut" instead of "close." People think they know how to talk, but they don't. You don't know how to talk in *that* environment without being very, very formal. The time when you need it most is in a fast paced evolution or in response to a casualty. You won't do it then unless you always do it that way, unless you train to do it. There's a great submarine saying that goes "you'd better train the way you're going to fight, because you're going to fight the way you trained." Don't ever believe you can change the way you do things when you go from one situation to another. Especially when you're under pressure.

DG: You made me think of something. Jim Watkins said that the Rickover influence of making sure everything was designed properly, all the things you just ticked off a while ago, were adopted by all other parts of the Navy as well, over time.

MB: Yes, it was.

DG: Was that because they saw how effective that was? So the aviation guys and the black shoes got on board?

MB: Well, I think you have to give the aviators a lot of credit for operating safely. Maybe it's if you're operating in three dimensions, as opposed to two, that you're probably likely to be more careful. The aviators, I think, have always had their own formality and way of doing things. Now, it was different than ours, but they have procedures and they *have* to follow those procedures. The maintenance has to be very, very formal or else an aircraft is going to fall out of the sky. But I do think a lot of what made the nuclear power program the quality program that it is *has* gone into the rest of the Navy, and the big thing—maybe Admiral Watkins talked about this—was SIZEMARK, and I forget what that stands for, but

DG: No, that's new to me.

MB: It was after the Vietnam War. It was when Admiral Holloway was CNO. I think he was CO of ENTERPRISE, a nuclear aircraft carrier, at one point. He recognized the material condition of the surface Navy was bad. It was too common that the way to get to be a CO, and to go on to bigger things, did *not* go through a tour in the engineering department. And so, understandably, people shied away from getting into the engineering area. I'm probably overstating it, but it was hard to be a superstar if all you were doing was turning the shaft and producing light, electricity, and water. So people stayed away from that, and as a result the material condition of the ships was poor. Of course, the ships had been run pretty hard in Vietnam which didn't help. So Admiral Holloway went to Admiral Rickover and asked for help. He wanted to train surface COs and senior people how to run a ship so that the material condition would be reasonable. Such a school was set up out in Idaho and prospective surface COs, squadron commanders and materiel people went through it. It was essentially nuclear power training tailored to the surface Navy, as I understand it.

DG: The engineering aspect?

MB: Well, it was more than just engineering; but certainly that was the focus. I've talked to people who have taught there. It was more about achieving and maintaining materiel readiness with the emphasis on engineering, but the principles would apply to the ordinance aspects of a ship or the electronic support measures part, or elsewhere. The school also taught an understanding of how propulsion plants and electrical systems and hydraulics worked and why they worked that way. It made a big difference. It infused a formality in the surface Navy and people didn't always like it.

DG: Oh, there was a resistance to it?

MB: Oh, yes. You can understand that there would be resistance. I've talked to a number of officers who went through that course. Almost uniformly they said they didn't want to go, they didn't like it, but when they finished they knew they needed it.

Jeff VanBlaracum raised an issue I was completely unaware of. I found it particularly interesting that none of the officers interviewed mentioned this. There were not only differences between diesel boats and nukes and their crews to some extent, but he speaks about the large differences between fast attacks and boomers and the adjustments crews had to make going from one to the other.

DG: Everybody I talk to seems to have had some time on boomers, some time on fast attacks, and their missions are really different. But if it's homogenized, I mean, if you guys spent a couple of tours on fast attacks and a couple of tours on boomers, then I would think that the personnel really aren't any different.

JV: Actually, they are. They are night and day different.

DG: Really. Well, how do you account then, because you were on a boomer; now you're fast attack. Did you change?

JV: I changed.

DG: So tell me about that, that's interesting.

JV: It's very interesting in that I'll tell you that today we have a lot of guys, especially in the torpedoman rating, they spend their whole career, until they make chief, onboard a Trident submarine, one of the boomers. They don't have chief torpedomen on Tridents, so they send that guy to a fast-attack submarine where it has absolutely nothing the same—it's night and day different. As you said, complete and totally different mission. More sea time, not the rigid schedule, that kind of thing. A fast attack is constantly changing. And it's very hard for them, and, in fact, recently there's been a very high failure rate of those guys. And it's not just torpedomen, but a lot of guys who spend their whole career, up until they're senior, on boomers and they try to come to a fast-attack and they have a very, very hard time.

DG: Does anybody go their whole career on boomers and sort of wrangle that? I mean, is that possible?

JV: Yes, it is.

DG: But it's also common to move like you said; there's no billet for chief torpedoman on a boomer, so they put you on, and then they can't hack it. Can you get more specific about that? The adjustment, I mean.

JV: The adjustment is that now they have the same number of torpedomen in their division, and their job is ten times more. And their knowledge of the systems on a fast-attack, first of all they're different, way different than they are on a boomer. And so he comes in, this chief, and he doesn't know as much as probably his qualified third class does about the systems. So he's already under the gun, kind of, and a lot of them don't make it, just because they don't spend the time because they're used to that rigid, predictable schedule that they had in the boomer Navy. And it was not easy for me, either, to make the conversion, but I spent the time and a lot of guys do. There are guys who spend the time onboard and learn what they have to learn to succeed.

DG: It seems like we're talking about the mission being completely different. The boomers go and just cut big circles in the middle of the Pacific someplace and wait. And you guys are up in the littorals snooping around. Doing all kinds of stuff and then hauling ass to the next mission.

JV: And our schedule always changes.

DG: So you have a whole different mindset on a mission.

JV: Yes.

DG: And then you said that a lot of the systems and equipment are different on boomers

JV: Night and day different.

DG: So which is the most difficult to accommodate?

JV: I think if I had to pick one, I would think it would be the difference in the equipment, because now the chief is supposed to be the expert. He's the man. But he is not really the man because he doesn't know enough. Vertical launch and the weapons handling system are completely and totally different. And it's just a sheer amount of extra things that you have to know and deal with. So that's probably the biggest burden, the single point, but it's a combination of things that cause these guys to fail. That's probably the biggest one. The next one is the uncertinty…oh, we're supposed to pull in today, but, nope, you're extended. You're going to stay out here for two more weeks. And then you're going to come in for two days and you're going to take off again for another three weeks.

DG: Because you are over tasked?

JV: Because that's the way we are.

DG: It's the nature of a fast-attack boat—because you can't get the other one to go snooping around, big damn Trident submarine. So they just do their cutting holes in the water thing and you guys are doing all kinds of things.

JV: Right. We have a very wide spectrum of missions, and it's very hard for these people to convert over and get out of the mindset of this is what I have to do, because their schedule is pretty well set. You do the same thing every upkeep, pretty much. You know, other than equipment may fail, this, that, and the other, minor differences, but it's totally different on a fast-attack. Totally different.

DG: So you were talking about the differences between both the missions and the tasking of fast-attacks. You guys are overloaded, basically.

JV: Absolutely. There's not enough of us to do the job, and so our schedule is very, very, very much like Jell-O. That's what we say. Our schedule is Jell-O, because it's never firm. And even since we've been here in Santa Fe (on a three day namesake city visit), our schedule has changed.

DG: You mean the boat schedule?

JV: Yes. And it's okay. I mean, there's nothing we can do about it. There's things that we have to do, and so we've got to go do it. And that's a very hard thing. And I'll tell you, the diesel boat guys, now they transition into the nuclear fast-attack Navy much easier than they did with the boomer.

DG: Really. Why was that?

JV: Because that was their ship. That was your boat.

DG: Oh, right, you're talking about the blue and gold crews?

JV: Right, right. Very, very hard for them to get accustomed to that mentality.

DG: Could you explain what the blue and gold thing is just for the non-sub-mariners?

JV: Sure, it's two crews. Every boomer has two crews and that's so that the ship can stay at sea as much as possible and not wear down the crew. In the big scheme of things, the boomer, the ship itself, spends more time at sea than the fast-attack.

DG: Yeah, but with two crews.

JV: But two crews. I'm not going to say that the boomer guys do not have pride in ownership in their ship. They do while they're there, but it's only part-time; it's not year-round. They go to the boat half of the year. We go to the boat every day of the year. The diesel boat guys had that mentality; that was their ship, all the time, twenty-four, seven. And so they transitioned into the nuclear fast-attack Navy much easier than they did with the boomers. Much easier.

With the permission of The Day, *I include the following article who's basis is an assessment by RADM Mark Kenny. It seemed that a good way to wind up this chapter called* Apples and Oranges *would be the persuasive argument against the US Navy regressing to buying 'apples' (diesel boats) again.*

Admiral Throws Cold Water On Diesel Sub Proposals

Nuclear-powered Boats Have Speed, Stealth That Cannot Be Matched, He Says

By Robert A. Hamilton, New London Day, 13 Mar 05

Groton—When the Pacific Fleet needed an additional submarine, the USS Alexandria headed out from the Naval Submarine Base, went up under the Arctic ice, and arrived was in the western Pacific "very quickly," said Rear Adm. Mark W. Kenny.

"A diesel submarine would have probably taken six to eight weeks, and a lot of that time would have been snorkling, so it would have been detectable," Kenny said. "And it couldn't have gone under the ice. That's probably the most glaring contrast between the two platforms."

As some top military and civilian analysts push the Navy to at least consider diesel-electric submarines as a less-expensive alternative to nuclear boats, Kenny, the commander of Submarine Group Two and the Navy Region Northeast, said submariners are skeptical.

"It's something we certainly will look at, because we've been asked to look at it, but I think the answer will come out the same, that it's not worth it to invest in diesel submarines," Kenny said.

Diesel submarines are limited to slow speeds while submerged on battery or air independent propulsion or AIP systems and are noisy when they're charging their batteries on the surface, he noted. And even advanced AIP systems only give submarines a couple of weeks underwater.

Nuclear submarines can maintain high speed and stay submerged for months at a time, making their own air and water. They're the best platform for a Navy that often has to sprint to trouble spots to protect U.S. interests, he said.

"If we had to worry about undersea superiority off the east and west coasts of the United States, diesels would have a huge part in that," Kenny said.

"But our focus is forward, our focus is speed. If you read anything from (Defense Secretary Donald) Rumsfeld, you're going to always see speed mentioned: speed of operations; speed of action; speed of options. Then you'll hear stealth.

"We don't want to have a large footprint overseas, we don't want to have forward bases," Kenny said. "The submarine force has always been about forward, stealth, endurance and speed. Diesel submarines are very capable adversaries, quiet, but their weakness is their inability to transit."

Even the most capable diesel or AIP submarine is designed to be quiet at about 3 to 5 knots, and the faster they travel the less time they can spend underwater, so if you spot a conventional submarine on the surface, you can be pretty sure it's within a 500-mile radius a week later.

A nuclear submarine, on the other hand, could be more than 5,000 miles away in the same week.

In addition, Kenny said, diesel submarines on the open market are less expensive because they're smaller, which means that they can't bring as many weapons or sensors to a fight.

"To build a diesel submarine with the payload of a 688 or Virginia, you'll start to get up to the same cost," Kenny said. "Even if you powered it by diesel you're going to be up in the price range of a nuclear submarine, if you want to have equivalent capability—and I would argue that you would never have equivalent capability, just by the nature of the diesel submarine."

Kenny said the submarine force instead should look at expanding its capabilities through technologies such as "leave-behind modules," a package that could be placed on the ocean bottom near a trouble spot to monitor a situation and possibly take action where necessary.

"A leave-behind module could have sensors…It could have unmanned underwater vehicles that could be sent out based on a sensor trip wire, to go out and search and possibly attack," Kenny said.

Kenny said he favors technologies that would allow a submarine the size of the current Virginia class to carry more "payload," either inside the hull or externally. "It's not so much the size as the bang for the buck," he continued. "We could get a submarine of equivalent size and put twice the payload or twice the volume for war-fighting capability. That's really I think a better goal.

"People focus in on the size, but we are really looking at capability for the buck," Kenny said. "We think you're going to need a certain size if you're going to take weapons to the fight, and that's going to drive your payload volume. But cost is a driver, and that's what we need to look at, capability for the cost."

Full Circle

"When you get your ship on station, if you are not alone, surrounded and outnumbered, you're in the wrong place"
Admiral Kinnaird R. McKee's instructions to his submarine commanders

The advance to nuclear powered submarines would, in my opinion, have happened naturally. It was the natural progression of technology. However, it happened rapidly and in large numbers due to the Cold War between the United States and the Soviet Union. The kinds of submarines the U.S. developed and built were #1 attack submarines with the main task of surveillance and trailing Soviet boomers and killing them if necessary, and # 2 SSBNs with the task of disappearing into the oceans and launching ballistic missiles if necessary. Since the dissolution of the Soviet Union and the end of the Cold War, the missions have changed considerably and, oddly, now are more like those missions of the WWII fleet boats including surveillance, recognizance, sinking of enemy ships and the insertion of SEALS. Today, instead of deep, blue water operations, our fast attack SSNs are operating in shallow littoral waters within cruise missile range of the vast majority of the world's population. Should a potential adversary of the United States happen to read this book, my advice to them would be to move inland—way inland.

It is interesting that on a simple actuarial basis, in this year 2005 most active duty submariners volunteered after the implosion of the Soviet Union. They never trailed a Soviet boomer and their diesel boat processors are, like me, old men.

Jim Watkins as Chief of Naval Operations naturally had the big picture and commented on this topic.

They (commanding officers) had a new machine under them, totally new capabilities unheard of in diesel submarines. The machine was going after sophisticated intelligence gathering, learning to employ longer reach weaponry; it was going after a lot of other things that didn't equate well with World War II submarining. That was a totally different era, and it's going to be different as well in the future. You still need stealthy vehicles in this world of satellites that can see everything down to a few feet of resolution, and those newest nuclear submarines are going to be there fifty years from now. They're launching missiles; they're doing all kinds of things. And the big boomers are going to get converted to missile launching capability, and who knows what role they'll play in strategic defense. I think it will be significant. These days of exploding technologies, all things are possible, and submarines will remain a great, flexible, stealthy, fast-moving platform with unlimited maritime utility.

So the culture from diesel to nuclear has been an incredible story, 50 years of conversion. It took about half that time to get over the fits and starts of why nuclear and, "gee, do you need all that?" Why don't we have, a la Norman Polmar, more diesel submarines? I said, 'Norman, you've got 160 diesel submarines—they're called the allies—that work in their own territorial areas, their littorals.' Forget it. We don't need them here. What we need are these long-reach capabilities to go all over the world and go with our battle groups, be part of the battle group. They were on their own during World War II. They weren't connected with battle groups. They might have been out there where our forces were, but they were pretty much lone sharks doing their job, and they did a hell of a job. It was a different world then, and this is the new world now.

So that whole interaction between the submarine corps and the battle groups, that came about really in the mid-seventies, started coming on very strong. They were hooked up officially as of the late seventies, another big change. And it was good for submarining, too, because I think it gave them a perspective that they didn't have before, about how they operated and so forth and how important they were in context with what the air arm was doing and the surface arm was doing. That interconnection became very valuable. And obviously you want survival of that battle group, and they became a watchdog, a scout out there looking for potential predators.

DG: Haven't they adapted marvelously with the dissolution of the USSR? They do different tasks now.

JW: They do different tasks now. All the supporting aircraft like the S-3s have been converted to tankers, you know. Antisubmarine warfare is still there, but it's focused now on the foreign littoral areas. While the Russians had some idea where some of our submarines were during the Cold War, the other nations of the world didn't have the sophistication to know. The transition from World War II to the Cold War was a significant transition. But now, from Cold War to post-Cold War is a whole new ball game because the Russians aren't there, and that was previously the sole focus. You remember the call "the Russians were coming." Every year we put out a thing, "the Russians are coming, the Russians are coming." And hence, the growth of a major program to build all these SSNs and SSBNs. We're now down to, I don't know, half of the force we were, certainly when I was around. And we were up over a hundred SSNs and all the SSBNs. And I don't know that we need any more than we're building, but we need to keep going. There's no question about it, and there's always such a long lead time, a long lead time for building and deploying the next series of Virginia class for example. And that's good, but one of these days we're going to need them, and you need them fast and you can't build them fast. And nuclear is the only way to go. They've always handled it beautifully in terms of their environmental interests and so forth. So that's basically the kind of a story I see. I see the SSBN as continuing to be *the* strong powerful leg of the triad. During the Cold War period it won the war finally because the Russians couldn't beat our technology lead. They just couldn't do it and they knew we could get them. Our technology developed an information flow of useful data to the battle groups as to where the Russians were and what they were doing—we could get them every time with our aircraft, with our submarines, with our intelligence. We were out there, we knew where they were. We trailed them. You couldn't do any of that with a diesel submarine. You're constantly having to come up and snorkel and charge those damn batteries. They're really a drawback to meet today's needs. Of course it worked in WWII. The technology of the enemy wasn't sophisticated enough to do much about it, and we excelled after we got off our duffs in the early forties and really started building a large submarine force. I mean, we brought Japan to its knees without any question. And we stopped the German nonsense in the Atlantic. In the latter days of the war, the Germans would go to sea and recognize that they had only a 20 percent chance of coming home. That does not do a lot for crew morale. So we were really good by the end of WWII. But to maintain that superiority, I think, it was absolutely essential that we develop a power source that could have unlimited duration, save for satisfying the crew's eating habits. You can now go anywhere for long distances and not come up for a month. I mean, you'd take off from San Diego when I was skipper of the Snook, dive at the entrance buoy and pop up in Naha, Okinawa seven weeks later. You know, that's amazing.

DG: It was. It was a completely different vessel. I mean, you think that we just made this marginal change like you went from adolescence to being 26. That wasn't what it is at all.

JW: Oh, no, no, no, no. That's a major, major, major step change, and everything that went with it then changed, so when you talk about the cultural changes, they were significant. Significant throughout the Navy. You always spend a lot of time in any kind of change like this living through an antagonistic period of time. In this case the naysayers would say, oh, it's a terrible idea. It's so expensive. What are we doing this for? We could build 50 diesel submarines for this. Why are we doing that and that and that? Pretty soon, however, you get to the point where transitional negatives are not an issue anymore. And then when Reagan came in with a 600-ship Navy, we really started moving out with some of the new technology that was essential because we had allowed ourselves to deteriorate during the prior administration by the mid to late seventies because of the Vietnam War syndrome. So when Reagan came in, he said, By God we're going to get going here and get our "peace through strength" up. When we got our strength component up it then changed a lot of things. And we scared the hell out of the Soviets, and they knew it. They knew we were on a race that they could not keep up with. And that's why they gave up at Reijchevic, you know. I really believe that it was because Reagan, in at the last minute, said no to Gorbachev's request to cancel SDI. He said I'm not going to change my program. And it wasn't long after that that the whole Soviet Union collapsed. They couldn't keep up the pace. They didn't have the dough to do it and they didn't have the technical capability to beat us. So that's why I like the idea of keeping this pressure on them even now. We should never let our defenses down because there's no assured peace even in a mono-polar world. I mean, look at what we've got now. The uncertain world is demanding more of our forces than ever before. And we don't fight wars as they did in the 17th and 18th and 19th centuries. We just don't do it anymore. It's another world and it requires the most sophisticated stuff. So, again, I think the transition to nuclear submarines was a step in a direction that can now continue to be fine-tuned to meet the emerging technological challenges of this crazy world we live in today.

And I think Rickover's nuclear program has given us some very fine officers, too. I think this pressure to do well academically and to perform well and so forth is all built into it. You can set high standards for your people and they will respond well. You don't fool around with it. You get the very best you can to run a complicated machine like a nuclear-powered ship. It has paid off and we've not degraded our operational capabilities.

It's a different kind of a war. It's not fought the same way. Do you have to have everybody in *Top Gun* or can you put some people in long-range bombers, can you put some people in ballistic missile submarines? That's a different ball game. It's like a different kind of a person and a different kind of a culture than we had before. I mean, I was in the middle of the cruise missile program when we started. I served on *Barbero* with its Regulus cruise missile. We also had Loons and various kinds of missiles and payloads. We thought we were really hot shots, where we could drop it somewhere within ten miles of the target. Of course we had to surface and had to open that big hangar on Barbero since one could not launch submerged in those days.

DG: It was the only thing at the time though—a stop gap.

JW: It was a stop-gap but it was known to be that way. It was a developmental program, and it was terrific. Jim Osborne and all that gang were in it. You know, there was a whole cadre of people that focused on submarine-launched missiles. And they were pretty impressive. These missiles could be nuclear-tipped, and so that really opened the door to the tactical nuclear game. And now you put that responsibility on an unlimited-duration submerged vehicle and you've really got something that is very useful for the defense of the United States, an early version of the ballistic missile program. Of course all this was accelerated by the technology explosion that we've had since the 50's. GPS positioning changed everything. Remember when the first submarines were fitted out with these systems, we were using inertial navigation. We thought that was terrific in those days, say, compared to a magnetic compass near the North Pole? Wow!

So, anyway, I think the submarines are going to continue to play a huge role, particularly in the Arctic as the ice thins out. The Defense Department's ice-free study of the Arctic 50 years from now is an indicator of more changes to come for submarines. Who knows what the role will be? It'll be substantial and it'll stay there for a long time, for years.

DG: It seems to me that there have been time periods where a particular vessel was pre-eminent, with the battleships and then the carriers, and now it's almost—would you say submarines are the preeminent ship now?

JW: I think they're the exclusive owner of stealth, you know. Yes. Save the stealth bomber, which is stealthy from certain kinds of radars and that kind of thing, not necessarily stealthy for the highest technology that you could bring to bear on it. For example it's very hard to hide from heat seeking sensors.

DG: I was going to say that's really temporary.

JW: And, you know, how temporary the opaqueness of ocean is if we do what we're recommending on the Ocean Commission, i.e. to wire up the ocean to learn about environment and climate. And we're filling the ocean full of fiber optics. Well, those things can be converted to all kinds of new devices. So at some point the oceans are going to be more transparent than they are today. But they are still opaque if you know the science of sound. I see the submarine in the next hundred years as still being a very viable platform.

Jim Watkins has the unique perspective of having been CNO, Secretary of Energy and for a number of years deeply involved in the World's oceans. I was comforted by his views concerning national defense generally, and the US Submarine forces in particular. All this on a current 2003 basis.

JW: The United States should be credited for staying up with technology and the changing times throughout the world, and I think they have. I think the military has done a superb job, better than we have in any other non-military venture, I'll tell you that much. They stayed with it and they coordinate. They're forced to coordinate. We have no choice in the modernized world. And so I think that has forced the services to come together and share a heck of a lot more and it's a much more powerful and integrated force. And that's the way things are taught today, and I think it makes a lot of sense. To try to get my nine Federal Agencies that are in ocean businesses coordinated just in research will take a ten-year program and it will be only partially done. We now manage by vertical standpipes, very specific missions. That's okay, but so many of those issues are common because nature integrates horizontally beautifully. Yet we manage vertically, pieces of nature, and it doesn't work well. And we're finding out now that we can manage horizontally as well as vertically through modern computer capabilities and information interchange and all that kind of stuff. And where we're doing it, we're making a lot of new inroads. Where we don't, we're stumbling; we're counterproductive of each other, doing a lot of dumb things.

The Defense Department, in my opinion, has never been in that mode, despite the negative comments on inter-service rivalry which I thought were way overplayed and nonsense. Of course you want a service chief to fight for his own forces. At the right time, they'll come together and they'll fight together just like we have frequently demonstrated. It doesn't take a rocket scientist to get good people together who will fight together, but they'll also fight for what they think their component of the forces needs to have in hand. I always thought that it was nonsense to accede to the Goldwater/Nichols Bill for that reason. Why? Because it took out the interaction between service chiefs that could be equally important to that of the Chairman. The Chairman was the coordinator and the Chairman was the spokesman, but the Chairman always spoke for the Chiefs. Now, the Chairman alone spoke for the Secretary of Defense. That's the way it appears. And that's the way the law reads. I think it's a mistake because each Service Chief represents a component of society, each of which is a different culture—the Navy has a different culture from the Marines from the Air Force from the Army. They come from different backgrounds. They're made up of different ethnic mixes, different ways of life. Those are important inputs to get separately. And I can remember when Reagan, at one of the Security Council meetings, asked each one of us. I want to hear from each Service Chief now. With all the information we have here, should we go into Grenada next week? Well, I thought that was terrific. We weren't prepared for that question. Nobody had briefed us that he was going to ask that question, and each answer that came out was totally different but always at the bottom line was "I think we ought to do it," even though we did not know what the students in Grenada wanted. We had never asked the students, "Do you want to get out of there or not?" We didn't know until they came home and kissed the ground. But all the other information was so strong, we said, Yeah, we should go, Mr. President.

Okay, another one was SDI, and Secretary Weinberger was big enough to say, "Mr. President, you've heard from me on how we should base the MX missiles. You've heard from Secretary of State, and now I want you to hear from the Service Chiefs. They have a different opinion. They think we should modernize the forces that we have today but we should move aggressively over the next 20 years to Strategic Defense. And Reagan said, That's what we're going to do. I agree with that. It's time to get out of this mutually-assured destruction concept for this country. And that's why this preemptive strike strategy is so critical right now. This preemptive strike is a whole new way of doing business. It's a very different psychology. It's presently going too fast. It really is, in my opinion. It's a slippery slope. Maybe we're right and maybe we aren't, but we've never done this before. It's always been deterrent, it's always been defense, it's always been a deterrent kind of thing. Unfortunately, we too often wait till the Pearl Harbor has taken place. Or we wait till the Jews are exterminated. Okay, I know, but then we move, like 50 years of the Cold War. We stayed out of WWIII because of that deterrent—and you can argue whether nuclear weapons are moral or immoral, but in my opinion they were moral for that purpose. Everybody had them, so what are you going to do? We all think they're bad, get rid of them. Every president said that. But how to do it once you've got the glue on your hands, how do you get rid of it?

So I think that the submarine forces played a huge role in the winning of the Cold War. It played a huge role in winning World War II, and they're going to play a huge role in winning this weird war against terrorism in the world. Because they can move forces fast and stealthily. They can move into areas nobody can see them, so they don't have any problem. And the surface ships don't have any problem with violating sovereign rights of the states that they're near. I mean, North Korea can challenge us 150 miles off the coast in the Sea of Japan, but if they step out of line very far they're going to get their ass beaten. We're not going to put up with that crap. If they really take on one of our RC-135s or something, we'll take them on if outside their territorial air space. And so I think that the whole stealthy business of being there, and people know you're there, and that you're gaining the kind of information—the ground truth information is so important to correlate with everything else, and only submarines can do that. I mean, you know, you read *Blind Man's Bluff.* Well, nobody confirms or denies the thing officially, but it's a pretty good story of what went on, but it's even more exciting in actuality than that, much more exciting.

And, again, the submarine played a huge role in analyzing where we stood, vis-à-vis the Soviet Union, all the time. That information was incredibly valuable. And you can't do it by a national technical means alone. You have to have two forms, people on the ground and national external sensor capability. Really, you have to have human intelligence. We had a sound and capable human intelligence corps that was stupidly knocked out in the 70's. I mean, if we had the human intelligence today that we should have, we'd be in a far better position to assert ourselves with real knowledge based on much more than a defector or two or whatever. You can't get by with only satellites; you have to have people on the ground to verify what all other external sensors are telling you.

DG: I had a conversation with the former skipper of the Santa Fe. He told me one day, on the last deployment they spent the vast majority of their time in water less deep than the length of the boat. I was amazed. They must be really up close.

JW: They are up close and personal because, you know, you can do that. There are risks associated with that, and their operational orders should tell you under what circumstances you can do that kind of thing. But these boats are so beautifully built. They're like a fine tuned automobile; highly, highly responsive to you. And so you can do things that you might not have been able to do earlier. You can get out of trouble fast. You couldn't do it before, when on batteries you can't get very far before your batteries are down. You can go 25 knots—or 20 knots but for only about a half an hour. And now, with nuclear power you can go over 30 knots as long as you want. That makes a huge difference in your tactics and what you can do.

Submariners have always been remarkably adept at fixing things and responding to situations. In these interviews and among the many submissions to this project are references to submariner resourcefulness. Some think that ability was lost with the introduction of nuclear power and the accompanying 'procedures.' Jeff Vanblaricum spent a lot of time in his interview on the subject, praising the diesel boat guys. Mike

Barr took issue with the premise that submariner resourcefulness was lost in the nuclear power submarines.

DG: I was told that in a lot of cases the manufacturers don't want you messing with their products. Just give it back and we'll give you a new one, or plug in this whole replacement part.

MB: And that works fine if you've got one on the ship when you're at sea for 60 days, but if you don't then submariners are still going to try to fix it if it's going to end the mission. The exception to that is if a repair might degrade an important safety feature.

DG: So would you say that that talent is *not* lost?

MB: I don't think it's lost. I don't think it's lost at all. I can't really talk with any authority for the last seven years since I've been retired, but the things that submariners have continually done when the chips were down is just amazing. They get in and they fix things. It's mostly the enlisted guys, which is just a wonderful credit to the quality of the people. They have great intelligence, training, perseverance and dedication. In one case a submarine in the middle of the South Pacific had a reduction gear problem. The crew fixed the reduction gear so they could get to port on their own; otherwise they would have needed a tow. Normally that would have been a repair facility job and a tough one at that.

DG: That's good. They know how it works. I assume that's fairly big stuff, too.

MB: Oh, yes, they know how it works, and that's the key. They understand the theory well enough to understand how equipment works. There is good documentation in most cases so you can determine what needs to be done. With the planning that the chiefs and officers do, the crew can go in and fix things safely and efficiently. This capability is not limited to the propulsion plant. I will readily admit that as things get more computerized, either you've got the replacement component or you don't, and the ability to fix some components is limited, even with our talented people!

Our people are as good as they ever were, maybe better. I got to my first submarine, which was USS SNOOK (SSN-592), in January 1963. It was a new ship, one year old, and the material condition of the ship was certainly perfectly adequate. My first commanding officer tour was on USS SCULPIN (SSN-590), a sister ship of SNOOK, fourteen years later. The material condition of SCULPIN at age 15 was significantly better than that of SNOOK at one year. And that has nothing to do with any lack of ability of the crews. We the Navy and the Submarine Force got much better at maintaining our ships so the condition of the force got better and better. It continues to be very, very good. Supporting lengthy submarine at sea operations with no external support. It is continuous improvement at its best!

Jeff VanBlaracum addressed this issue in his interview.

DG: You had mentioned, and I don't ever remember any chief I ever knew doing this, but you had mentioned that you got sonar qualified. So you've learned a lot of other jobs. You were a torpedoman basically and your main job now, of course, is Chief of the Boat, which is a big important job. But in your various tours you went to the trouble of learning other skills. Which ones?

JV: I qualified auxiliaryman of the watch on my first ship—that's the "A" division watch, machinist mates. I qualified to stand their watch.

DG: And what motivated you to do that? Were you just curious?

JV: I did it because I'm the type of guy who needs something to do. Otherwise I get stale, you know, and I didn't want to get stale. And it also increased my knowledge of the ship, and that was good. I wanted to know more.

DG: I think it was great. I admire you for it. I just don't remember people back on the diesel boats learning other stuff. We all got qualified naturally, but then everybody had their particular job and nobody came up and tried to learn about torpedoes or go back with the engineman.

JV: Right. You see it a lot more in the nuclear Navy, the cross-qualification. And what it does is for a department, it broadens their—it makes them more flexible. Now, I can send, if I've got a guy, a sonarman, let's say, that's qualified torpedo room, I can send one of my torpedomen on leave and this guy can cover if he's there. It's that kind of thing. It's flexibility.

DG: It sounds like it's also a little better attitude. Didn't Bob Patton, my other COB friend, do you remember him getting other skills?

JV: Oh, yeah. It's very common nowadays and Bobby was a diesel boat sailor. And it was kind of, this mentality on a diesel boat where you knew just about everything there was to know about that submarine, you know what I'm saying? Nuclear submarines, it's very hard to know everything about that submarine because there's a lot more of it to know. So the cross-qualifications help out.

DG: What I'm trying to do, is to get people who had no nuclear experience, the old guys like me, before they die, and then people who were in during the transition, like you and I talked about a minute ago, and then points of view from people who were not influenced by the old diesel boats, you know, what they thought of it, and see if there's any difference. And there may not be a lot of difference, actually, in terms of the culture. Attitudes and esprit, élan and things like that.

JV: I believe there is a difference between diesel boat and nuclear submarine personnel, then and now. And I think the biggest thing is that you get personnel involved, say electricians involved in weapons handling, and there's a lot of that going on. That's the biggest thing for me because even when I first came in the Navy, we wouldn't allow anybody else but torpedomen to be juggling fish. Now it's a different mentality—we have to, because of our tasking.

DG: Because there aren't enough guys to handle the weapons?

JV: That's right.

DG: Do you have battle stations positions? Battle stations, torpedo or toma-hawk or whatever the heck they call it? And guys aft will come forward to help?

JV: Absolutely. We have nuclear-trained personnel handling weapons during battle stations. And they're great weapons handlers because they're very procedur-ally compliant.

DG: So in the case of battle stations there'll be the senior guys back there in the reactor compartment, so the junior guy in the reactor compartment can come forward and help out.

JV: Yeah.

DG: Okay. Now I know what you mean.

JV: And actually even some of the senior guys. In fact, *the* senior nuke onboard the *Santa Fe* just recently was our battle stations conventional weapons handling supervisor, on one side. The difference is you have two sides on a fast attack. And it's a huge torpedo room, and you've got two teams of personnel working, basically reloading or loading, whatever, so you need a lot of people.

NUKE HUMOR

One guy posted recently that Soviet surveillance ships would be stationed so as to observe the boomers as they made their way out of port prior to their dive. If anything were thrown over the side they would retrieve and examine it for intelligence purposes. So, the sailors on this particular SSBN built a floating device and stuck some cheap Radio Shack antennas on it, released it and then blew their saved up sanitary tanks at the spot of the bogus device. They all had a big laugh because the Soviet snoops would have to motor over into the middle of the sanitary tank slick to retrieve the Radio Shack device.

"We would be followed by them out of Holy Loch on every trip. Never under-stood why we didn't go out in the dark. We always went with a tug and a large power boat which were there to mask the prop noise we made."

Glen Keiffer—a.k.a. Eric VonZipper

My only direct exposure to submariners was during my service on Barbero *from 1958 through 1961 where I found many colorful and humorous shipmates. We had several cooks who were hilarious and provided entertainment during chow. I suspect all the other boats were similar in this respect. The diesel submarine navy was loaded with characters and they were a lot of fun to be around and to go ashore with. My recent experiences with nuclear power sailors and officers leads me to think they are far more serious. But the more I discover about them the more I think that they are not much different in the color department than we diesel boat sailors. Confirmation of my theory is the presence of Glen Keiffer, a nuclear sailor and a friend of mine, whom I met on a submariners BBS, whose* nom de guerre *is Erik VonZipper. As they say in New York City, "Don't ask." He once told me a story about liberty in Rota, Spain, which I'll attempt to relay.*

Glen told me about going ashore on liberty in Rota, Spain. He never confided in me what came over him—surely it couldn't have been alcohol and pretty ladies, he must have simply forgotten that liberty was up at midnight since the submarine was scheduled to get underway in the morning. He awoke in the early morning, startled to realize that he was dangerously close to "missing ship's movement," one of the cardinal no-no's in the Navy. If the ship leaves port without you and you can't quickly develop an advanced case of pneumonia, you are toast. Anyway, my friend Glen wasted no time with an *adios,* leapt into the nearest cab for a high-speed run to the pier, like something out of *The French Connection.* When he reached the head of the pier his heart dropped as he saw his submarine backing away from the dock. Our Glen, being an exceptional athlete sprinted toward the end of the pier, peeling off his civvies as he ran. Then he dove off the pier and fast-swam toward the submarine with his shipmates in headphones on the Maneuvering watch cheering him onwards. As he approached the submarine they threw him the eye splice of the mooring line lying on the deck still un-stowed and pulled him up over the tank tops like a wet rat and hurried him below as if no one had witnessed it. He recalls during the swim seeing the CO watching this spectacle from up on the sail and slowly turning to avert his view.

I think the real reason he told me this story was a commentary on what a splendid Captain he had on that submarine. The unavoidable consequence of his transgression was Captain's Mast—a ships judicial proceeding. A day or two later, following all the evidence he was sentenced to confinement to ship for 60 days—normally an onerous punishment. Glen then said with a smile that that was the exact amount of time his submarine would be at sea.

Von Zipper's second story is about gilly and says as much about Glen as it does about his CO on U.S.S James Madison *SSBN 627*

"PREFACE; On nuclear subs, especially boomers, there was a Petty Officer, that was in-charge of the gilly, which is 100% pure alcohol and used to clean electronic equipment. Actually, it was harder to get near the gilly than to approach the weapons.

"About the third or fourth patrol, the Supply Officer, says I would be the gilly Petty Officer. Me, the number one drunk or at least one of the biggest drunks on the Madison, was to be gilly king. See, being the PO in charge of the gilly, I only needed the supply officer's signature on the chit. Now, if you are not the gilly king, you need your Leading Petty Officer, Division Officer, and such to get at the gilly. Now, MCC, Missile Control Center, my watch station, had PM's, (preventive maintenance), that needed the gilly to perform and so did other divisions. Now, remember, this is not the torpedo gilly. It is twice as good. There can be no impurities in the gilly because the equipment it was use to clean could not have things on the contacts you were cleaning.

"Now I draw a pint of gilly, probably for another division, and Swede, Rich, and I go to lower level missile compartment. This is not a level people travel going through the sub. Rich is a new FT on this patrol and he qualified on his watch station, MCC Supervisor, which means Swede and I would stand fewer watches. This Rich is sort of good type guy and not someone that would get in trouble much, where Swede and I are pros at getting in the shits. Well, after about three or four highballs of gilly and coke, we go to the crew's mess.

"Now, I must also, preface this, too. See, Swede and I rode bike together. On this patrol, we started to wear our leather motorcycle jackets and sunglasses. We are wearing them all the time. After about a week we are told we can no longer wear our leather jackets. Then about a week later, we are told that we can not wear our sunglasses, either. Now, to get around this last straw, the sunglasses, we just push out the sunglass and wear the rims, with no lens in them.

"So back to the crew's mess. Rich, Swede, and I are talking and I am feeling no pain and Swede is pretty much the same way. Now on a boomer, the Captain rarely walks all around without people telling you ahead of time. He doesn't want to see everything that is going on, especially since the Madison's weapons department was the tops of the Atlantic Fleet. Well, this is just before the night's movie. Well, I am sitting on one side of the table that sits six. Swede and Rich are sitting across from me. The Captain comes into the crew's mess and walks right back to our table and sits down. Now, remember we were ordered not to wear our jackets and sunglasses, but never knew where that order came from. This Captain was the greatest. Well, he starts the conversation out by congratulating Rich for qualifying at his watch station and being ahead on ship's quals. Then he starts to stare at me. He says 'look straight at me' and then puts his two fingers through the rims on my face and pokes my eyes. It reminded me of the Three Stooges. I start to laugh, at which time Rich decides to pass out. Rich's head hit the table, breaking his rims. He had put them on, too. His face is flat against the table. Swede says real quick,"Cap, Rich has been working around the clock on his quals and has not slept in two days. I guess he decided to sleep right now." Swede picks Rich up and throws him over his shoulder and walks out of the crew's mess with everyone watching us. That leaves me there with the Cap and me laughing so hard, that I am actually pissing in my poopie suit. The Cap says,'I guess you can just work a man too hard.' He then gets up and leaves.

"Now, I am laughing so hard that I slide down to the deck under the table. Up comes my Chief, who is still friends with me, and says, "Tipping into the gilly again, Erik?" The whole crew's mess was rolling and I figured it was a good time for me to leave, too.

"Now, I am sure the Captain knew what was going on, but he was a good leader. He knew that none of us had to stand a watch for sometime and what good would it do to say anything after two months at sea?

"'Till this day, when I think about this story, I laugh out loud. I keep thinking of this full Bird Captain putting his two fingers through the lens rims and at the same time have a guy pass completely out right across from him.

Dan, I think that was one of the funniest happenings on the boat."

As this book project is winding up I thought it important to the subject of "full circle" to mention that the Navy is in the process of converting four Trident submarines. Florida SSGN-728, Ohio SSGN-726, Michigan SSGN-727 and Georgia SSGN-729. (Interesting they chose consecutive hull numbers for this). The initial reason is compliance with the most recent SALT Treaty which dictated the elimination of the subject submarines with respect to their 'deterrent capability' (read ballistic missiles). Presumably it was assumed they would be scrapped. Not so. They now are designated SSGNs, just like the old pre-ballistic missile boats of the 50's Barbero, Tunny, Growler and Grayback. (With the exception of the "N" of course.) Why get rid of perfectly good nuclear submarines with ample life left in them?

The converted submarines will be, I believe, more valuable to the Navy than in their original configuration. Each one will have SEAL capability. Their ability to launch scores of Tomahawk missiles and other reconnaissance and intelligence vehicles makes them extremely useful and suitable for today.

Ron Gorance served on five or six boats from 1958 to 1975. His funny story appears in the "Are You Crazy?" chapter if you recall.

Here's something else I wrote some time ago that might be useful:

The W.W.II sub vets I served with in the '50's were courageous, confident and cool (in every sense of the word). I respected them so much that I tried to mimic their behavior and attitudes. Regrettably, my conduct often came across to them as bravado (Dictionary—A disposition toward showy defiance or false expressions of courage). In later years, the young Nukes came along and mimicked my generation. This appeared, on the surface, to have produced obnoxious, boisterous and incomplete copies of those men I had tried so hard to emulate.

I have always felt somehow inferior to the W.W.II submarine heroes, but knew in my heart that I could have been one of them if only I had been born earlier. My gut tells me that Nukes are having the same difficulties living up to our honorable heritage, and appear to use bravado as a cover for each perceived failing just as I did. But one thing is certain: a diving alarm drowns out the loudest blast of bravado, and false courage can't survive submerged.

The Cold War and nuclear power changed the whole world, so it is just as impossible to measure the caliber of today's submariners as it would be to compare General Washington's men to General Frank's. I think the men have not changed. I have experienced three distinct generations of one family. Silver and Gold Dolphins symbolize the invisibly thin line which connects us all.

USS Parche SS-384 1943 to 1946   USS Parche SSN-683 1974 to 2004

It was always my intention to include this part on Red Ramage since he came up in the interview with Bob Gautier. I thought Ramage's simply stunning, white knuckle WWII attack of a Japanese convoy which appears below was a great example of the many other diesel boat COs submarine exploits. Then, last fall, 2004, USS Parche SSN-683 was decommissioned in Bremerton, WA and the news surrounding the event listed that submarine's awards. Parche was the most decorated ship in US Navy history! Parche, in over 19 deployments, was awarded nine Presidential Unit Citations (PUC), thirteen Navy Expeditionary Medals and 10 Navy Unit Commendations among other awards! Most people never even heard that name before. Not surprisingly, about the longest group of entries in the index of Blind Man's Bluff is under the name Parche. In this book, which attempts to compare the old diesel boat culture to the nuclear powered navy of today, I can not think of a better or more appropriate example than the two Parches.

The first Parche had a short war of about a year and a half. Commissioned in November 1943. In both patrol numbers one and two, under Red Ramage she was awarded the Presidential Unit Citation (PUC). Trout's fifth patrol under Red Ramage also was awarded the PUC.

From the Bob Gautier interview and the genesis of this section;

DG: There was another guy that I ran into at that Nixon Inauguration in 1969, one of the many crowded parties. And I literally bumped into somebody and I turned around and he turned around, he was in blues, an admiral, wore the Medal of Honor and his name tag said RAMAGE! I nearly had coronary arrest.

BG: (Bob Gautier) Yeah, Red Ramage.

I said, "Red Ramage, holy smokes!' You know that is a name straight out of Central Casting. Anyway, we shook hands and I told him I was a submariner—had a nice little visit. What an honor. Some of those guys are just, you know, really special to me.

BG: Well, I'll tell you a story about Red Ramage. When he was Commander First Fleet here and I was chief of staff of the flotilla, and we had a boat come back from West Pack with a fairly good run. I told the boss, Bob Setterford, I said, You know, when the guy comes to debrief us, we ought to invite Admiral Ramage over here, let him hear the debrief. Of course, he was with First Fleet, and he had no need to have the clearances, and so he didn't have a clearance. But I told the boss, I said, 'This is stupid.' I said, 'He certainly has done enough to be able to sit and listen to one of the briefings.' And the boss agreed with me. And we had Ramage come over and sit through it and he thought that was great. He liked that, but he didn't have a clearance. I thought, you know, we overdue this stuff about the damn clearances. And here's a guy, you know, with a Congressional Medal and all that stuff that we were going to deny him listening to a guy making a run.

DG: Because it was secret.

BG: Yeah. It's stupid.

The following article appeared in The Sun newspaper of Bremerton, Wash., on Oct. 20, 2004. Chris Barron generously agreed to let me use it. His email to me in part read, "It's interesting that I've received more response from that Parche story than any other story I've ever done in my career. And I've done some big ones."

A silent warrior's final day
By Chris Barron
Sun Staff

On a dark and gloomy rain-filled day, a shroud of secrecy permeated the air on the Bremerton waterfront.

It was the perfect setting for the final day in the top-secret career of the Bangor-based USS Parche, one of the world's most prolific spy submarines.

By the time its life ended Tuesday in a decommissioning ceremony at the Bremerton naval base, the Parche was the most highly decorated ship in Navy history—even though most Americans have never heard of it.

Commissioned in 1974, the Parche spent 30 years and 19 deployments as America's top espionage sub, reportedly tapping the undersea military communication lines of the Soviet Union during the Cold War, plucking lost Soviet weaponry from the ocean floor and gathering intelligence on other enemies afterward.

The Parche was officially designated by the Navy as a "research and development" submarine. And it did plenty of that, testing new sonar and undersea warfare technologies.

But its highly classified missions, none of which have ever been officially confirmed, are the most intriguing aspect of its history. Many of those missions were deemed to be of "vital importance to U.S. national security," earning the submarine an unprecedented nine Presidential Unit Citations. The vast majority of ships never receive even one.

For being the most decorated ship ever, shouldn't more people be made aware of what it accomplished?

"Those that need to know, know," said a matter-of-fact Rear Adm. Ben Wachendorf, who commanded the Parche from 1988 to 1993.

Wachendorf, now U.S. defense attache in Moscow, traveled from Russia to be at Tuesday's ceremony.

"I wouldn't have missed it for anything," he said. "It means a lot to be able to say goodbye to an old friend."

In fact, all but one of the Parche's nine former commanders were present at the Parche's decommissioning. In addition, about 130 former crew members, most belonging to the USS Parche Association, were on hand to witness the sub's inactivation.

Those who returned to see their sub one last time said it was not only the camaraderie of submarine life that made Parche special, but also the exotic and extremely challenging missions it completed, which often involved excruciatingly long periods spent submerged with dwindling food and supplies.

"It's the end of the life cycle," said Manchester resident Will Longman, chairman of the Parche Association. "It's very meaningful. The camaraderie does not go away. And the uniqueness of Parche imparts its own special camaraderie."

The Parche also was the last of the Navy's 37 Sturgeon-class fast attack subs to be deactivated—though it barely resembled any of the other ships of that class.

That's because its hull was extended by 100 feet to accommodate extensive classified modifications in a four-year stay at Mare Island Naval Shipyard near San Francisco in the late 1980s and early 1990s.

In 1994, the Parche and its crew of 190 moved from Mare Island to Bangor. It had already earned six Presidential Unit Citations by that time and earned another three after its transfer to Bangor, including a ninth for its final deployment that ended in late September.

The Parche's final resume also included 13 Navy Expeditionary Medals and 10 Navy Unit Commendations—all unprecedented numbers.

"Parche has had a career unmatched in the annals of submarine history," said Rear Adm. Paul Sullivan, commander of the Pacific Fleet submarine force.

"Parche has gathered enough citations that are just truly remarkable…based on her superb performance in critical national tasking.

"She now ranks among the most legendary vessels to ever have sailed under our flag."

Sullivan compared the Parche's storied past to other historic Navy vessels, such USS Constitution, USS Monitor, USS Missouri and USS Nautilus.

"And now there is Parche," he said.

The ship figured prominently in "Blind Man's Bluff: The Untold Story of American Submarine Espionage," a nonfiction book published in the 1990s, which described how it spent its Cold War days spying on the Soviet Union.

It's also been reported the sub, with a claw-like device, was able to pick up lost Soviet missiles or bombs from the sea floor. Later, it reportedly deployed unmanned drones to complete many of the espionage tactics.

Following the Cold War, the Parche continued its highly classified missions, with many observers citing an even higher sense of secrecy. It's said the Parche spent plenty of time in the Persian Gulf, gleaning intelligence on Iraq and Iran, and traveled through the Western Pacific keeping tabs on China and North Korea.

Capt. Richard Charles, the Parche's first commander, traveled from Mobile, Ala., for Tuesday's ceremony. He took command while the sub was being built and went on its first deployment, a five-month journey in the Mediterranean Sea. After that, the sub transferred to the West Coast and began its spy missions a few years later.

"Those guys in the Pacific had all the fun," Charles joked. "I just built it.

"It's always sad to see a ship retire, but after a while, they are like you and me; they wear out."

Ironically, the name of the Parche's last at-sea commander, Capt. Charles Richard, was a mirror image of the sub's first. Richard was relieved in a change-of-command ceremony Tuesday after leading the Parche on two post-September 11th deployments, including one that lasted 122 days in 2002.

"Being commander of this ship was an extraordinary experience and I was fortunate to be given the experience," he said. "I hope that each man who has served aboard this ship will look back and swell with pride knowing that he answered his country's call."

Following the ceremony, the Parche, probably one of the least known subs to the general public because of its highly classified missions, silently shifted over to Puget Sound Naval Shipyard. There, it will be torn apart and recycled over the next few years.

And it's probably the first time in the Parche's history that its whereabouts will be known.

"That just proves our success that nobody knows what we do," said Bremerton resident Curt Mathews, who retired off the Parche last year. "It's kind of fun. People say, 'The Parche? I never heard of it?' Well, that's good.

"And we like it that way and that's why we were successful in all of our missions."

Reprinted by permission from The Sun newspaper in Bremerton, Wash.

The following is from a monograph (found in the excellent book, U.S. Submarine Operations in World War II) by the Submarine Force Board of Awards recommending the Congressional Medal of Honor to the CO of U.S.S. Parche SS-384, Commander Lawson P. "Red" Ramage. I had never read it before. I was stunned by the boldness and aggressiveness of this action and as a former Torpedoman, I could only imagine the fierce activity in both the Forward and After Rooms as well at the Conn! If a Hollywood script writer submitted a story like this he would be laughed out of Tinsel Town!

The personal bearing and outstanding skill displayed by the commanding officer in this series of attacks against a large heavily escorted enemy convoy, consisting of tankers, transports, and freighters, contacted on 31 July, is one of the outstanding attacks in the submarine warfare to date, with action-packed into every minute of this 46 minute battle against the enemy. Attaining the ultimate in aggressiveness exceptional courage, personal heroism, and bearing, the commanding officer sagaciously and with consummate skill, fired 19 torpedoes in 46 minutes to obtain 14 or 15 hits in this brilliant night surface attack.

By a brilliant act of stratagem the commanding officer penetrated the strong escort screen; and, although hemmed in on all sides by ships and escorts trying to maneuver and deliver counter attacks, he daringly closed to the favorable firing position from which to launch his torpedoes. With a well executed stern shot, he succeeded in damaging a freighter. Following up with a series of bow and stern shots, he sank the leading tanker and damaged a second tanker. Despite the grave problem of machine-gun fire and flares from escorts, near proximity of vessels, some as close as 200 yards, he successfully delivered two forward reloads to sink a transport.

At the same time, he commenced maneuvering to avoid nearest escort's gunfire and obtained a stern shot at damaged tanker that had now manned her guns. As he reached a firing position, the first fusillade of tanker's 4" or 5" shells passed close overhead and slightly forward. Because of the accuracy and intense firepower of additional enemy 20 mm and 40 mm increasing the possibilities of casualties, all lookouts and spare hands were sent below, with the exception of the bridge quartermaster who volunteered to remain on the TBT.

The commanding officer, with utter disregard for personal safety, courageously remained at his station on the bridge, despite the hail of bullets and shells, in order to maneuver the ship more effectively and score hits with his stern tubes. Simultaneously, with his sinking the damaged tanker and while trying to close a large transport, he was forced to commence evasive maneuvers to avoid a fast transport or freighter bearing down, apparently intent on ramming him, and also in order to avoid concentrated machine-gun fire of the two nearby escorts. With bullets and shells flying all-around, he ordered emergency full speed ahead and swung the stern of the Parche as she crossed the bow of the on rushing transport or freighter, clearing this enemy ship by less than 50 ft.!

Although now boxed in by escorts and the large transport dead ahead, the commanding officer delivered three smashing down-the-throat bow shots and stopped the target. With high-speed and expert seamanship, he tenaciously attacked again, scoring a kill hit with a reloaded stern torpedo.

At break of dawn, with enemy escorts counter attacks becoming too accurate to justify further attack and risk, Parche cleared the area thus having damaged one enemy ship and sunk four others in 46 minutes in another encounter, a 300 ton patrol vessel was sunk by gunfire.

The counter-attacks of the enemy against the Parche during her series of aggressive surface torpedo attacks upon the convoy on 31 July 1944 were probably the most intensive and thorough counter-attacks ever encountered by a submarine engaged in surface approaches and attacks against the enemy. Only exceptional seamanship, outstanding personal heroism and extreme bravery of the Parche's commanding officer saved this submarine from serious damage if not total destruction by enemy gunfire and ramming.

The commanding officer's courage and fearless action in remaining on the bridge of this submarine during the intense and accurate enemy gunfire in order to maintain the offensive at all times, enabled him to control his ship skillfully and efficiently launch his torpedoes effectively and evade the enemy's vigorous efforts to destroy Parche.

I am proud to say that Captain David Marquet is my friend. We first met when he was CO of U.S.S. Santa Fe *SSN-763. I had been contacted and informed that the ship had no 'point of contact' here in their namesake city. I agreed to do 'it' which was a milestone in my life as it turned out. David and his wife Jane, Bob Patton the COB, a JO and a Third Class Petty officer visited the city. We had a dinner party for them and a good time was had by all. We even had a plan for a three day trip to sea which, due to the ever fluid schedules of our fast attack submarines, had to be scrapped. Then the Greenville 'accident' shut down civilian visits for some time. Regrettably, I as yet, have not had the pleasure of dropping down their hatch.*

David called me late in 2003 and asked whether I was still working on this project and would I be interested in a well received presentation he had made about the respect, admiration and similarities his crew had for their diesel boat forbearers from WWII. I was delighted and agreed to include his written version of his original presentation since it is my conclusion that we have come full circle from the diesel boat era through the transition, growing pains and adolescence of nuclear power submarines to today's outstanding forces.

David's 'One Brotherhood' assessment is an entirely fitting way to finish this project.

He is currently Executive Assistant to the Chief of Naval Personnel.

Diesel Boaters and Nuclear Submariners—One Brotherhood

By David Marquet

With the cryptic message "Underway on Nuclear Power," the Captain of the USS Nautilus, Commander Eugene P. Wilkinson, USN heralded a new age in submarine warfare.[1] Freed of the need to periodically come to the surface or periscope depth to run diesel engines and recharge their batteries, submarines could now remain submerged indefinitely, creating a true submarine, rather than a part-time submersible.

The periods of the next two decades were ones of dramatic technological achievements for the submarine force—starting with the nuclear power plant, and later extending to submarine launched ballistic missiles, advanced torpedoes and acoustic quieting. Together, these revolutionized submarine warfare and created a discontinuity in the history of the force.

At the time, this technological transition was combined with a cultural transition. Admiral Rickover hand-picked men to attend his nuclear power training programs, and inculcated them with a belief in disciplined and deliberate operations based upon intimate technical knowledge. There were shifts in training and in responses to monitoring and reporting problems (today we'd call it transparency). Combined, these changes resulted in tension as the cultural transition was made to a nuclear-powered submarine force.

Despite the technological rift and initial cultural divide, submarine operations today strongly resemble the operations of our World War II predecessors. World War II submarine commanders like Dick O'Kane and Gene Fluckey would quickly feel at home on board the control room of a modern fast attack submarine. More significantly, the spirit that drove them to victory is infused in today's submarine force. This connection with our predecessors is an important link for our heritage that has not been decoupled by the shift to nuclear power.

Return to Shallow Water

Following the dissolution of the Soviet Union in 1991 and the first Gulf War, Operation Desert Storm, our nuclear-powered submarines shifted operational emphasis from the deep water contest with the Soviet Navy to operating in the littorals. This coincided with a new naval strategy, "…From the Sea," published in September 1992.

While it is true that this was a new role for the *nuclear-powered* submarine force, viewed in the longer lens of history, it was a return to our diesel boat roots. In a broader sense, the deep water missions of the Cold War were a departure from a norm that we have now returned to.

Onboard nuclear-powered submarines operating in the Western Pacific, one will find charts of World War II war patrols and Plan of the Day notes commenting on how the ship will be operating near a certain submarine's war patrol area.

The modern nuclear-powered is significantly heavier than the World War II submarine. However, the current 688-class submarine at 360 feet long is only 15 percent longer than the 312-foot long World War II fleet boat. Place the silhouettes side by side, and the difference looks trivial. Just as our predecessors learned to handle a 300-plus foot long submarine in shallow water, we are doing the same.

Photographic Reconnaissance

As I would practice photo-reconnaissance around the Hawaiian Islands, I would remind my photo team that this was born of a legacy starting with USS Nautilus (SS 168) in September 1943, during the Gilbert Island campaign.

Nautilus conducted the first full-scale submarine photo-reconnaissance mission in support of the amphibious landings at Tarawa and the Gilbert Islands. During this first photo-reconnaissance mission, the team aboard Nautilus found the 2 navy-supplied cameras to be wanting and ended up successfully using a Primarflex single-lens reflex camera volunteered by one of the officers. Today's photo-reconnaissance teams would find this excerpt from her patrol report quite familiar:

> The method used in photographing the beaches was to take a group of pictures at one time. One officer turned the periscope between each exposure. Another took the pictures. The average time to take a roll of twelve pictures was a little under two minutes. The time required could be shortened some by special equipment. The greatest cause of delay was spray on the lens, vibration, or rolling of the ship. Unfortunately No. 2 periscope, which was used because of its larger field, turned with great difficulty and was occasionally responsible for some delay between exposures.[2]

Throughout the remainder of the war in the Pacific, submarines were called upon to conduct photo-reconnaissance missions prior to the amphibious landings. In all, submarines completed 13 missions. (The last mission, tasked to USS Swordfish against Okinawa was not completed as Swordfish was lost.) These missions reconnoitered landing sites including Saipan, Palau, and Iwo Jima—saving the lives of Marines going ashore.

Rocket Launches

Today's submarine force is armed with long range and highly accurate ballistic and cruise missiles. In fact, the first weapon launched in Operation Iraqi Freedom was a submarine launched Tomahawk cruise missile from the USS Cheyenne.[3] These Tomahawk missiles provide an important stealthy striking force and submarine-carried missiles can comprise a third of a carrier strike group's Tomahawk missiles. Accurate and secure submarine-launched ballistic missiles have formed a vital leg of a our strategic nuclear deterrence capability.

Launching missiles from submarines is a continuation of trends in weapon systems inaugurated by our World War II predecessors. Indeed, at 0150 on the 22nd of June, 1945, the word was first passed aboard an American submarine to "Man Battle Stations Rockets." This was Gene Fluckey's Barb. They launched rockets with a 5000 yard range and 9.6 pound warheads against industrial targets in Hokkaido and Karafuto (the southern half of Sakhalin island). The procedure for Fluckey was cumbersome. First, he needed to be on the surface. Then, after announcing battle stations, the rocket launcher was brought on deck and loaded. The only control on the rockets was the range. Hence, aiming needed to be done by pointing the bow of the ship in the direction of the target, accounting for deflection. In all, it would take about 30 minutes to get the salvo off.[4]

Today's submariners had significant advantages—being able to launch submerged and on any course, the missiles having their own steering and guidance systems.

Torpedo Firings

During World War II, the U. S. submarine force sank 55% of Japanese merchant tonnage although they comprised only 2% of the U. S. Navy's personnel.[5] One of the key reasons the submarine force was so effective was the effectiveness of their torpedoes. It was not always so, however. The initial Mk 14 torpedoes were plagued by run depth and exploder problems. The new Mk 6 combination magnetic and contact exploder, introduced in the summer of 1941, was temperamental and unreliable. Sometimes the torpedoes would explode prematurely, sometimes they passed under the target without exploding, and sometimes they would even hit the target, but not explode.

It was not until the Rear Admiral Charles Lockwood, then COMSUBPAC, and Captain (later Vice Admiral) "Swede" Momsen, conducted their own testing in 1942—firing torpedoes into nets to accurately measure their run depth—was the submarine force able to convince the Bureau of Ordnance that there were serious problems with the torpedoes. Eventually, these problems were solved, with the more reliable Mk 18 torpedo introduced in September 1943.[6] The submarine force learned the hard way that realistic test firing was the only way to ensure our torpedoes would work.

We have not forgotten that lesson and today's submarine force shoots hundreds of exercise torpedoes in realistic scenarios against other submarines and surface targets each year. These exercise torpedoes are equipped with data-gathering capabilities that can by thoroughly analyzed. Additionally, we shoot unaltered warshot torpedoes against hulks, testing the torpedo's entire capability up to and including detonation. Some of these torpedoes are tested in locations most likely to be subjected to potential conflicts. We have fired our exercise torpedoes in each of the 5th, 6th, and 7th fleet Areas of Responsibility (AORs).

Operating with Battle Groups

Following the demise of the Soviet Union, today's nuclear-powered submarine force has emphasized a shift toward operations with Carrier Battle Groups. Just as the 688-class submarine was designed with the speed to keep up with today's fast carriers, escorts, and resupply ships, the World War II diesel submarines were called "fleet boats" because they were originally designed to operate with the fleet. Although the majority of submarine operations in World War II were conducted independently, submarines did operate with battlegroups on several occasions.

One such occasion occurred during Commander Dick O'Kane's second patrol with Tang in March and April of 1944. He was assigned to Admiral Marc Mitscher's Task Force 58 in support of Operation Desecrate. This operation was designed to damage Japanese shipping in the Palau Islands as much as possible. The operational plan was for the carrier-based airplanes to strike ships in the harbor, and those that fled would run into submarines stationed at the outlets of the main channels.

Tang was assigned a position 60 miles from the outlet of one such channel, Toagel Mlungui. This required a transit of 3500 miles from her previous operation for a position that O'Kane felt did not optimize the strengths of his ship. To make matters worse, O'Kane later discovered that the channel he was guarding was mined on the first days of the operation. Needless to say, Tang did not sink a single target during this time.[7]

At the end of any operation, in the enduring legacy of the post-deployment debrief, submarine skippers tell all to their operational commanders, including the good, bad and ugly. Following this operation, O'Kane reported to Rear Admiral Lockwood that "...if a senior submariner had been ordered to Admiral Mitscher's staff, and if operational control of the submarines had passed to the task force commander for the strike on Palau, *Tang* and *Trigger* would not have been left guarding mined channels." [8]

We have learned these lessons and are now detailing senior leaders to the battle group staffs. Operational Control is being passed to the battle group commanders more and more. During my 1999 deployment in Santa Fe, operational control of my ship was assigned to three different carrier battle groups: the Constellation's; the Theodore Roosevelt's; and the Kitty Hawk's.

The Spirit is Alive

More important that these operational parallels, today's submarine force continues traditions that keep the spirit of our World War II predecessors alive.

On modern submarines, one will find World War II Presidential Unit Commendations and Medal of Honor citations being read when dolphins are awarded to our newly qualified submariners. On my ship we altered the language when shooting torpedoes, replacing the suggested language with the "hot, straight, and normal" of our predecessors. Instead of "night steaming boxes," we had areas designated "Wahoo" and "Tang." For my crew, these were more than mere words, but served as a tangible reminder every time we fired a torpedo that we were continuing an important legacy from our predecessors.

Operating out of Pearl Harbor allows one to develop a special connection with our submarine forefathers. Departing from the Pearl Harbor "Sierra" piers, and passing the USS Arizona, now a memorial, gave me and my crew a sense of comradeship knowing that these were the same piers and sights our World War II predecessors saw as they turned their bows west, heading for uncertain times. Yet, thanks to the actions of those men, we now pass the battleship Missouri as well, upon whose decks the surrender of Japan was signed.

And we know that it is with the Sailors that the spirit is strongest. Men like O'Kane and Fluckey were able to operate independently thousands of miles from home port because of the ability of their crews to persevere, and the innovation they used to keep their ships operational. The same is true today, and we would not be able to operate for 6-, 7-, 8-, and recently almost 9-months from home port without the untiring efforts of the Sailors who make up our crews.

More than the equipment and the operations, the men of today's submarine force are acutely aware of the awesome legacy we have inherited. We are keeping the spirit alive—that heritage of:
Patriotism
Sacrifice
And relentless pursuit of the enemy until he is on the bottom.

Captain Marquet at the time of this article, was serving as a submarine squadron commander in Pearl Harbor. He Commanded USS Santa Fe from 1999–2001.

Ditty Bag

"Enemy submarines are to be called U-boats. The term 'submarine' is to be reserved for Allied underwater vessels. U-boats are those dastardly villains who sink our ships, while submarines are those gallant and noble craft which sinks theirs."
Winston S. Churchill PM

I wrote a book, along with two of my brothers called SPINDRIFT—Stories from the U.S. Sea Services. *My portion, naturally, was about diesel submarines with chapters named* Watches, Heavy Seas, The Loop's Too Big! *(about movies at sea),* First Do No Harm *(about medicine on a diesel boat) and several others. My problem was that I had things to say about life on a diesel boat which fit none of the chapter themes and which were too short to warrant a chapter. These interviews also have anecdotes, interesting comments and facts which are hard to pigeonhole, and which fit none of the chapter themes in this book directly. My solution with* SPINDRIFT *was to create a chapter called Ditty Bag. Every Navy man reading this needs no further explanation, but for those who never heard the name, a ditty bag was where you kept your 'stuff' aboard ship. Every sailor for 500 years had one. I am confident the Navy still issues one to every recruit today. The Webster's dictionary on my desk defines it as, "a small bag used esp. by sailors to hold sewing implements, toiletries etc." Well, that's what they think. The far more authoritative 1950 edition of my* Blue Jackets' Manual *says, "A small bag or box used by sailors to stow personal articles."*

Originally I had planned to print the entire interviews in the back of this book but concluded it would be redundant since much of the interviews have been used in the preceding chapters. Instead they can be found in their entirety on my web site "subpowershift.com". This chapter is the repository of the worthwhile parts of the interviews I have not included so far.

Nuclear Power School

DG: What was the point in doing all that moving around of the Nuclear Power School location?

MB: (Mike Barr) Well, as I understood it, it was *not* Admiral Rickover's idea. Admiral Rickover was happy to have a Nuclear Power School any place there was a chalkboard and a piece of chalk. When existing facilities got too crowded, when bases hosting a Nuclear Power School were shut down, or when financial efficiencies were needed, the Navy would propose new locations. Admiral Rickover would, of course, have to agree with the new location. When the schools were finally combined in Orlando, there were about four or five hundred faculty and staff and about twenty-two to twenty-three hundred students. We were running four enlisted and four officer classes essentially all the time. The enlisted classes could be 500 or so and the officer classes 100. There was also a preschool to help enlisted students get ready for the six month course. It wasn't that they weren't intelligent, most were very smart, but they needed to brush up on some fundamental math and physics concepts. The preschool was six or twelve weeks, so you actually had another 600 there.

DG: I know a lot of people who had never taken physics. I went to a Catholic boys' school, and you had to take Latin, you had to take physics, a lot of math. The best physics I ever had in my life, the best school I ever went to was Submarine School. It was fascinating, and I remember—and I'm going to be 64 next month—and I remember all of that stuff. I remember hydraulics—why is it that I remember all that stuff after all these years? And I don't remember anything. But submarine school was really something. It's all about how the Navy taught. I think that people in academia could learn a lot about how to teach kids from the Navy.

U-boats, Hollywood, Rounding the Horn and Liberty in the Falklands

Pat Hannifin had the unique distinction having started on an S boat and ending up on an SSBN. Who better to talk about the topic of this book? I was amazed to hear him discuss his time on a U-boat!

DG: After the *Balao*, did you end up a CO of a diesel boat?

PH: Yes, I had command of a diesel boat here in San Diego in the early fifties. *Diodon* SS 349. Before that I had served in a German U-boat. Yeah, in '46. U-858. It was a type 9C. We operated three, I think—and the two others were the type 21s, the 3008 and the 2513 down at Key West.

At the end of World War II we took over several boats and we operated for quite some time the 2513 and 3008 and the 858, (it had surrendered off Cape May in New Jersey at the end of the German war). They brought it in to the Philadelphia Shipyard, and with the help of the German crew translated a bunch of the operating manuals and we got to know it, did some repair work on it, and then took it to Key West, and we operated it down there, firing their torpedoes and comparing their equipment with our equipment.

In sonar they were so far ahead of us in underwater listening. So far ahead of us. At radar they were very far behind us, but their sonar was outstanding, I served in that for, I guess it was until about July of '46 when we took it up to Portsmouth and put it out of service. In fact, they used it as a target, sank it off of New London. But it was an interesting experience. Well, it helped me a lot because I later was the technical director of "U-571", the submarine movie. It helped because I'd served in both—there's an old S-boat and a U-boat, and I'd served in both those submarines.

DG: Wow. Was that fun?

PH: It was fun. It was a blast, it really was. Good time. It's a very noisy movie. The first time I saw it, after we got back to the states—we filmed in Rome and then Malta—and the first time I saw it with sound in it was back in the editor's room with the director. And we got through and I said, Jonathan, you know I was depth-charged in the Yellow Sea in shallow water in World War II, and I remember being scared as hell, but I didn't remember it being that loud. And he said, Admiral, this is a movie, it has to be loud. And it was. Anyway, I served in a number of diesel boats. Oh, let's see, went to Sea Robin in Panama, put the Grampas in commission, put the Rasher back in commission as an SSR radar picket, and was exec on there, brought it to San Diego and then took over the Diodon as CO.

Go back to the U-571. My job was to train these actors to be sailors and then submariners, and so I really had to teach them what a submariner was and this business of being able to depend on your shipmate and all that sort of thing. But, as you remember the story is that Matthew McConaughey's character is the XO on the S-boat, and he gets turned down for a command.

DG: Right. I remember that scene.

PH: And as the movie moves along, all of a sudden he ends up on that U-boat as the commanding officer. But he was turned down for a command because the skipper didn't think that he really understood the difference between being a good officer, a good XO, and being a commanding officer.

DG: And that point was made well.

PH: Well, that was my point and I worked on the script for 18 months before we started filming that scene.

DG: So they would submit drafts to you?

PH: Oh, yes, the guy who wrote the screenplay was the Director and had a good background where he knew all about the Enigma machines. He really had a good background, but he didn't know anything about submarines. He really didn't, and that's why I was asked to come out to help him on the technical aspect of it. So he didn't know how submarines dived, why they dived, how they surfaced, how they shot torpedoes. He didn't know anything about it. And so we went through that whole thing.

DG: So you must have effectively written some of the script.

PH: Well, I helped an awful lot, but it was basically his story. And we talked a lot about this business of—because when he first wrote the story, it was not about an XO being turned down. It was about a guy who had lost his boat during the war and was sort of drifting around and came back, and he had Michael Douglas scheduled to play the part of an older guy. And we talked with Michael about it and he said, You know, I'm 50 years old. He said, I can play 45; I can't play 35 very well. Besides, he was busy, so they got Matthew McConaughey and we changed the story around to fit that.

DG: Well, I didn't know. That is interesting. That is a very interesting story, but I think the greatest submarine movie I've ever seen, was *Das Boot*, and it was because it was so authentic.

PH: Absolutely.

DG: There was one scene where they were up behind a splinter shield, you know, and they were going through this North Atlantic big, heavy weather, and they had the sou'westers on, water was coming over. And I said to my brother, you know, I remember exactly that same thing. I used to stand lookout watches and in big seas we had to lash ourselves to the splinter shield.

PH: We had a German crew, as you know in the U-571. The guy who played the part of the German skipper was great, Thomas Kreshman. He's an outstanding actor. So I was trying to help the German crew out in their stuff. I had to be on the set on every scene. But we got a German guy from the German Navy who had been in the post-war German submarines, so he didn't know anything about U-boats. What he really liked to do was to drink beer.

We were filming over in Rome because it was the largest sound stage in Europe, and they built a full-scale U-boat and most of the S-boat on that sound stage. And the guy who built the set for *Das Boot* built our set. It was actually about 15 percent larger than the U-boat. Absolutely identical, because they had all the information. Hell, I couldn't find that much information about S-boats at all, but he had it down cold. This German technical director that they had for that crew we finally had to fire him. And we got hold of Captain Hans Krug, who was the technical director for *Das Boot.* Eighty-one or eight-two years old, he came down and he and I had a ball. We had a great time. It had been 50 years since I'd been on a U-boat. So we had to school the crew on the U-boat. He took me all through the thing and it all started coming back, showing me how the trim systems operate and all that sort of thing, so that my guys knew what the hell they were doing. For Harvey Keitel—he was the Chief of the Boat—he really wanted to know.

DG: He is a consummate actor.

PH: Oh, absolutely. He called me when he got asked for this thing. He called me and he said, "What the hell's the Chief of the Boat?" So I said, "Harvey"—he lives in New Jersey—I said, "You're going to find out because I want you to go up to New London." And I called the Admiral who was the group commander, who was the son of my roommate at the Naval Academy, Johnny Padgett, and I said, I'm going to send Harvey up there. Put him with your Command Master Chief and teach him what a Chief of the Boat is. He spent about three days up there with all the chiefs and then went back to New Jersey, came back up the next week because there was a meeting of the submarine veterans of World War II up there, so he wanted to get up and meet those guys, too. Harvey was great. Absolutely great.

DG: Did he become taken—was he taken by these guys?

PH: Oh, absolutely. Yeah, absolutely.

DG: That would be hard not to. I mean, that's a special group.

PH: I was able to get Matthew McConaughey and Bill Paxton both on some of the SSNs down here, but we didn't get to go to sea. But I walked them through and then they sat and talked in the chief's quarters and in the ward room and all, to talk with the guys to sort of get a feel. Harvey was the only guy who had any military experience in that crew. He'd been a Marine for two years during the Lebanon crisis. Well, he said it was the turning point in his life. He said, "I was a kid wandering around Brooklyn getting in trouble. But suddenly two or three of my friends and I decided to join the Marine Corps," and he said "I have no idea why we did that," but he said it changed his life.

DG: Oh, sure. That's not unusual at all.

PH: No. It was interesting.

DG: Oh, so did they have an opening? I mean, you worked 18 months on this project.

PH: Oh, yeah. Well, 18 months before we started filming. This started in the summer of '97 until January of '99 when we went over to Rome and started filming. And filmed there until April or May, and then down to Malta. And in Malta they had built a full-scale U-boat in a shipyard that we took to sea. It didn't submerge, but we did all of the surface shots from that. There was nothing inside it except some diesel engines. But it had the gun up there and the whole thing.

DG: Did they build a set for the control room scenes?

PH: Oh, they built the whole submarine, the entire submarine for the control room area. Yeah. So you filmed it all in the set. And they built a gimbal system that you could take two compartments and put on this gimbal system and a tank in there and do the shakes and rolls and all that sort of thing, full of water. The way they build those sets you can take a whole side out and get the camera in from there. Or you could take the other side out and get it from that angle. Yeah. It's amazing. The way those Italian workers over there built those sets is just absolutely astonishing. It is so realistic, you couldn't believe it.

DG: Are they made out of metal?

PH: Metal and plastic and—but piping is all plastic, and their painters are so good that it looks like metal. It really is astounding. I was so impressed with that bunch. I've got the DVD for U-571.

In Malta there's a big tank that was built for the movie the *Gladiator*. We used that. One side of it, a side along the Mediterranean was a flat wall, so it looked like the water just continued on out into the sea. They built two submarines in there, the old S-boat and the U-boat, and they used that for the boarding scene. You remember when they rode over in the rubber boats from one boat to the other? And they used that. And they had 200 foot pipes going up with water coming down, rain, so that they created rain. They had big machines to create the wind. One of the actors was John Bon Jovi, and he played the part of the engineer officer, the friend of McConaughey's.

DG: Oh, I didn't know that's who it was.

PH: Well, we cleaned him up. He looked real good. [Laughter] He's a great performer, but he's a damned good actor. And he loves to do these things. He's acted in five or six movies. But he came from New Jersey, married to his high school sweetheart, absolute regular guy. But, you know, we cut his hair and cleaned him up and put him in a uniform, and he's really very good. But he wanted a much larger part in this thing. He gets killed in the scene when the S-32 is blown up. At any rate, Jon wore a wetsuit under his uniform when he was doing this rowing across it, because they did it at night and it was cold and wet and pretty miserable. And he said, "God damnit, I make several million dollars a year. Why the hell am I doing this kind of stuff?" [Laughter] But he was good and a fine actor.

DG: You know, I'm going to go rent that movie or buy the DVD because I want to see your work. What a fun thing.

PH: You know, the Brits were very pissed off at us about that movie because they had actually done this. Not in the same way. The way they got the Enigma machine is that a British destroyer and I think it was the Canadian Corvette, depth charged, the U-110, I guess it was. And they thought they had sunk it but it actually survived and got on the surface. And so the HMS Bulldog skipper was going to ram it and sink it. But decided instead to come alongside and put a boarding party over under a young sub-leftenant named David Balme, and they rowed over in a whale boat and got aboard. He told them, "Pick up anything that's loose, equipment, documents, anything you can, and then get the hell off because there may be scuttling charges set." And so David took this group over and they went down there and they found, among other stuff, the Enigma Machine. But while they were down there, there was another submarine scare and Bulldog took off. And David said he was afraid that they wouldn't find their way back to him, but they did. They didn't know about the Enigma Machine, anyway, except the very high level. And they didn't know that they had it until they got back and the intelligence people got a hold of it. And so they swore them all to silence. I don't know what they did with the German crew, but they were never heard of after that, as far as I know. They were taken prisoner.

DG: And they must have been put in the slammer somewhere.

PH: They didn't want the Germans to know that the U-110 had not been sunk. And David got, I think, theVictoria Cross. Anyway, when this hit the news that we were making this movie. The headlines in the English papers were, We did it but the Yanks have taken credit and Hollywood is now the hero. People in Parliament were writing letters about it. It finally got up to the Prime Minster and the President talking about this business. What happened in this movie, and the reason why it was set the way it was, is that after the U-110 incident and they got the Enigma Machine, the Germans put another rotor in the machine and so, for a period of time, they weren't able to break anything. And it was during this period of time that the "U-571" scene was set. So we needed to get another Enigma Machine, and so this is why this whole story was written in the way it was. But we brought David Balme down to Malta, he and his wife, to watch the filming down there. And then Universal brought him and his wife over to the States and brought him out to Universal. And, in fact, the DVD has an interview with him and one with me on the background stuff, which is pretty interesting. But the one with him is particularly interesting. He got out of the Navy after the war was over and took over his family's cotton importing business. A wonderful man, a delightful man, and he said he thought this was a great movie. He said, "We Brits would never have made a movie like this anyway." [laughs].

DG: So he remained friendly, I mean after you showed him what you were doing and everything?

PH: OH, yeah, he liked it.

DG: Was he reticent at first?

PH: Oh, no, not at all. Not at all. He was very interested in relating the story and things that happened, and he does this on the DVD. Yeah, it's worthwhile. Take a look at it. And there's a big interview with Jonathan Mostow of *Das Boot*, who was the director and also wrote the screenplay, too; a short one with me. But it was a lot of fun.

Jack McDaniel allowed me to use this funny piece which I thought was particularly apropos following Pat Hannifin's comments about advising on the film U 571. Jack was concerned that I leave the impression that he thought all these up. In fact, he gathered them from various people.

Submarine Movie Clichés

With the help of a few friends, I've been collecting a list of things you can expect to see in submarine movies. Most of them will slip right by the average viewer at the same time they're causing those who know to groan in agony.

1) The Fathometer will be operated continuously from the moment the boat leaves the pier until it returns. Everyone aboard will hear it, but the enemy never will.

2) No matter which torpedo tube the captain orders fired, when we go to the cutaway shot it will come out of tube # 2.

3) There are no fuses or circuit breakers anywhere in a submarine, so if there's a short you will get spectacular sparks. (This also applies to Star Trek.)

4) The CO and XO will never get along. If the XO happens to like the CO, the CO will develop an unreasoning dislike of his former best friend.

5) The awkward, very-lovable young seaman will die.

6) A Mark-14 torpedo weighs about 3300 pounds, and has a warhead containing 10,000 pounds of Torpex. If it hits it will make a truly spectacular explosion.

6a) If this is a "serious" movie, at some point one of the torpedoes will fall off the rack on top of someone. (Probably the kid in rule 5.)

7) Depth charges have to touch the hull to sink the boat.

8) The above notwithstanding, if a depth charge explodes anywhere within 500 feet of the sub, every light bulb and gauge face in the boat will shatter.

9) You can tell you've reached your proper depth when equipment starts falling off the bulkheads.

10) The radar is broken.

11) The civilians in the audience can't tell one ribbon from another, so pick the most colorful and pin them on. How many people in the audience are going to notice that an admiral in 1993 has medals for service in the Spanish American War?

12) Fairbanks-Morse diesels should always be run with the upper crankshaft covers open, because it looks cool to have stuff moving.

13) Angle on the bow and target bearing are the same thing as far as most of the audience knows, so why worry about which is which?

13a) It is perfectly normal to fire a bow tube at a target bearing 175°.

14) Someone will get appendicitis, and the PhM (the sub's Doc) will operate using a scalpel a MMC made out of an old spoon.

15) World War II subs were perfectly able to shoot it out with each other while both were submerged at 150 feet.

16) The captain's family will inevitably be aboard the Japanese transport he has to sink.

17) The knob in the middle of the (WWII era) torpedo tube breech door is the lock.

18) COB is a crusty sea dog who knows more about submarines than any officer who ever lived. (Okay, so once in a while they get something right.)

19) All Japanese freighters will be hit in the one hold that contains the entire artillery shell inventory of the 4th Imperial Marines.

20) When the dive officer reports, "steady at 300 feet, sir," the depth gauge in the background will indicate the boat is on the surface.

21) If a film tosses out the entire plot of a famous sub novel, the one thing it will keep will be the QM operating the periscope with a pickle switch. The periscope they show will, of course, be hydraulic.

22) Submarines are steered by the planes operators.

23) On the rare occasion when an actual position is mentioned, the coordinates will be somewhere on the outskirts of St. Louis.

24) Female submariners don't have to qualify to wear dolphins.

25) When racing through the water at the enemy, war shots have bright yellow warheads.

26) The technical advisor on a submarine movie will ideally be able to append the designation (SW...Surface Warfare) to his rank. Any technical advisor who has an (SS) qualification will be ignored.

I sent the above to Pat Hannifin. Here was his predictable response.
Dan
They are great! I hope that you did not see any of them in my "U-571"!
Pat

Diesel boat COs

Chuck Grojean was one of a handful of diesel submariners who did not go through Nuclear Power School.

DG: Well, you were a CO. And then you were, I guess, recruited for nuclear power school?

CG: I sought out nuclear power. I didn't go to nuclear power school, those of us who had had command of a diesel boat went directly to Admiral Rickover's staff, and we served for one year, all of us who had had command of a diesel boat all went to Washington, D.C., for a year and served on Rickover's staff. When I was there there were about eight of us that were in that category, and we were tutored from 8:00 in the morning until 5:00 every night with a staff of about six or eight brilliant PhDs, post-graduate mathematicians, physicists and chemists—thermodynamics, nuclear physics, nuclear engineering guys. And we took those subjects at a very compact, heavily pushed course. We went to classes all day long and then we were given about five hours of homework every night.

DG: So this was before there was an actual nuclear school.

CG: The nuclear power school was there, but that was for all of those who had not had command. If you came from a command capacity—I had command of the Angler when I was selected, so I went directly to that, along with about seven other ex-commanders.

Jacuzzi in Silo 15

Master Chief Jeff VanBlaracum, as I write this, is COB (Chief of the Boat) on USS Santa Fe SSN-763. Here he is talking about the conversion of USS Kamehameha SSBN 642

JV: I became a torpedoman on *Stimson*—a striker, left there as an E5, did nine patrols onboard her, went to Orlando for instructor duty, and then I went to the USS *Kamehameha*. And that was after she was converted from being a boomer into a fast-attack, for SEAL deployment.

DG: Did they take out the silos?

JV: No, they left them in. In fact, we made use of them for our trim system to help compensate for the weight and buoyancy that was added by the dry-deck shelters that we use with the Seals. And so there were some of them tied into the trim system, some of them were used as magazines and smaller-end stowage for the Seals, and then we actually had a Jacuzzi in tube 15. Yeah, pretty interesting.

Note: I inquired and found out the hot tub was not for recreational purposes, but to warm up the Seals following cold water operations.

The Fifty Ton Gyro Rotor

Chuck Grojean's, I am sure, little known fact.

DG: You know, one of the aspects of being on a diesel boat that I liked was the fact that we were really a surface ship and subject to storms, seeing whales and sunsets and being salty and all that. I mean, a mariner, really. And that was absent from the nuclear power submarines.

CG: Yes, yes. Because you went out and as soon as you got in deep enough water you dived. You didn't come up until you got to your destination. You were never really associated with being on the surface of the sea. You were very much associated with going where the bottom was, of knowing salinity, temperature gradients, and all of that. But you didn't have the weather to contend with except if you were on a missile submarine and you get an order to fire, and it's very rough; you've got state seven or state six seas, and you've got 20-foot waves. That wave action, of course, is felt down at a hundred feet, and so you sway a lot back and forth. On the first three missile submarines we had a big fifty-ton gyro that stabilized the ship, so that we could fire missiles from a stable platform.

DG: *Fifty tons!!??*

CG: Yeah, fifty tons. Oh, it was a huge thing—size of this room. And you spun it up and the idea was that it would keep the ship from rolling back and forth so that you could fire missiles. We found that we didn't need it, and so we didn't put it on any subsequent ships. It was a horrendous monster. If it had ever broken free it would have ripped through the ship and torn everything apart. It was a dangerous thing.

DG: Fifty tons. The whole thing was fifty tons?

CG: Fifty-ton rotor.

DG: *The rotor!!??* Wow. And it was high-speed naturally.

CG: High-speed. Yeah. And we had a lot of things, of course, in the first missile submarines that were highly technical, like trying to hover. We finally developed an automatic hovering system, but we didn't have it initially. The same way with inertial systems, we had three huge monsters, but why you had three instead of two was because if one was bad and you had two, you wouldn't know which of the two was bad. So you had to have three to—if the two were right and one was different from it, you knew it was wrong.

Test Depth

Test depths of nuclear submarines are secret. Those of the old diesel boats are, I am confident, no longer so. Obviously the modern, nuclear power submarines can dive much deeper than my old boat—U.S.S. Barbero *SSG-317, made in 1943. The thing which most of us have considered often, particularly following an 'episode', is at what depth does the submarine crush and kill everyone? What margin of safety did BUSH-IPS add to determine the test depth? Two hundred percent? One hundred percent? Fifty percent? What does the age of the submarine do to that number? Does it diminish with age? I never met anyone who knew or would tell. It is obvious that if they let that 'safety factor' be known then submarine operators would be fairly comfortable going deeper than they should, confident that they can get away with it. In the Preface I mentioned an incident my shipmates and I experienced. I have the feeling that similar losses of depth control happened often. I am confident of this since the depth ranges were narrow for the old diesels—for example in our case it was 412 feet, a mere 100 feet more than the length of the submarine. It was fairly easy to get out of control particularly if you were deep and going fast. Like flying an air plane at 200 feet…no margin for error. The following are two other depth 'episodes' I found interesting. One is from Walter Bell on* Rasher, *the other is by Don Walsh, also on* Rasher *who experienced a completely unique 'episode.' Two stories from the same boat is coincidental and indicates to me that such things were not uncommon.*

Walter Bell YN1 (SS)
1960–1962

Rasher was my first submarine, and like a first love holds a special place in my heart. I recall the time that we were operating out of San Diego and at two in the morning we dove and almost lost her.

I was asleep in the FTR (Forward Torpedo Room) and woke up thinking I was standing up. I was not; Rasher had one hell of a down angle and was headed down. The door to the Control Room was open and I could hear Albie Ness, the COW (Chief of the Watch) give orders to blow Safety, blow Negative, blow the Forward group and the after group, all back emergency and we were still going down. All of us in the Forward Room were watching the depth gauge in total silence. Somewhere around 1200 feet, far below our test depth, metal was groaning and the boat was shaking. I figured we had best ask God for forgiveness for our sins one last time since it looked like the end was imminent.

BUT, then she started back up stern first and popped out of the water. Inspections revealed that there was no damage to the boat, and not a man left the boat as 'no longer volunteer.'

Investigations indicated that a valve had malfunctioned in the forward group and had allowed water to fill the tanks making her heavy forward when the dive started. The Good Lord was looking out for us that night.

Since 1200 feet sounded unbelievable to me, I emailed Walter to be sure he remembered that episode correctly, being careful not to offend him. We both concurred that such an emergency would probably remain in anyone's mind crystal clear for life! Walter later emailed me the following;

"Thinking about the incident, I remembered that Albie Ness did a wonderful job that night and I am sure the stress was tremendous. Right after the incident, a young reservist who was on board for training walked up to Albie and said, "Hey Chief, that was fun. Let's do it again." Albie smooth decked him—I'm sure as a reaction of that stress. As I said in the article, God was looking out for us that night."

Don Walsh is a good friend who was kind enough to agree to an interview and write the Foreward to this book. His incident, which he relates here, surely is unique among submarines and belongs here, just following "Test Depth."

Those Stout Manitowoc Boats: A Personal Testimony

By Don Walsh, former C.O. Bashaw (AGSS-341)

During WWII the Manitowoc Shipbuilding Company built 28 submarines at Manitowoc Wisconsin. The first 10 were Gato Class, "thin skin boats" with test depths of 311 feet. Initial sea trials were done in Lake Michigan, they were then sent down the Mississippi River to New Orleans for final completion and loading out.

Founded in 1902, Manitowoc was an old and well-established shipyard with a long history of building excellent ships for Great Lakes service. By 1940 they had built 306 ships of various types, but never a warship.

As the Navy's fleet buildup began in the late 1930's, the yard hoped to find work building small warships up to destroyer size. They were turned down as work went to larger shipyards on the Atlantic, Pacific and Gulf coasts. However, top Navy officials certainly knew about Manitowoc's fine reputation for quality work. In early 1940 Manitowoc was asked to undertake building of the most complex ship: submarines. This was a radical, almost unimaginable, proposal for a company of shipbuilders most of whom had never seen a submarine. Initially, the yard's management did not want to do it but the Navy insisted. In September 1940, the yard was awarded a contract for an initial run of 10 subs.

Teams of experts from the Electric Boat Company came to Manitowoc under contract to the yard to help with the early stages of this program. Also some Manitowoc personnel visited Electric Boat and the Portsmouth Naval Shipyard to observe submarine construction underway at those sites.

The first "Manitowoc boat", USS *Peto* (SS-265), was laid down in June 1941. She was launched in April 1942, 228 days ahead of schedule and went off to war just a year after the Pearl Harbor attack. Early delivery of subs was to be a way of life for this fine shipyard. And as they got out into the fleet, their crews began to send the yard thank you letters for the quality and strength of those subs. Satisfied 'customers', the best kind of praise for the Manitowoc employers who won Navy Department production "E" awards every year during the war.

USS *Rasher* (SS-269) was the fifth sub from this yard. Her keel was laid down in May 1942, four days after Peto had been launched. Commissioned in 1943, she became the second highest scoring US submarine in WWII. She missed the top spot, earned by USS Flasher, by only 750 tons of Japanese shipping.

In 1956, fresh from sub school, I reported aboard *Rasher*. A few years earlier she had been converted to a radar picket submarine of the "Migraine III" type. Now SSR-269 would be where I would qualify for my dolphins and be my home for the next two years.

The Migraine III subs, *Rasher*, *Raton* and *Rock,* had a 30 foot section inserted forward of the control room to hold the combat information center (CIC). The long bow was great for the bridge watch on the surface. However, you had to watch it when diving as that long bow could pitch you down quicker than a conventional length hull. When your test depth was 311 feet, you could get there in a hurry.

In February 1957 *Rasher* was deployed to a wintry Bering Sea to assist with a firing test of a Regulus I missile. The idea was to test it in the worst possible weather conditions.

Tunny the launching sub was located in the ice near the Pribilov Islands; I believe *Carbonero* was the guidance vessel. She was downrange towards the Aleutians. As a radar picket sub, *Rasher* had the capability to track the missile flight from launch to impact area.

The test went well and mission completed, *Rasher* headed south through Unimak Pass in the Aleutians. The seas were heavy in the North Pacific so the captain, Commander 'Flag' Adams, ordered the boat submerged to test depth so we could all get a good night's sleep.

It was about 0300, with chief engineer LT Gib Carter as conning officer, when the boat was shaken by a substantial blow. The diving gage quickly went to 700 feet though the sub remained at its same distance beneath the surface. Gib called the captain who had slept through the whole thing. Flag's opinion was that we had hit a whale. While that did not make much sense, it was the best 'theory' we had at the time. All compartments reported to control that everything was o.k. so we resumed our previous course and depth.

The 'what' of it was answered the next morning when we surfaced and were able to get radio traffic. *Rasher* had been right above the epicenter of an underwater earthquake just south of Unimak Pass in the Aleutians. The overpressure (like a depth charge) made the depth show 700 feet and the hull did experience that depth. It was exciting and the first reported case of a submarine experiencing this type of natural event.

But that was life on board *Rasher*. During my two years on board I saw more diverse casualty events there than all the rest of my subs put together. It is not that it was a hard luck ship, we just did a lot of different things with a high operating tempo during my time there. Fires, flooding, etc., all were experienced. It was great 'school of the boat' for me. We had a magnificent crew and wardroom and all casualties were handled quickly, efficiently and safely. I never had the feeling that personnel error was ever an element. Much of our equipment and 'plumbing' was old, worn and broke easily. But we fixed and move on. I don't think we ever missed a commitment due to material problems. *Rasher* was always "on station and ready for work'. We even got a couple of "E's" doing it. She was a great ship.

In 2003 I went to my first *Rasher* crew reunion. It was at Manitowoc where we celebrated the 60th anniversary of her commissioning. I took some time away from the celebrations to drive down to the weed covered and abandoned site of Manitowoc Shipbuilding. All was quiet, the last ship built there was nearly thirty years ago. Many of the buildings had been pulled down but you could still see the large covered assembly building where the hull sections had been fabricated. Nearby were remnants of the building ways and sideways launching sites. I may not have been exactly at the point where Rasher had been launched six decades earlier but I was close. Close enough for me to offer a silent thanks to those men and women who long ago built those tough Manitowoc boats.

Leak Proof Valves—A Class A Oxymoron

When Chuck Griffiths mentioned 'leak proof' valves I began to laugh.

DG: Admiral Grojean told me that in the early, early days the training was eight guys around a table with PhD's teaching. When was the school more formal?

CG: Well, it was after my time. I went to school in Rickover's headquarters, in his offices, not necessarily with PhD's but I guess maybe most of those guys were. For example, I worked out of the shop of the guy who was in charge of valves for the whole program.

DG: Valves?

CG: Valves. And you can imagine. Well, you know, we had a whole new industry because they needed leak-proof valves, which didn't exist then.

DG: [Laughter] I don't even know how to define that.

CG: It didn't exist, and so you can imagine when you're handling steam and when you're handling the radioactive water, when you're stopping radioactive water, you just needed absolute foolproof zero leakage valves.

DG: Nothing like old valves.

CG: Oh, no. Nothing like that existed anywhere. So all the materials, everything was different and that was a whole industry.

DG: Was this guy a civilian? You're talking about the valve guy.

CG: Oh, yeah, he was a civilian at the time but had been a naval officer. Actually, it was a guy by the name of Rick Clayter whose brother later was the secretary of the Navy. His brother was the head of Southern Railroad, and later he was brought in to be the Secretary of the Navy. But Rick Clayter was the valve guy. One guy was in charge of each of these various segments of the program.

DG: And while they were conducting their job, they were also training you?

CG: Yeah, we had a syllabus to follow. I'd spend so much time in Clayter's office, so much time in Griggs' office on the electrical plant, so much time in Rakowski's office on the core, you know, that sort of thing. But we were trained by the guys that were in charge of each aspect of the plant. Then, of course, we took our exams like everybody else, and then we also went out to the prototype. We had to go to the prototype. Then it was Idaho. And we all had to qualify on every position in the prototype just like everybody else does in the program including enlisted guys. So we had a year's training program and it was different. They had started a nuclear power school by now but the PCOs weren't going to it. And Grojean and all of the PCOs went to PCO school in those days.

Nuclear Safety

Apart from commenting on the rigid procedures Rickover initiated and insisted upon, there was very little discussion in either the interviews or submissions concerning nuclear safety and accidents—surprising given the civilian record including Chernobyl and Three Mile Island and the Soviet's loss of several nuclear submarines due to reactor problems/disasters. Below is a comment from the only contributor who chooses to remain anonymous.

"My initial impression of "nukes" was they were too serious about their jobs, and didn't really "enjoy" their occupation. With the passage of years I came to understand that they were probably reacting to the extreme amount of "damage" that they could cause if things didn't go properly. As a diesel boat CO about the worst thing that I could do would be to kill some 100 crew members if I screwed up. As a nuke CO I could be responsible for contamination of somewhere like Pearl Harbor with enough Cobalt 60 to screw that place up for 30,000 years. Quite a different order of worry."

The following came up in my interview with Mike Barr. He was not responding directly to the above comment since he was unaware of it. Mike Barr's comments on the subject gave me considerable comfort and I thought the juxtaposition of the two points was interesting and informative.

DG: This is another thing that comes up and I was never aware of it, but some people were very, very conscious of the fact that somebody in the program could screw up and cause a nuclear accident.

MB: It would have been very, very difficult for a single person to do that.

DG: I don't mean by sabotage or something, I'm talking about just not handling it properly.

MB: Right, and that's what I meant. Even by some failure, advertent or inadvertent—and I'm not talking about sabotage—to do things correctly.

DG: Was that because of mechanical, procedural or both reasons?

MB: Well, I mean, it would take hours to explain what made it so that our ships then and now operate so safely. It is a careful design that takes into account what might happen, and then protects against problems by the design. It's the fact that the ships are constructed to the design and constructed well and checked all along the way. It's very careful configuration control throughout the life of the ship. It's modernization when appropriate, as-built drawings and technical manuals and procedural manuals so that the crew and support people know how things work and what you need to do to repair or operate them. It's the careful selection of people, the training of the people, continuing training of the people, the qualifications that you have to go through, the rigor of the formality of the way you operate the ship. All of that, and many other things, make the ships safe. There is "defense in depth" at every turn so that if any one thing, or several things, don't work right, the chances of you having a serious problem are very slim.

DG: What about THRESHER?

MB: The loss of THRESHER was *not* a nuclear issue. It was almost certainly a failure of piping in the engine room. At that time, Admiral Rickover's organization (called Naval Reactors) was not responsible for the engine room design. They took responsibility for it shortly thereafter, and there hasn't been a problem like that since.

Now, of course, we also lost SCORPION, but that had nothing to do with the engineering department at all. One person making a mistake could not cause a significant reactor accident.

DG: Well, that's nice to know.

MB: Now, you can have a series of people making mistakes. Things don't always go perfectly, but even in such circumstances, a serious reactor plant problem is not going to happen.

I've now had six years working in the civilian world as a support service contractor at the Laboratory (Los Alamos), and I also had a tour at DOE headquarters, 1989 to 1991, and I will tell you that there is just no comparison. I mean, you can't even start to compare the professionalism and the way that the nuclear Navy operated to what I observed.

I'm not saying that the civilian area doesn't have dedicated people. There are many dedicated, intelligent, talented people. I know a lot of them. But you need somebody like Rickover to pull it all together. To have the vision, the intelligence to get good people around him and to make all the necessary things happen: proper design, construction, configuration control, maintenance, training, qualification, procedures etc. The Admiral's long tenure leading the Navy nuclear propulsion program (about 30 years) was a major factor in setting consistent policy and then following it. Changing policymakers every year or two makes consistency difficult. The nuclear program did have enough funding to do things right (Admiral Rickover saw to that) and that helped. You *did* get bright people. Even with the rigorous selection of personnel, there *were* off-ramps as you went along. Not everybody made it. For example, when I was CO at Nuclear Power School, only about half the enlisted people who entered the Navy in the nuclear power program actually made it to a submarine or nuclear surface ship. Many who didn't get through nuclear training stayed in the Navy, and went on to be very successful in other parts of the Navy. There were check points all along a career in the nuclear Navy, and at every step there were people who didn't get through.

You know, I had something to do with Rocky Flats when I was at DOE (Department of Energy), and one of the buildings where they did plutonium operations had been in operation since 1954 or thereabouts. They were still trying to operate. It had lots of problems and eventually got shut down and didn't start up again. Now look at the nuclear Navy. The first nuclear powered warship, USS NAUTILUS (SSN-571) went to sea for the first time in 1955. By the time I was at DOE (Department of Energy), NAUTILUS had been in a museum for several years. You can't pull together an operation that works the way the nuclear power Navy does in a few years. It takes a commitment to begin with and continued effort for years and years and years. And I watched that happen. I wasn't always smart enough to recognize what was happening at the time, but the standards that we operated to when I started on SNOOK—and they were very, very high at that time—much higher than anybody else's—would have been unacceptable 20 years later.

DG: Really?

MB: Oh, absolutely. From a formality point of view, from an operational capability point of view, from a propulsion plant operation point of view, from a maintenance point of view. From almost any point of view.

DG: So you did things way, way better years later.

MB: Yes. It was the continuous improvement as you went from year to year. And the product of that, as I mentioned earlier, was exemplified by the ship that I commanded first, which, at 16 years old, was in substantially better material condition than my first ship was when it was 1 year old. The improvement came from various sources, but a lot of it came from the people who manned the submarines and surface ships, saying "We can do this better. Here's how."

Sanitary #1

No book involving diesel submarines is complete without a story or an explanation about the Sanitary System. Interestingly, for the layman at least, here is where diesel and nuclear powered submarines are alike. Both types need to, while submerged, get rid of the accumulated sanitary waste. So, I will explain the logistics, procedures and problems surrounding, as we diesel boat sailors called it, "Blowing Sanitary #1."

The following is from an earlier piece I had written.

Sanitary #1 was a large tank inside the pressure hull topped by a pair of stainless steel commodes. There was a lever on the side of each commode controlling a spool valve in the bottom and a seawater valve to help flush. When you finished your business in the head, you had to open the door since you could not turn around otherwise. Well, you may be able to turn around and face the commode, but you could not bend at the waist due to the size of the tiny "compartment." Then you would *slowly* pull the lever toward you until the holes lined up and everything dropped into the tank.

When the tank was close to full the man on watch would open a high pressure air valve and put a pressure in the tank until it exceeded that of the surrounding seawater—specifically at the keel. The deeper we were, the more pressure was needed. The watch was aided by two pressure gauges right over the commode. One displayed the pressure inside the tank, while the other displayed the pressure of the sea just outside the pressure hull. Once having put a higher pressure in the tank than the sea, he opened a large valve at the bottom of the tank and the contents would be expelled into the sea. When he heard air escaping through this valve, he knew the tank had been completely blown. So he would close it and shut off the high pressure air to the tank. Part number one…so far, so good.

The second part was a problem since now there was a greater pressure in old Sanitary Tank #1, than what existed inside the submarine. The commodes could not be used until *we equalized the tank and the atmosphere inside the boat* by venting it into the submarine. In spite of charcoal filters at the vent, the air bleed back into the boat smelled VERY badly.

There was a problem—I believe unique to diesel boats—with Sanitary Tank #1 and snorkeling. This part requires a quick primmer on snorkeling.

When snorkeling we ran our big diesel engines which sucked huge * quantities of air out of the boat. The replacement air was drawn down through the snorkel just above the surface of the sea above us. This worked well until either a wave would cover the head valve or the diving party on watch would inadvertently dip the boat and the snorkel head valve under water. When that occurred the head valve would automatically slam shut with the main engines still running, thus pulling a vacuum in the boat. This was very hard on the ears and would wake you from a deep sleep. When that wave receded or the snorkel was back where it belonged—above the surface, the head valve would open up and the pressure ride of seconds before would reverse back to normal. We even had airplane type altimeters throughout the boat which displayed our "altitude". One in the engine room would shut down the diesel engines at the equivalent of 6000 feet as I recall. I wondered at the time how civilians would react to an elevator in a mile high building which got you to the top in a few seconds!

The problem with the ears paled by comparison to that which the cycling back and forth had on the sanitary system. Every time the snorkel head valve would slam shut, creating a vacuum in the boat, it also created a differential pressure between the sanitary tank and that inside the submarine, with a greater pressure inside the sanitary tank. If you did not keep your wits about you when you went to the head while snorkeling, you ran the risk of vaporizing what you had just left in the commode all over yourself and the head. This, of course, would not kill you, you would just wish it had.

* Gene Robinson of Becuna SS-319 *commented on snorkeling:*
"I knew when the order to snorkle was given that the After Battery was not a good place to sleep. On several occasions my blankets were ripped away from my rack and deposited in either the passage way or on another rack. Also, when the water tight door was opened in the Forward Engine Room the air was so cold I gave up sleeping and joined in a card game."

Fred Starr
EM1(SS)
USS Rock SSR-274
1953–1958

In April or May 1958, the Rock paid a visit to Vancouver, British Columbia. After operating with the Canadian Navy, we moored in Vancouver and held an open house where thousands of Canadians stood in long lines to visit the boat. After an exhausting two days of liberty and sheparding visitors through the boat, we got underway for Mare Island, CA. When we got out to sea, the sea was really rough and there were quite a number of hung-over, seasick sailors in the stern room who desperately needed to use the head. Unfortunately we found that we couldn't flush the head! We blew the sanitary tank and still the damned toilet bowl wouldn't flush! Finally the auxiliarymen figured out that there was something jammed beneath the flush flapper valve and the only way to clear it was to blow the sanitary inboard! The auxiliarymen found some wood or metal, covered the toilet and had an unsuspecting sailor stand on the cover. Then they opened the toilet flapper valve and opened the air valve! There was a hellacious roar of air pressure accompanied by an indescribable smell and the distinct thump of a solid object striking the improvised cover beneath the sailor's feet. When the inboard blow terminated and the temporary cover removed, there was a lovely glass perfume bottle resting in the toilet bowl! That occurred fifty years ago and I can still smell it and get a queasy feeling in my stomach when I think about it! I'm sure it was an unforgettable experience for the sailor who stood on the cover. Just another day at sea in a good old diesel boat!

Jake Laboon

I am including this one out of respect for a WWII submariner—Mike Walsh. Also because this fellow Jake Laboon was a colorful submariner and a buddy, life long friend and football teammate of my big brother John at the Naval Academy—class of 1945—and a navy aviator. It seems odd that my deceased older brother John's name should come up in a book about submarines.

As I prepared for the interview with Pat Hannifin at his home, we passed some small talk while I hooked up our lapel mics and put a tape in my machine. I asked him what class he was in. He replied class of '45. I responded that that was my brother's class too. He looked at me for a second, snapped to the connection of the last name of Gillcrist and said two words, "Big John". Naturally I had tears in my eyes thinking that after 63 years, this fine, successful submarine warrior remembered the nick name of his classmate—my brother.

The second connection with Jake Laboon was that in some rather spooky coincidence Jake Laboon and John Gillcrist both died of the same thing—esophageal cancer—in the same hospital—Walter Reed and within 30 days of one another.

Michael Walsh
RM2/c
U.S.S. Peto (SS 265)
January 26, 1943 to January 6, 1946

During our 10th & last patrol while on lifeguard duty we picked up a downed flier who informed us his wingman was also downed but the area he landed at was in a minefield. A young LT. by the name of Jake Laboon volunteered and with a rope tied to his waist swam to the area of the downed airman and pulled him to safety. LT. Laboon was given the Silver Star for this heroic deed. This same LT. was a Naval Academy graduate of the class of 1944 and excelled at football at the Academy and was also an All American Lacrosse player. After the war he joined the Jesuit Order and was ordained a priest in June 1956. He then entered the Navy and served as a Chaplain with the 3rd Marine Div. in Vietnam. He became North Atlantic Fleet Chaplain and after retiring became pastor of St.

Alphonsus Rodriguez Church in Woodstock, MD He passed away Aug. 1, 1988. On March 18, 1995 a destroyer, the U.S.S. Laboon (DDG 58) was commissioned at Norfolk, VA in honor of this outstanding man.

I was honored to attend his first mass after his ordination in 1956 and have videos of the re-enactment of his rescue of the downed flier and of his appearance on the old T.V. program, "To Tell The Truth" way back on April 21, 1959, along with a video of the U.S.S. Laboon commissioning ceremony in 1995. I've made many copies of these events and passed them on to some of my former U.S.S. Peto shipmates. An interesting footnote is our Captain Hugh Caldwell is still living with his wife in Chapel Hill, NC.

Regards and Good Cheer, Mike Walsh

Ship Christening

During my interview with Chuck Griffiths at the Army Navy Country Club in Arlington, his wife interrupted us briefly to say hello.

CG: My wife has a meeting today, a board meeting of the Society of Sponsors. She's president of the Society of Sponsors. These are ladies who have cracked the bottles and christened ships of the United States Navy. And so she's got a board meeting today and then she's got a luncheon here that she's throwing for her board. So she and her crowd are here today.

DG: So there's actually a society of those people who've christened ships?

CG: Oh, yeah. Teddy Roosevelt started it. So it's pretty old. It's a very distinguished group of ladies. All the presidents' wives and some members of Congress, senior members of the Navy who are lucky enough to have had their wife christen a ship.

DG: Has that been traditionally a womans function?

CG: Hundred percent. Only women.

Submarine Tour

David Barry Vanderhoff
STS/SS RET
Hawkbill SSN-666, Kamehameha SSBN-642, Daniel Boone SSBN-629, Swordfish SSN-579,
September 1977 to December 1998

On the brow stands a young man with a forty-five-caliber pistol and a giant book full of security clearances. "You won't have to worry about those because I'll vouch for you!" As we crawl down the ladder, you realize the drop to the deck is about fifteen feet. There are meters, levers and a bunch of pipes and contraptions, which tell you we are no longer in Kansas! About halfway down, you detect a strange smell. Don't worry; it's just amine and hydraulic fluid! (Amine is the chemical used to collect CO_2, and the smell will wash out of your clothes in about two months.) Looking forward, you will see the Control Room. At the very front is the Ship's Control Panel. To the left of that is the Ballast Control Panel (the place where the Chief of the watch moves the fluids and gases to ensure a smooth ride). To the right is the Fire Control area. The guy sleeping on the locker is the one responsible for flipping the switches required to launch an attack.

See that guy hunched over the chart table to the back on the port side of the control room? He's responsible for the navigation of the ship. Ok! In the center of the control room is the periscope stand; that's where the captain makes his safety sweep prior to diving the ship or coming to periscope depth. Watch out! The periscope rings (a circular metal bar used for raising or lowering the periscope) will catch you in the forehead if you're not careful. You can see a number of repeaters in the overhead and at the back of the stand. The one that looks like a small television is the "periviz" (short for perivision, a monitor for the periscope) and the ones in the back are for sonar (short for Sound Navigation and Ranging) The captain can double-check on most of the major evolutions from his station here.

Let's head towards the back of Control (we're going aft now.) Down the stairs, and you notice that there is barely room for two people to squeeze by each other. Yeah, it gets pretty funky in here after a couple of months under the water. Not everyone showers as frequently as they should.

OK! Heading forward and to the right, we can see the galley; that's where we eat. Can you imagine squeezing two football teams' worth of guys into these tables? It looks pretty small, but when you have only a couple of minutes, complaining about the space is the last thing on your mind. Meals here are served every six hours around the clock. And you were wondering why so many of us have a weight problem? Have you ever tried to work a six on—twelve off schedule? Especially, when most of your off time is taken up with paperwork and drills? (A drill is an exercise where you practice for an emergency situation.) Didn't think so! The best thing about the galley is that no matter what time of day it is, or what's going on, you can always have a semi-intelligent conversation about current affairs. You probably didn't realize that most of the guys here have an above average intelligence.

OK! Keep going back, and duck down through this watertight door. Watertight door? Oh! Between every major compartment there is a door, which can isolate each compartment from the other compartments. What's the little window in the middle called? It's called a Deadman! Ha Ha!

In case of an emergency, you can look through the window to check for survivors or floaters.

Moving on, notice that little board with all the slimy–looking globs on it? It's called a booger board! Our Machinist Mates like to keep themselves amused on long patrols by seeing who can come up with the longest booger. Gross, huh! Most of the forward equipment for keeping us alive is in this space: The O2 generator, the COH2 burner, the CO2 scrubbers and some of the smaller motor generator sets, etc.

You're look'n a little sleepy, so to the right and down that hatch and we'll be in twenty-one man berthing! Watch your head 'cause this space has a low overhead! Notice how this space is shaped like a giant U? It covers the battery compartment. If any seawater gets in here, we'll be the first to die. How do I sleep? Get used to it! The next mission is going to take place in water so deep, that if we have any emergencies, we won't be able to recover, anyway!

Yeah! That's your bunk on the bottom, about the size of a coffin, and no room to move. Hey! You better get some sleep! I hear we're having a major drill in a couple of hours. Sweet dreams!

Dolphins, Wings, Pins and Medals

Bob Gautier interview.

DG: Can I tell you a quick little anecdote that Admiral Hannifin talked about? There were just three admirals who were qualified to wear the War Patrol pin *and* a Deterrent Patrol pin, you know that Polaris thing? And he said there was a regulation that you could only wear one device down there under your ribbons. And these three got together and said, 'We're just not going to pay attention to that regulation.' So I guess they wore both. But he said there were only three of us, so it was a pretty easy decision.

BG: That's right. As a matter of fact, about the time I got to be an amphibious squadron commander, they came up with the Surface Warfare pin. So I had my yeoman check into it and they said, 'Yeah, you rate the Surface Warfare pin. Yeah, you can wear that, but you have to give up your Dolphins.' I said, 'Screw it. You're not going to get my dolphins.' And today they let you wear both. As a matter of fact, there are a few guys—a few submariners—who have wings and dolphins, and for awhile you had to wear whichever one that you were—whatever service you were in.

DG: When it related to your job.

BG: Yeah, related to the job. So Chuck Larsen, who later became Superintendent of the Naval Academy, he was an aviator and a submariner. So when he got to be—I guess he was CINCPAC, he came to make a speech, and Chuck, he'd had the DEV group—he'd been the DEV group commander about four or five after me, and so he came to do the speech and I talked to him and everything, and he had both his wings and his dolphins on. And we got this one guy in town, Jack Bennett, who was my XO on a submarine. And Bennett was on a boat with Elliott Laughlin when they sank the Red Cross ship. So Bennett told me, he said, 'You know, Larsen has got those dolphins and wings interchanged. He's got them wrong.' I said, 'I think that's a good idea. Why don't you go tell him that?' I mean, what the hell difference does it make?

DG: Did you ever hear why? I mean, what would possess someone to go from pilot to subs?

BG: Most of them go the other way. Most of them go from submarines to flying. I don't know why it is. Yeah, but Chuck has both of them. But I figure for a four-star, if he wants to wear—Christ, he can wear them on either side as far as I'm concerned.

DG: Or on his shoulders.

BG: Yeah, or put them in his pocket. This is like the new commandant of the Marine Corps. Evidently, there's two or three medals that he wears, but he can't find the authorization to wear them. I mean, he's got a whole chestful of ribbons. And when Gene Flucky was SUBPAC, Gene Flucky used to wear three ribbons. He wore the Congressional Medal, the Navy Cross, and a Silver Star. That's all he wore, just those three. So I thought, that's pretty cool. So when I got a personal decoration, and I got three, that's what I'd wear. I wore the three. So I figured the Commandant of the Marine Corps, he didn't—you know, all you got to do is take them off.

DG: Yeah, it didn't look any different.

BG: Nobody knows what the hell they are, anyway. But I think that Commandant is the first guy who doesn't have a World War II Victory ribbon. That's how young he is. Yep. I'm to the point that I've got almost as much retired time as I did active duty time. And that's pretty good.

DG: Count your blessings.

Pancake Diesels

Chuck Griffiths on the 'lousy' design. In this part of the interview I could detect the frustration still in his voice after 40 years!

CG: You remember, they re-engined that whole class, the whole *Tang—Trigger* class. They all got new engineering plants because the ones they were designed with were failures. I was XO of 563, which was *Tang*, and she had the old engineering plant. And, for example, we didn't have an electrician that shipped over on the *Tang* because they figured they would spend all their time swabbing generators and working around the clock

DG: Trying to make them work?

CG: Trying to make them work. And because it was a lousy design, BUSHIP's design, and it was a terrible failure. They changed the whole plant to the *Barbel* plant on all those ships, which was a very good design. And, again, the bad design was those high-speed pancake engines, which were high-speed diesel engines built to reduce weight and size so as to be able to make the engineering plant smaller.

DG: But what did they sacrifice?

CG: They sacrificed everything and it was just lousy. It was a terrible failure. We carried spare crankshafts in our torpedo racks when we went to WestPac because we were changing crankshafts so frequently in the engines. We never had four engines up. You were lucky if you could get two up. Almost every boat in that class was towed back to port at some time during their career. It was that bad a design.

DG: How embarrassing. Do you remember that ditty, "*Harder, Darter, Trigger, Trout*. Never came in 'cause they never went out"? Were they examples of this?

CG: They were all examples.

DG: I never did understand, until now, why they never went out!

CG: They were examples. Along with *Wahoo* and *Tang*. And so I was an XO of *Tang* with that horrible plant and then CO of *Wahoo* with a wonderful plant. You know, there couldn't have been a happier ship. It was just a wonderful ship and, of course, everybody shipped over on *Wahoo*. Yeah, it was great. I even had Bill Crow as my XO, for example.

DG: I never thought of a relationship between a mechanical thing and retention rates.

CG: Oh, tremendous. Tremendous correlation, and very understandable, totally understandable.

DG: I could certainly understand the negative side. Why somebody would just bail and get out as soon as he could.

CG: Well, he just wouldn't ship over. Electricians just wouldn't ship over because it was a miserable life on that class ship. It was not just that ship, it was the whole class. Of course, after they were all re-engined, it was a totally different picture because they were re-engined with three Fairbanks Morris engines, and the ships had to be lengthened by 40 feet to do that. They were end to end, just like they were in the old diesel boats. The only thing is they were all three in the same room, and one was in the center down in a well and the generators were in tandem, like they were in the fleet boats. But with the pancakes, the engine sat vertically on top of the generator and, of course, they never could design a seal that would hold oil in a situation like that. And so that's why the generators were flooding out all the time with the oil from the engine. Well, it was a vertical connection, you know, went right through from the crankshaft to the engine, right through the seal into the generator. And so the generators were flooding out all the time, *all* the time.

Jim Watkins

Jim Watkins had an amazing career which went way beyond the Navy portion where he reached the position of CNO. When I asked his long time assistant for a biography and a picture for this project, she asked, "Do you want the one pager, or the five paged one?" He was my XO on Barbero *SSG-317 and he generously agreed to an interview in his office in DC. I was struck by how many people I interviewed who had a very high opinion of both his leadership abilities and his personality. Many comments among the submissions spoke favorably about* Snook's *morale (Watkins was XO on this submarine) and the lack of friction between the diesel and nuke crew members. So, I decided to include these accolades and anecdotes.*

  Bob Gautier

DG: Did you know Watkins well?

BG: He put the Snook in commission in Pascagoula. This is right after I was down there. And so he and his family lived down there and one of my younger cousins saved Charlie from drowning. They lived right next to him down on the sound at Ingals. Jim was a great guy. He really was.

DG: Well, he went all the way. I mean, CNO, that's not chopped liver.

BG: No, and they had several children, and the girl, when the Prince of Wales came over here, they lined up and had him dating Watkins' daughter back in Annapolis. But his wife died about five or six years ago.

DG: I'm going to interview him. I'm going to D.C. next month and I'm going to see several people, three, actually, and he's one of them. He was my old XO on Barbero.

BG: No, let me tell you, he's a fine speaker and he presents well and he's alright.

Mike Barr called him,"an unbelievably fantastic CO"
DG: So you went aboard SNOOK as a JG and Watkins was then the CO?

MB: No, he was not. Actually, the CO when I got there, for about three weeks, was a CDR Howard Bucknell. Then, for the first roughly half of the three years I was on that ship the CO was CDR Bill Yates, who was a wonderful human being and an excellent CO. For the last half of my tour, the CO was CDR Jim Watkins, who was also a wonderful human being and an unbelievably fantastic CO. So I was very lucky. I had people as COs and XOs who were great people, and our Ward Room was great too. For example when CDR Watkins was CO (he later became CNO and Secretary of Energy) the XO was LCDR Ron Thunman, who became a three-star, and the MPA was LT Bruce DeMars, who became a four-star admiral. There were six future flag officers in the ward room while I was there.

Watkins, Trost and Kelso—Twelve years in a row as submariner CNOs

The following letter from me to those I interviewed speaks for itself. It is a question which did not occur to me until all the interviews were finished. I list their responses after my letter.

Dear Admiral (sent to all those interviewed),   2–11–04

I hope I am not wearing out my welcome but I had a subject which I wanted to ask you about concerning the disproportionate number of CNOs who were submariners—particularly in that string beginning with Admiral Jim Watkins (followed by Trost and Kelso). If you could, let me know if you wished to opine and then through which method. Either you can write your response or let me know and I can call you and interview you over the phone.

My thoughts may be a bit naive and romantic, since I take considerable pride in this. I assumed that since submariners did such a splendid job and had such a profound effect particularly during the Cold War, that it was perfectly natural that they be put in that position in spite of being from a tiny naval community. I mentioned this to a friend who responded, perhaps a bit cynically, that it was more a function of Rickover making sure there were a disproportionate number of submariner candidates for the position. The second person I posed the question to disagreed and had yet another slant which was that Rickover had such a fine filter that only the very, very best submariners made it to the top echelon and were, therefore, the best candidates for the CNO position.

I think it is an extraordinary circumstance that a community of 2% of the Navy could produce a string of some 12 years of CNOs. I intend to work this into the project but I am, once again, way over my head and simply speculating. It is a worthy subject and I would love to have your views on the matter.

Thanks again.

Mike Barr's response via e-mail;
Dan,

I'm not sure what I can add about the three submarine CNOs. Certainly they were all absolutely superb naval officers and superb people as well. As you know I know Jim Watkins fairly well. I have never met a finer man or naval officer in my life—and I've known a lot of **very** fine ones! There are many people who feel the same way about ADM Trost and ADM Kelso. It is certainly true that ADM Rickover had a good deal to do with selecting great people for his program and then helping those he felt were worthy to reach flag rank and beyond. I do not know how effective he was in the latter effort. For most of his tenure there were many senior officers who detested him and would block his efforts out of spite, if for no other reason. Also remember that Rickover left active service reasonably early in Watkins' term as CNO and died relatively early in Trost's term. Thus, at least for Trost and Kelso becoming CNO, I would think Rickover's input would be marginal at best. It is much more likely that they had the support of people like SECNAV.

I think the truth is more that Rickover choose excellent people, which should lead to a proportionately higher fraction of "his" people reaching high rank, but the people who rose to the highest positions did it on their own merits. Undoubtedly all nuclear trained officers learned a great deal about how to be effective from Rickover, which helped. Also the fact that submarines were so important in the cold war helped. However, all three CNOs (and lots of other submarine flag officers) performed in non-submarine billets (e.g. fleet commands, senior OPNAV positions) and competed with flag officers from other branches directly and successfully. Also, one should remember that there are superb non-submarine flag officers too. Rickover did not get them all.

So, at least from my point of view, the three submariner CNOs earned the job themselves and it was an unusual combination of events that put them in that job in sequence. Don't try to make too much of it. I'd be happy to talk more about this if you wish, as long as you keep in mind I was not privy to what really happened!!

Mike

Bob Gautier called me on the phone to respond. His conclusion was simple, "They were selected for CNO because they were just good naval officers. Had nothing to do with their submarine background. Look at Vern Clark (the current CNO. A surface warfare officer). He is doing a hell of a job and is not squirrelly like Tom Haywood."

Bob took this opportunity to point out that sometimes the great candidate is not selected. He mentioned Mike Moore, class of '43, who had earned his PhD in nuclear physics, being turned down by Rickover, "because he was too smart and would be dangerous for the program." *I am still unclear as to what that meant exactly.*

The other example was Jim Bradley class of '45 who was an intelligence specialist, debriefing returning patrols. According the Gautier, Hal Shear, then Vice Chief, asked Bradley for intelligence for which he had no clearance. Bradley properly refused to give the information to this very senior admiral, and was told, "As long as I am in the Navy you will never make flag." *It is disturbing that the man kept his promise.*

I interviewed Chuck Grojean on the phone. Here is his take on the matter.

DG: It seemed, on the face, that that was an extraordinary thing for a community that represents two percent of the Navy to produce three CNOs in a row.

RG: Prior to that you'd had Bob Long, who was a Vice CNO. And you had an inordinate number of four stars who were submariners.

The situation arose during the seventies that the submariners had had more admirals selected than they ever had in the past. And this was directly related to the importance of nuclear power to the Navy and the importance of Rickover in terms of controlling. Ultimately he was the supreme controller of everybody who had anything to do with nuclear power. So he was instrumental in getting more people selected for flag rank.

The next part of the equation is the fact that they were all very good men, not that there weren't equally good men in other areas such as Naval aviators and surface Navy and in the Seals and all the other, but they were good men and they were representing what had become in the Navy a brand new powerful part of the Navy. And because of that these guys rose to the top in terms of power, and a lot of it had to do with—as it always has in the Navy—how much money in the Navy budget goes to what. And a lot of the money in those days went to the submarine force, whereas previously it had not gone to the submarine force. The money prior to that had always gone to the carriers, and that's the reason that you found so many flyers getting the money because there was much more money that went there. So I think that the control of the Navy, to a great degree, goes to the allocation of money that's in the Navy budget.

But, Watkins, Trost and Kelso—those guys were superb people. They all stood very high in their Naval Academy class. They all were outstanding submariners before nuclear power came along, and they shone when the nuclear power era came into being. And that's my take on it.

DG: But it seems to me that during the Cold War the Marine Corps wasn't asked to do much, nor was the Army, except just practice over there in Germany. But the submariners were the ones who were really producing the effect of deterrence and scaring the hell out of the Russians. Is that fair?

RG: The day-to-day war was fought by the submariners, doing all that they did. From the time when you had a hot spot and when you had crises here and there, you found the aircraft carriers going to the spot, as they do today. But conducting the day-to-day operations, and when I was Commander of the Submarine Force Mediterranean, I found that the Secretary of the Navy, the Secretary of Defense, they wanted to know what was happening in the Mediterranean vis-à-vis Soviet submarines. We were the ones who had most of the answers.

Once again Mike McLane had an interesting slant to offer concerning the disproportionate power and influence of the tiny submarine community which I, as a recovering Catholic, found amusing:

The fellow I had coffee with today, Dr. Bill Browning, is a brilliant analyst who has worked with the submarine force for years. Probably has more time submerged than any other analyst. Very involved in sonar search theory and optimum allocation of sonar trackers based on the environment and the possible threat. Used to work for Dan Wagner Associates many years ago then branched out on his own. When I was Director of Tactical Analysis at Development Squadron, Bill was there under contract. Excellent man. He is working on the capture of unclassified submariner oral histories from a number of people like Adm. Joe Williams. Active in Navy Submarine League and well known in the "community". I have a feeling he will be very interested in your book when it comes out and MIGHT end up being a contact worth cultivating.

Last year, when Subase was on the BRAC list, I asked Bill, "how can they do this?" and Bill very wisely said, "The 'big' navy doesn't like submariners because they are very smart, arrogant, AND only 6% of the navy." Today he drew a parallel between submariners/navy and the Jesuits/Roman Catholic church relationships (they are only 5% of the holy orders). Said there might be material there for a book. I asked him who he thought would be the more pissed-off, submariners or Jesuits. He laughed and said "probably both, equally".

Deterrent Patrols

Hugh Smith obtained the following statistics from Ms. Judy Hallmark—Strategic Systems Programs, Public Affairs Office:

Polaris—1245 patrols
C–3–1182 patrols
C–4–397 patrols
"41 For Freedom" total 2824 patrols

Trident I—387 patrols
Trident II—186 patrols
Trident total patrols—573
Assuming 65 days per patrol that is 604.9 years of patrols.

How quickly we forget. In 1995 or so, I found out what those little devices were which submariners wore beneath their ribbons. I was informed that they were Deterrent Patrol pins. Well, I asked the question, "Where the hell is my pin? Why didn't the people who came up with this device start from the beginning…with Barbero and Tunny both of which performed quite arduous patrols with the Regulus I missile, in old WWII fleet boats, probably in a lot more danger than any of them experienced?" In a dark and righteous mood I fired off a letter to the then Secretary of the Navy calling the oversight to his attention and admonishing him for not watching out for his men. Weeks later I received a letter from some four striper aide to the Secretary informing me that they had fixed that problem two years earlier by awarding the device to the crews of Barbero and Tunny for particular, stipulated patrols. Of course they had no way of informing any of us, having lost track of us decades before. I felt good about us receiving that recognition and for their having reached back and corrected the 35 year oversight, but I had the feeling that whoever initiated the device may have held us in some contempt in our rickety old diesel boats with our dinosaur Regulus I missiles. Maybe someone who reads this book can enlighten us via the web site. Stay tuned.

I decided to end this chapter—and the book—with the following Kipling poem. In a time when changes, particularly in the technical side of our society, are happening nearly at an exponential rate, it is refreshing to re-read a poem like this one. It describes us today the same way Kipling described our submarine predecessors in 1916.

"Unseen they work, unseen they win"...WOW.

The Trade

They bear in place of classic names,
Letters and numbers on their skin.
They play their grisly blindfold games
In little boxes made of tin.
Sometimes they stalk the Zeppelin,
Sometimes they learn where mines are laid
Or where the Baltic ice is thin.
That is the custom of 'The Trade'.

Their feats, their fortunes and their fames
Are hidden from their nearest kin;
No eager public backs or blames,
No journal prints the yarns they spin
(The Censor will not let them in!)
When they return from run or raid.
Unseen they work, unseen they win.
That is the custom of 'The trade'

1916, Rudyard Kipling (1865–1936)

Glossary

A Ganger—An "A" ganger is an Auxiliary division type. MMs, who are *not* nuclear trained on nuke boats, take care of auxiliary equipment such as ship's system hydraulics/pumps/engines/O2 generators/air compressors/fresh water/fuel oil, etc. On older boats they handled all mechanical systems.

Anchor Pool—A betting contest involving money where a sailor guesses the hour and minute his ship ties to the pier or "drops anchor" usually when returning to home port after a lengthy patrol. The CO would be shooting for a particular announced time, but the actual moment could vary due to a multitude of events.

Angles and Dangles—Radical vertical motions and horizontal turns, usually at high speed, used for training, demonstration of capability, or to assure the ship is properly stowed for sea.

Batteries—As one would suspect, a storage place for electricity. Diesel boats had upwards of 256 cells at one ton each, storing power for submerged operation without the diesel engines. Nuclear powered submarines also have batteries for emergencies. When fleet boats were converted, or "Guppied", they were given modern batteries with far more capacity.

Blue and Gold Crews—A system of manning an SSBN so that it is on station at sea as much as possible. When the submarine returns to port after a deployment it is turned around quickly, replenished with stores and spare parts etc. One crew is replaced by the other and the submarine can leave on another patrol.

Blue Suit—In the context ADM Watkins used it, refers to naval officers in charge of a program as opposed to others.

Boomer—Fleet Ballistic Missile submarine designated SSBN. There have been four classes up until now. Several have recently been converted to SSGNs.

BUPERS—Bureau of Personnel in Washington, DC.

Casualty—On a submarine it is a long list of bad things which can happen, most of which, if not dealt with fast and correctly, will kill the crew and put the boat on the bottom. Fire, exploding hydrogen gas, chlorine gas, flooding, bow planes/fairwater planes locked in the down position, reactor "problems" are just a few examples.

Class—Each new version of a ship type. The class is always named for the first ship of the class. A "688" refers to the U.S.S. *Los Angeles* SSN 688 and all following submarines of that class. The *Ohio* Class submarines are named after U.S.S. *Ohio* SSBN 726

Cigarette Deck—A deck as big as a small kitchen with a railing and bench seats. It is part of the sail of a WWII fleet boat and just aft of the bridge.

COB—Chief of the Boat. The head enlisted man on a submarine. A distinction of great honor and responsibility. He reports to the XO and CO and has many responsibilities with respect to the enlisted crew members. He is also the Senior Enlisted Advisor.

CO—Commanding Officer—the Captain. On diesel boat he was usually a LCRD. On nuclear power—fast attack boats he is usually a CDR. On SSBNs,—a Captain.

Core—The inside of a nuclear reactor—the nuclear material. A 'fuel tank' which does not need filling up for many years at a time.

Crush Depth—Not a popular topic for submariners. It is the depth at which the pressure hull and/or sea water systems are breeched and flooding occurs. Much deeper than test depth! (See Test Depth)

DBF—Stands for Diesel Boats Forever—an unofficial term. Many former crew members of diesel submarines have very fond memories of life aboard such "boats", and regret their passing.

Detailer—Officer in the Bureau of Naval Personnel whose job it is to fill fleet assignments with properly qualified people. Each of the three navy communities—Surface, Submarines and Aviation has one.

Dogs—Strong steel hooked pieces controlled manually by a crank in the center of a water tight door or hatch which locks the door or hatch shut.

Dolphins—The device a qualified submariner wears on his left breast. Two dolphins facing toward the middle with the bow of a diesel boat, bow on. Silver for the enlisted crew, gold for the officers.

Dry Deck Shelter—(DDS): A floodable, externally faired cylindrical chamber attached to a missile tube of an SSBN converted for submerged ingress-egress operations, usually SEALS. The large door to the outside allows carrying and using a SDV (Swimmer Delivery Vehicle). The DDS is accessible from inside the ship when drained down.

Enigma Machine—The cipher operating a system of three substitution rotors each spun 26 X the prior rotor's spin for a possible combination of 17,576 positions. The recipient of a message also had to know the pre-determined settings according to the date. The Americans and the British, being practical Yankee types, decided it was a lot easier to just secretly steal one from the Germans than to attempt to break their codes.

Fast Attack—Designated SSN. A submarine whose purpose is to sink enemy ships and submarines, fire vertical launched Tomahawk missiles, launch torpedoes, and gather intelligence among many other tasks. A highly versatile vessel.

Fast Cruise—Refers to exercising the ship in as close to at sea conditions as possible while made "fast" to the pier. The engineering plant is usually up to supply electrical power, underway watches are set, equipment is checked out, evolutions and casualty drills are conducted, etc. It is normally done after a long in port period or overhaul, before sea trails, etc. It can be from a few hours to several days in length.

Field Day—An all hands evolution to clean the entire ship or boat. Civilians call it a major house cleaning.

Gilly—100% pure alcohol—NOT denatured. On diesel boats it was used as fuel for the Mk14 torpedoes and occasionally consumed by enterprising sailors. With the passing of the Mk14 fuel burning torpedoes and the introduction of highly sophisticated electronic gear on the nuclear powered submarines, it was used for cleaning of sensitive electronic gear and occasionally consumed by enterprising sailors. *See 'Ditty Bag' for a funny gilly story.*

Goat Locker—Special quarters for the Chiefs on a submarine.

Green Board—There was a panel in the Control Room of diesel boats which indicated the positions of every hull opening. When every light was green, indicating that all hull openings were shut, "Green Board" was announced and the dive continued. It has evolved into an expression among submariners of good fortune.

Gun Sponsons—A waist high metal shielding surrounding a gun mount designed only to deflect shrapnel from the crews manning the guns. It was not armor and was of little use in a direct hit.

Guppy—(Greater underwater propulsion) The name for the modernization of the WWII fleet submarines. Among the changes were a snorkel, more hydrodynamic sleek sail and better batteries. A boat was "guppied" which went through this process.

Half Hour Rate—The discharge rate that a fully charged submarine battery can support for thirty minutes (when the battery will reach the low voltage limit). The term is generally not used for a nuclear submarine battery. It was common for a diesel battery.

Head Valve Cycle Syndrome—A humorous and completely un-official term used by Ron Martini in the Preface referring to an unpleasant condition experienced only aboard diesel submarines while snorkeling. (See Ditty Bag—Sanitary #1)

Heavie—A cotton rope, heavier than clothesline with a monkey's fist knot around a piece of lead at one end. It is used when a ship is docked. A sailor with a good arm holds the bitter end and throws the coiled up heavie like a discuss, toward the pier. The bitter end is then bent (tied) on the ship's mooring line and the workers on the pier pull the line ashore and drop the eye at the end over a bollard.

Hot Bunking—Sleeping accommodations on submarines are often inadequate—more crew than bunks. So, the more junior enlisted men share one man bunks, one after another so that the bunk mattress never cools off.

Hatch—Sealable, dogable openings for passage vertically. Between the Control Room and the Conning Tower—the Conning Tower and the Bridge, are hatches. They posses the same pressure integrity as the pressure hull. (See Watertight Doors)

JO—Junior Officer.

Jury rigging—When used in the Navy it means repairing equipment with unconventional parts and measures. Submariners are particularly good at it and do it often.

Littoral—This is a very often used word for modern submariners. It means the shore or edge of oceans and lakes. For submariners it means the regions close into the coast where they can operate submerged. Keeping an eye on possible new adversaries is now, since the end of the Cold War, more important than ever. A friend on a Fast Attack, referring to a deployment, mentioned only that they spent the majority of the patrol in water shallower than the length of the submarine. Obviously maneuvering a submarine in such shallow water demands great seamanship and leaves little margin for mistakes.

Main Induction—The air intake located in the sail of a submarine. It has a valve which naturally seats with sea pressure which is shut during each dive. The failure of the main induction to close was an often fatal casualty. As with every other "hull opening" such as all the hatches, there was an indicator light in the Control Room. (see Green Board)

NECP—Navy Enlisted Commission Program. Promising sailors are sent to college and upon graduation receive a commission as an officer.

Ned Beach—Renowned submariner in WWII as well the early transition covered by this book. Author of, among other books, *Run Silent, Run Deep*.

Noseconer—(as defined by Ron Gorence)
"Noseconers were the group forward of the reactor compartment, as in the nose cone of an Atlas Centaur rocket, i.e. front end, or where the payload was. That is, the most important part of, and the main purpose of the rest of the rocket.
Torpedo men were the most important (according to them) because they were the whole purpose of a fast attack boat—to deliver torpedoes to the enemy. Quartermasters were the most important (according to me) because the ship would wander around lost if not for us. Sonarmen were most important, because they were the only ones who could find the enemy. Cooks were most important, because you can't fight on an empty belly etc. etc. Snipes, nukes, electricians, etc. anyone aft of the nuclear power plant were not noseconers. They only pushed the important people to where they had to be. Of course, to nukes, noseconers were also knuckle draggers."

One MC (1MC)—The main announcement system on a submarine. Can be heard everywhere aboard.

ORSE—Operational Reactor Safety Exam. Periodically administered to nuclear trained crew members.

PCO—Prior Commanding Officer

PD—Periscope depth, measured from the keel to the surface. It is where a submarine needs to be so that its periscope, when raised, will be far enough out of the water to allow visual observation of the surface around the submarine.

Pinging—The first definition should be obvious thanks to Hollywood's usually corny submarine movies. The second is the practice, very common in every submarine's "After Battery" (crew's mess), of breaking someone's chops, (avoiding the more vulgar expression). On diesel boats there was far more idle time for the practice than on today's nukes. Diesel boat sailors raised 'messing with people' to an art form. It was a function of very smart sailors with too much time on their hands.

Poopie Suit—Coveralls worn by nuclear power crews. Once at sea, all hands shifted to "poopie suits." These were blue coveralls used because of their low lint content. This helped to prevent spontaneous combustion fires in the laundry dryers. A few boats had this problem prior to poopie suits being required. Plus they dried faster than dungarees. The laundry was kept going 24 hours a day. Diesel boat submariners wore what they wanted to on patrol—usually dungarees.

Presento—Gifts from the Captain to various big shots, politicians or supporters of the Navy who visit the submarine. Usually ball caps with the name of the sub. For the more important, some sort of wooden plaque or a framed picture of the submarine leaving port and signed by the Captain. For some odd reason it was always in hard-to-read gold ink.

Pro Pay—(more correctly "proficiency pay") is extra pay (above base pay—like submarine pay) for ratings where there is a shortage or which have special skills. It can vary from about $50/mo to $150/mo (when I last saw the numbers). It can vary for different rates within a rating (e.g. MM2 vs. MM1). The need is periodically re-evaluated and the propay levels are modified accordingly.

Qual—Qualification is the certification that a new member of the crew knows and can perform damage and fire procedures throughout the boat. It is also at least a rudimentary understanding and an ability to perform jobs other than one's specialty. Qualification permits a submariner to proudly wear Dolphins.

Ranks—Enlisted

E-1 = Seaman/Fireman Recruit
E-2 = Seaman/Fireman Apprentice
E-3 = Seaman/Fireman
E-4 = Third Class Petty Officer
E-5 = Second Class Petty Officer
E-6 = First Class Petty Officer
E-7 = Chief Petty Officer
E-8 = Senior Chief Petty Officer
E-9 = Master Chief Petty Officer

Commissioned Officers
-Ensign (ENS)
-Lieutenant Junior Grade (LTJG)
-Lieutenant (LT)
-Lieutenant Commander (LCDR)
-Commander (CDR)

-Captain (CAPT)
-Rear Admiral (lower half) one star (RADM)
-Rear Admiral—two stars (RADM)
-Vice Admiral—three stars (VADM)
-Admiral—four stars (ADM)

Ratings—

TM = Torpeodman
FT = Fire Control Technician
QM = Quartermaster
ET = Electronics Technician
IC = Interior Communications Technician
EM = Electrician Mate
EN = Engineman
MM = Machinists Mate
YN = Yeoman
HM = Hospital Corpsman
CS = Commissaryman/Cook
RM = Radioman
PN = Personnel Man very occasionally
GM = Gunner's Mate (when there were deck gun)
BM = Boatswains Mate back in WWII
CT = Communications Technician (now days called spooks)
MT = Missile Technicians
MS = Miss. Specialists
ST = Sonar Technician
*Your Navy has chosen to eliminate or consolidate some ratings such as
RM, ET, IC, QM, MS and, regrettably, as an old Torpedoman, TM.*

Reactor—The power source for nuclear powered ships and submarines. Produces heat which is converted to steam which in turn powers turbines for electrical generation and propulsion.

Retention Rate—It is a very high priority in the Navy in general, and in the Submarine Service in particular, to persuade talented and highly trained sailors to stay in the Navy. We called it 'shipping over' (for another 'hitch'). It was a measure of performance among Commanding Officers. A high retention rate on a submarine often, but not always (as Dave Oliver pointed out), suggested the morale was high.

School of the boat—Knowledge gained aboard—not through books or in a class room. A submariner learns a great deal through word of mouth and by example from his shipmates. This was particularly true on the diesel boats

SSK—Six submarines in the 240 hull number range (*Angler, Bashaw, Bluegill, Bream, Cavalla* and *Croaker*) were converted to 'killer' submarines whose mission was to find, monitor and if necessary, sink Soviet submarines. The modification was a large, bulbous rubber bow filled with hydrophones.

Shipmate—"Shipmate is a wonderful word. It refers to people who are thrown together by duty but bound together by shared experience and common affection." *Linton F. Brooks*

Shore Power—Submarines and other ships tied to a pier usually get their electrical power from a connection on the pier.

Shipping Over—When an enlisted man, toward the end of his enlistment, decides to stay in the Navy at least for another four years, or whatever the prevailing commitment period is at the time. It is usually a sign that the man is happy. Chuck Griffiths says in "Pancake Engines" (see Ditty Bag) that not one person on *Tang*, maintaining the engines, shipped over.

Snorkel—It is an air duct which extends upward as a mast allowing the air breathing diesel engines to operate while the submarine is still submerged. It has a head valve at the top designed to shut when sea water covers the opening.

Test Depth—The maximum operating depth for which a submarine is designed. This is classified. (See Crush Depth definition and Ditty Bag for actual stories)

Vents—The valves at the tops of ballast tanks which allow the trapped air to escape and the boat to loose buoyancy and dive.

Welded to the pier—Generally a derogatory comment referring to a ship which rarely moves to sea. Submarine tenders seldom get underway and some ships always seem to be under repair. Many Navy ships are now decommissioned museums, not unlike the French navy.

Watertight Doors—Provide horizontal passage between compartments. They can be sealed and 'dogged' tight. In many emergency situations on a submarine, watertight doors are shut and dogged.

WestPac—Often means an extended patrol period in the Western Pacific.

XO—Executive Officer. Second in command.

Contributers

Ackerman, John

Arnold, George

Bachman, Thomas

Barbee, Bobby

Barbieri, John

Barr, Mike

Barron, Pat

Bay, John

Beeghly, Richard

Bennett, John

Benton, Gene

Birkle, Joe

Bliss, Jerry

Blonigen, Jerry

Blount, Robert

Brockingham, Gene

Brown, Dick

Bufis, John

Byrne, Wayne

Byrnes, David

Chwaszczewski, Richard

Cook, Stan

Craig, Anthony

Crooks, Paul

Curtis, Tom

Damato, Glen

Day, Wynne

Duncan, Clifford

Eckard, John

Emerson, Mike

Enneis, William

Ennis, Don

Ferrell, Larry

Flege, James

Forgit, Roger

Gautier, Bob

Gee, Jim

Gordon, David

Gorence, Ron

Goron, Ronald

Griffiths, Chuck

Grojean, Chuck

Guille, Les

Haight, Gary

Hannifin, Pat

Harmouth, Robert

Harris, Glenn

Harrison, Charles

Hartnagel, Paul

Harvey, Charles

Hester, Jack

Hill, Frank

Jarvis, Stan

Jones, Larry

Kail, Robert

Keiffer, Glen

Kimmel, Ronald

Lawton, Jim (Red)

Leonard, Tom

Lynn, John

Marquet, David

Martini, Ron

McDaniel, Jack

McGovern, Matthew

McLane, Michael

McMicken, William

OKeefe, Dick

Oliver, Bob

Patterson, Steven

Patton, Bob

Price, Hank

Rarrick, Thomas

Robinson, Gene

Roos, Bob

Schuster, John

Seteroff, Wviatoslav

Shepherd, Ronald

Shipman, Scott

Smith, Hugh

Southard, Andrew

Spide, Bob "Spider"

Spoon, Tim

Starr, Fred

Stone, Ray

Stoops, Dave

Strang, Norman

Sullivan, John

Turley, Brian

Turner, Ric "Indian"

VanBlaracum, Jeff

Vanderhoff, David

VanVracken, James

Vincent, Morris

Wagner, Darrel

Walsh, Don

Walsh, Michael

Watkins, James

Wethington, Gerald

Biographies of those Interviewed

Admiral James D. Watkins, U.S. Navy (Retired)

Admiral James D. Watkins, USN (ret.), Naval Academy Class of 1949, is a 1958 graduate of the Naval Postgraduate School, with a master's degree in Mechanical Engineering. He served equally aboard surface ships and submarines. Throughout his naval career, which was capped by his assignment to the highest military position in the U.S. Navy, Chief of Naval Operations, Admiral Watkins has always been recognized for his outstanding administrative ability.

President Reagan selected Admiral Watkins to become the 22n Chief of Naval Operations on June 30, 1982, capping a distinguished career spanning nearly four decades. While Chief of Naval Operations, Admiral Watkins spoke out about various national issues including the sad decline in effectiveness of the American educational system, the growth of international terrorism, technology transfer and the evolution of nuclear deterrence from an offensive to a defensive strategy. He also authored and published the first unclassified version of the U.S. Maritime Strategy in 1986.

Admiral Watkins' tours as a flag officer included Chief of Naval Personnel; Commander of the Sixth Fleet; Vice Chief of Naval Operations; and Command-in-Chief of the Pacific Fleet. His military decorations include several Distinguished Service and Legion of Merit medals, and the Bronze Star with combat "V" and other medals, campaign and service ribbons.

After retiring from active duty, Admiral Watkins served as Chairman of the Presidential Commission on the Human Immunodeficiency Virus Epidemic (AIDS) from 1987 to 1988 and the sixth Secretary of Energy under President George H. W. Bush, from March 1989 through January 1993. Admiral Watkins' accomplishments at the Department of Energy (DOE) were highlighted by the development of the first comprehensive National Energy Strategy, which provided a foundation to coordinate all aspects of energy supply and demand, while maintaining proper respect for the environment and our economic well being. One of the major achievements of the Admiral's tenure at the Department was passage of the Energy Policy Act of 1992. This 940-page law was the most comprehensive energy legislation ever enacted.

In September 1994, Admiral Watkins led the historic effort to establish an expanded partnership between the Federal Government and the more that 60 U.S. marine institutions. The effort resulted in a public-private corporation known as the Consortium for Oceanographic Research and Education, CORE. In September 1996, as a result of the CORE's efforts, Congress authorized and funded the *National Oceanographic Partnership Act, which* implemented a new, broad ocean science and technology agenda for the nation. Admiral Watkins served seven years as founding President of CORE, stepping down in March 2001 to join the U.S. Commission on Ocean Policy.

Elected as Chairman of the Commission in September 2001, he served in this capacity for three years. The Commission's report, entitled "An Ocean Blueprint for the 21st Century," was submitted to the President and the Congress in September 2004. This report contains the new national ocean policy as demanded by the enabling legislation.

For his work with CORE, Admiral Watkins was awarded honorary doctor of science degrees from the College of William and Mary and Oregon State University in 1999. In March 2001, he was given the title of President Emeritus of CORE, and was awarded the Navy's Distinguished Public Service Award by the Secretary of the Navy for his contributions to the nation in ocean science and technology matters.

Vice Admiral Charles H. Griffiths, U. S. Navy, (Retired)

Charles H. Griffiths graduated from the United States Naval Academy at Annapolis and was commissioned Ensign on 6 June, 1945.

After graduation from Submarine School in December 1945, he served in several diesel submarines before assuming his first command, USS Wahoo (SS-565) in August 1957.

After nuclear power training he served as executive officer of the pre-commissioning crew of USS Robert E. Lee (SSBN-601), the first of many submarines to be built at Newport News Shipbuilding and Drydock Company. Upon completion of his executive officer tour he fleeted up to command of the Lee, completing a total of seven deterrent patrols prior to being assigned as commissioning commanding officer of the Blue Crew of USS Simon Bolivar (SSBN-641).

His next assignment was in Washington, D.C. as Head Submarine/Nuclear Power Assignment Distribution Control Branch and Program Manager of Nuclear Power Personnel, Bureau of Naval Personnel.

He commanded Submarine Squadron Fifteen in Guam until September 1970 when he reported as Chief of Staff to Commander Submarine Forces, U.S. Atlantic Fleet. After promotion to Rear Admiral in August 1971 he became Commander Naval Forces, Southern Command with headquarters at Fort Amador, Canal Zone.

He next served as Assistant Chief of Naval Personnel for Enlisted Personnel Development and Distribution from June 1973 until September 1975, when he assumed duties as Commander Submarine Force, U.S. Pacific Fleet in Honolulu, Hawaii. In July 1977 he was promoted to Vice Admiral and assigned as Deputy Chief of Naval Operations (Submarine Warfare). He retired from active duty in the rank of Vice Admiral on 30 September 1980 after completion of thirty five years of Naval Service.

Upon retirement from the Navy he founded CHG, INC. for the purpose of providing Consultant Services to Industry on defense related matters.

He was one of the three co-founders of the Naval Submarine League and was the initial Vice Charmin of the Board. For nine years from 1986 to 1995 he was president of the Navy Marine Coast Guard Residence Foundation (Vinson Hall) in McLean, Virginia. He is currently President of his Naval Academy Class, Chairman of the Council on Naval Academy Class Presidents, a member of the Naval Academy Alumni Association Board of Trustees, a member of the Naval Academy Foundation Board of Directors and Secretary of the Naval Historical Foundation.

He formerly served on the Board of Directors of the Marine Mechanical Corporation and of the GNB Industrial Battery Company.

Rear Admiral David R. Oliver, Jr. US Navy, (Retired)

Dave Oliver is Chief Executive Officer of EADS North America Defense Company. In this capacity, Mr. Oliver has direct oversight and responsibility for all Defense activities of EADS North America. Prior to election to his current position, Mr. Oliver served in Baghdad in 2003 as the Director of Management and Budget for the Coalition Forces.

Following Senate conformation in 1998, Dave served as the Principal Deputy Under Secretary of Defense for Acquisition, Technology and Logistics through two Administrations until July 2001. He subsequently became a consultant (Dave Oliver, Jr., Associates). Mr. Oliver currently serves as a director on public and private boards.

In 1995, Dave joined Westinghouse Electric Systems Group in Baltimore, Maryland and directed a major international program. After Westinghouse was acquired by Northrop Grumman, Dave was Director of Technology and Business Development for the Naval Systems sector.

In the Navy, Admiral Oliver served at sea aboard both diesel electric and nuclear submarines. He commanded a nuclear submarine and two submarine groups. Mr. Oliver also directed significant assignments for the Navy, including requirement establishment and budget programming. His last Navy appointment was as Principal Deputy to the Assistant Secretary of the Navy for Research, Development and Acquisition.

His military decorations include the Defense and Navy Distinguished Service Medals as well as six awards of the Legion of Merit. His awards for public service include the Bronze Palm to the Department of Defense Award for Distinguished Public Service.

Born in Indiana, Dave graduated from the United States Naval Academy. He received a Master of Arts in Political Science and International Affairs (Middle East) from American University. In addition to many leadership articles, Mr. Oliver has written *Making It in Washington* (Trafford Press, 2003), *Lead On: A Practical Approach to Leadership* (Presidio Press, 1992), and the biography of his wife, *Wide Blue Ribbon* (Trafford Press, 2004)

Linda Bithell Oliver, the subject of *Wide Blue Ribbon*, is a career member of America's senior executive service.

Rear Admiral Jon Michael Barr, U.S. Navy (Retired)

A native of New Jersey, Rear Admiral Barr graduated from the U.S. Naval Academy in 1961. After graduation, he completed nuclear power training and attended Submarine School in Groton, Connecticut.

Rear Admiral Barr reported to USS SNOOK (SSN 592) in January 1963, serving in Operations, Engineering and Weapons Departments. Following duty on SNOOK, Rear Admiral Barr was an instructor for two years at the Naval Nuclear Power School, Mare Island, California.

In 1968, Rear Admiral Barr reported to USS TECUMSEH (SSBN 628) and served as Navigator and Operations Officer. In April 1972, he reported to USS BARB (SSN 596) as Executive Officer. Rear Admiral Barr assumed command of the Naval Nuclear Power School, Bainbridge, Maryland in 1974, and moved the school to Orlando, Florida in 1975.

Rear Admiral Barr took command of USS SCULPIN (SSN 590) in November 1977. In November 1979, he was assigned as prospective Commanding Officer of USS BOSTON (SSN 703). The ship was commissioned in January 1982. Rear Admiral Barr served as Commanding Officer of USS OHIO (SSBN 726) (BLUE) from February 1983 to August 1984. Following command of OHIO (BLUE), he served as Commander, Submarine Squadron SEVENTEEN, the Navy's first operational Trident submarine squadron, and commanded Submarine Group NINE as additional duty from July to September 1985.

From March 1986 to January 1988, Rear Admiral Barr served as Deputy Director of the Attack Submarine Division in the Office of the Assistant Chief of Naval Operations (Undersea Warfare). Following selection for flag rank in December 1987, he was assigned as Deputy Directory for Operations, National Military Command Center. In July 1989, he was named Deputy Assistant Secretary for Military Application, Office of Defense Programs, U.S. Department of Energy. From July 1991 to July 1993, Rear Admiral Barr served as Commander, Navy Recruiting Command.

Rear Admiral Barr was assigned as Commander, Submarine Force, U.S. Pacific Fleet from July 1993 to February 1996 where he was responsible for over 40 nuclear powered submarines, supporting facilities afloat and ashore and over 16,000 officers, men and women.

Following retirement from the Navy in March 1996, he joined Johnson Controls, Incorporated as President and General Manager of Johnson Controls Northern New Mexico, the major support services contractor for Los Alamos National Laboratory. Rear Admiral Barr retired in February 2003.

Rear Admiral Barr's awards include the Defense Distinguished Service Medal, Distinguished Service Medal (with Gold Star), Legion of Merit (with Gold Star), Defense Meritorious Service Medal, Meritorious Service Medal (with Gold Star) and several other personal and campaign awards

Rear Admiral Barr is married to the former Marcia Elizabeth Redston of Upper Montclair, New Jersey. They have three daughters, Susan, Diana and Jillian, and six grandchildren, Lindsay, Julia, Drew, Tessa, Sydney and Riley.

Captain Don Walsh, U.S. Navy, (Retired)

Don Walsh joined the US Navy in 1948 as an aircrewman in torpedo bombers and entered the Naval Academy in 1950. He served two years in the Amphibious Forces before entering submarine school in 1956. Don served on the submarines *Rasher* (SSR-269), *Sea Fox* (SS-402), and *Bugara* (SS-331) before commanding *Bashaw* (AGSS-241).

In 1959 Lieutenant Walsh became first Officer-in-Charge of the *Bathyscaph Trieste* at the Navy Electronics Laboratory in San Diego. Designated USN Deep Submersible Pilot #1 he was also the first submersible pilot in the US. In January 1960, he and Jacques Piccard dove *Trieste* to the deepest place in the World Ocean: 35,840 feet. For this achievement, Lieutenant Walsh received a medal from President Eisenhower at ceremonies in the White House.

From 1970–75, Commander Walsh was on duty in Washington DC serving as Special Assistant (Submarines) to the Assistant Secretary of the Navy for Research and Development (ASNR&D) and as Deputy Director of Navy Laboratories, his final duty before retirement as a Captain.

He retired to accept a professorship of ocean engineering at the University of Southern California (USC). There he was founding Director of the Institute for Marine and Coastal Studies (IMCS) with rank of dean. He left USC after 8 years to form a consulting practice, International Maritime Incorporated (IMI), a company he runs today.

Don Walsh was educated at the Naval Academy (BS in engineering), Texas A&M University (MS and PhD in oceanography), and San Diego State University (MA in political science). He spent 14 months as Resident Fellow at the Woodrow Wilson International Center for Scholars at the Smithsonian.

Dr. Walsh is author of over 200 ocean-related publications. He has given over 1,500 lectures, TV and radio programs in 64 countries. Since graduation from the Naval Academy, his travels have taken him to about 112 nations throughout the world.

For the past four decades, Dr. Walsh has also worked in both Arctic and Antarctic regions including the North (3 trips) and South Poles. To date he has participated in over 50 polar expeditions. His first trip to the Arctic was in 1955; the Antarctic in 1971. He made a circumnavigation of the continent November 2002—February 2003. It was only the 11th time this voyage has been made since Captain James Cook first did it in 1773–74. The "Walsh Spur" (ridge) near Cape Hallett is named for him in recognition of his contributions to the US Antarctic Program.

Among other awards, in February, 2001 Dr. Walsh was elected to the National Academy of Engineering. In March 2001, he was awarded the Explorers Medal by the Explorers Club. Both of these honors recognize his four decades of work in the design, construction and operation of undersea vehicles. In November of the same year the French Jules Verne Aventures organization awarded him its "Etoile Polaire" medal to celebrate "The Greatest Explorations of the 20th Century". In 2001 he was also cited as one of the great explorers in the Life Magazine book, "The Greatest Adventures of All Time".

He isn't slowing down. In 1999, he dove 8,000 feet to the Mid-Atlantic Ridge near the Azores at the Rainbow Vents hydrothermal vents field. In July 2001, he dove 12,500 feet to the wreck of RMS *Titanic*. And in July 2002 he dove on the WWII German Battleship Bismarck at 15,500 feet in the Atlantic. In all these operations, he used the Russian Mir submersibles that are rated for 20,000 feet. Also, he is currently working on two manned submersible projects, one in Dubai and the other in England.

Don lives on a ranch in rural Oregon with his wife, Joan. When not busy traveling he flies his experimental biplane around the area.

Captain Bob Gautier U. S. Navy, (Retired)

Robert Henry Gautier, Pascagoula, Mississippi was born June 29, 1923 son of Henry and Archie Quinn Gautier. He attended Pascagoula High School and Marion Military Institute, Marion, Alabama, prior to entering the U. S. Naval Academy in June 1942. Graduated with class of 1946, on June 6, 1945 (accelerated course due to World War II). He was commissioned Ensign and subsequently advanced to the rank of Captain and retired with 30 years of service in June 1975.

After graduation he served on USS Gansevoort (DD 608), USS Fieberling (DE 640) and USS Halfbeak (SS 352) prior to attending submarine school in 1948. Following graduation he served on USS Tilefish (SS 307), and was qualified for submarines, receiving his "Dolphins" in February 1950. He was later assigned as flag lieutenant and aide to Commander Submarine Forces, Pacific Fleet. He then served in commissioning crew of the new construction submarine USS Tang (SS563) in the engineering and operations department. In June 1953 was designated for command of submarines. He was assigned as Assistant Material Officer on the staff of Commander Submarine Forces, Pacific Fleet.

In June 1954 he reported to the Fleet Maintenance Division (submarines), Office of the Chief of Naval Operations. Returning to sea duty in June 1956 he served as Executive Officer USS Trout (SS566) and then commanded USS Conger (SS477). In April 1959, he reported to his hometown, Pascagoula, Mississippi as Commanding Officer, USS Blueback (SS 581). This was the first submarine built Ingalls Shipyard and the first submarine built is the South since the Civil War. He commanded Blueback during the final construction, commissioning, and made the first operational deployment, including the first patrol in the Western Pacific. He was relieved in August 1961 and then attended the Armed Forces Staff College, Norfolk, Virginia. After graduation he was assigned duty in the Inquiry and Liaison Division, Office of Legislative Affairs in the office of Chief of Naval operations.

In August 1964 he reported as Plans and Operations Officer, Staff of Commander Submarine Flotilla One, San Diego, CA. He then was Commander Submarine Division Fifty-three from June 1965 to June 1966. He then served as Chief Staff Officer to Commander Submarine Flotilla One.

He relieved as Captain, USS Montrose (APA 212) in June 1967 in the Philippines, returned to San Diego, CA in January 1969 During this tour he deployed to the Azores Islands, Atlantic Ocean as Commander Task Unit 42.2.1 (The on-scene operational commander for the at sea operations of USS Scorpion (SSN 589) Search Phase II). Using DSV Trieste II on nine successful dives to a depth exceeding 10,000 feet Scorpion was located, photographed and selected items were recovered. He was awarded the Meritorious Service Medal for this operation. He was relieved in January 1971, and awarded his second Meritorious Service Medal.

He was Commander Amphibious Squadron Six, Norfolk, Virginia from March 1971 to August 1972. In this tour he made operational deployments to the Mediterranean Sea and Caribbean Sea. When relieved he was awarded his third Meritorious Service Medal.

He commanded the Naval Undersea Center, a major research and development center, San Diego, CA from September 1972 to June 1975. He retired June 1975 and was awarded the Legion of Merit.

After retiring from the US Navy he worked as a consultant with Bendix Oceanics Division, Global Marine Development, Inc., Scientific Atlanta Governments Products Division He was director Lockheed Advanced Marine Systems, San Diego, CA for several years.

His hobbies are wine making, mainly reds, (Zinfandel and Cabernet Sauvignon) and deep sea fishing. He holds the world's record for 30 pound test line class with a 448 pound Giant Sea Bass caught April 1975.

In addition to the Legion of Merit, Bronze Star Medal with Combat "V", and Meritorious Service Medal with two gold stars he has the Navy Expeditionary Medal. American Campaign Medal, World War II Victory Medal, China Service Medal, National Defense Medal, Korean Service Medal, United Nations Service Medal, Vietnam Campaign Medal with device (1960) and Vietnam Forces Meritorious Unit Citation Medal with three stars.

Rear Admiral Charles D. Grojean, U.S. Navy (Retired)

Charles David Grojean was born on August 13, 1923 in Charleston, Missouri. He graduated from high school in Decatur, Illinois and attended Virginia Military Institute prior to entering the United States Naval Academy in July 1942. Upon graduating from the Naval Academy in 1945 he served in the destroyer and amphibious forces before entering the submarine service in November 1949.

After graduating from submarine school Admiral Grojean served in diesel and nuclear submarines in the Atlantic and Pacific fleets. He commanded the U.S.S Angler and U.S.S. Barb (a nuclear attack submarine). During the years of 1969,

1970 and 1971 he was Commander Submarine Flotilla Eight and Commander Submarine Force Mediterranean in Naples, Italy. His shore assignments included duty at the Naval Academy and on the staffs of the Secretary of Defense, the Joint Chiefs of Staff and the Chief of Naval Operations where he served as the Director of Political Military Affairs. He retired from active duty 30 April 1975

Since 1976 Admiral Grojean has resided in San Antonio, Texas where for eleven years he was a venture capital investor and partner in the firm of Southwest Venture Partnerships. In July 1987 he joined his son Peter, formed Admiralty Management Company and engaged in a number of entrepreneurial businesses. On July I, 1990 he became Executive Director of the Admiral Nimitz Foundation in Fredericksburg, Texas providing support of the National Museum of the Pacific War and other elements of the Admiral Nimitz Historical Center.

Admiral Grojean is married to the former Joan Stewart of Springfield, Ohio. They have two sons, Peter and David, two daughters Charlotte Grojean and Margaret Donley, and ten grandchildren.

Admiral Grojean's awards include four Legions of Merit from the United States Navy, the Legion of Merit from the Brazilian Navy, the Legion of Merit from the Venezuelan Navy, the Meritorious Service Medal from the U.S. Navy and various campaign medals. While Executive Director of the Admiral Nimitz Foundation he received the Secretary of the Navy's Distinguished Public Service Award.

Vice Admiral Patrick J. Hannifin, U.S. Navy, Retired

Patrick J. Hannifin was graduated from the US Naval Academy and commissioned Ensign, USN in June 1944. Following Submarine School he joined USS *Balao* (SS 285) and participated in three combat war patrols in the Pacific.

After World War II he served in the ex-German submarine U-858 and a number of US submarines. He commanded the USS *Diodon* (SS 349), and was the first Executive Officer of the first Polaris submarine, USS *George Washington* (SSBN 598). He commissioned the USS *Lafayette* (SSBN 616) as Commanding Officer. Assignments ashore included Deputy Director Submarine Warfare, OPNAV.

Following graduation from the Industrial College of the Armed Forces and a MBA degree from George Washington University in 1968, he took command of Submarine Squadron 15, the Polaris squadron in Guam. In 1969 Hannifin was promoted to Rear Admiral, USN.

His first flag assignment was as Commandant, Thirteenth Naval District in Seattle, WA. He later served as Commander Submarine Group Eight in Naples, Italy and as Commander Submarines Mediterranean, commanding the NATO Submarine Force. Returning to Washington, D.C. in 1973 he was assigned as

Deputy Director for Strategic and Nuclear Plans, Joint Chiefs of Staff, and later to the Navy as Assistant Director, Plans and Operations.

In 1976 Hannifin was appointed as Director Plans and Policy for the Joint Chiefs of Staff and promoted to Vice Admiral. In 1977 he was appointed Director of Joint Staff for the Joint Chiefs.

Admiral Hannifin from the US Navy in 1978 and lives in Solana Beach, CA. He is President of HANESCO, INC. a company involved in the exploration of oil and gas.

His son, Captain Steven P. Hannifin USN, (Ret) and grandson Lieutenant Commander Patrick J. Hannifin, USN continue the Navy tradition.

Master Chief Jeff VanBlaracum, US Navy

Master Chief VanBlaracum has served on four submarines. One SSBN, one special operations, and two Los Angeles class fast attack submarines. His last assignment onboard submarines was Chief of the Boat onboard USS SANTA FE (SSN

763). In his twenty years of service he has had two shore assignments. First as an instructer at Torpedomans Mate "A" school and the second as the Force Torpedoman on the staff of the Commander Submarine Force Pacific Fleet. He currently serves as the Command Master Chief Submarine Squadron Three in Pearl Harbor Hawaii.

CAPTAIN LOUIS DAVID MARQUET
UNITED STATES NAVY

Captain L. David Marquet, a native of Berkeley, California, graduated with distinction from the United States Naval Academy in 1981, with a Bachelor of Science Degree in Physics. Following commissioning, he completed nuclear power school and the Submarine Officer's Basic Course, where he was recognized as the honorman.

Captain Marquet has served in four submarines, two assigned to the Atlantic fleet and two assigned to the Pacific fleet. From 1999–2001 he commanded the USS SANTA FE (SSN 763). During his tour, USS Santa Fe made two 6-month deployments to the Western Pacific and Arabian Gulf. Additionally, USS Santa Fe was awarded the 1999 Arleigh Burke award for the most improved ship in the

Pacific Fleet, the 2001 Battle "E" for combat effectiveness, and three unit commendations.

Captain Marquet's shore assignments have included serving as aide to the Director, Research, Development and Acquisition in Washington, DC. From 1992 to 1994, he served as Mission Captain at the On-Site Inspection Agency, where he conducted inspections in the Former Soviet Union and Europe, and delivered humanitarian aid to Moldova, Armenia and Georgia. Following command of USS Santa Fe, Captain Marquet served as the head of the Tactical Readiness Evaluation team for the Pacific submarine force.

Captain Marquet served as a Military Fellow to the Council on Foreign Relations, in New York City, from the summer of 2003–2004, and has since become a member of the Council. From August 2004 to September 2005, he has served as the Commander, Submarine Squadron Three.

Since October 2005, Captain Marquet has served as the Executive Assistant to the Chief of Naval Personnel.

Captain Marquet holds the postgraduate degrees of Master of Arts in National Security Affairs and Master of Engineering Management.

Captain Marquet's awards include the Legion of Merit, Joint Meritorious Service Medal, and the Meritorious Service Medal (four awards).

Captain Marquet and his wife Jane live in Arlington, VA. He has three children, Michael, Emily, and Bryan.

Endnotes

1. This message was sent at 1100 on January 17, 1955 as USS Nautilus got underway for the first time on nuclear propulsion from the Naval Submarine Base, New London, CT.

2. USS Nautilus (SS 168) Patrol Report for patrol number 6, reprinted from the Full Fathom Five web site at http://www.geocities.com/pentagon/1592/nautilus6.htm.

3. COMSUBPAC press release, http://www.csp.navy.mil/news/cheyennereturn.html.

4. Eugene B. Fluckey, <u>Thunder Below</u>, University of Illinois Press, Urbana and Chicago, 1992, p. 324.

5. Theodore Roscoe, <u>United States Submarine Operations in World War II</u>, Naval Institute Press, Annapolis, MD, 1949, p. 493.

6. Roscoe, p. 146.

7. Richard H. O'Kane, <u>Clear the Bridge!</u>, Presidio Press, Novato, CA, 1977, p. 136.

8. O'Kane, p. 199.

978-0-595-38574-4
0-595-38574-5

Printed in the United States
55849LVS00004B/213